A LEGACY of LOVE

VOLUME TWO

A Journey to the East

A LEGACY of LOVE

VOLUME TWO

A Journey to the East

With

Saint Germain

As Channeled Through

Philip Burley

*A Legacy of Love, Volume Two, A Journey to the East
with Saint Germain as Channeled through Philip Burley*

Mastery
Press

For information about this title, contact the publisher:

Mastery Press
P.O. Box 484
Laveen, AZ 85339
United States of America
Email: PB@PhilipBurley.com
Website: www.PhilipBurley.com

ISBN: 978-1-883389-41-3

Printed in the United States of America

Cover design: Philip Burley and Jennifer Fleischmann
Interior design: 1106 Design

ACKNOWLEDGMENTS

To editors: Anne Edwards, and a private co-editor

To bring a book into existence requires a team effort. **A Legacy of Love, Volume Two, A Journey to the East *with* Saint Germain *through* Philip Burley**, is no exception:

Thank you, Anne Edwards, and a private co-editor, for your editing skills and their application to making *A Journey to the East* a success. Editing such detailed, very personal, heart-filled dialog, while making the presentation meaningfully captivating, is no small or easy task.

I am exceedingly grateful for your excellent, professional oversight and careful, exacting editing. You have helped turn the spoken, recorded, transcribed word into a piece of inspiring, entertaining, and compelling historical spiritual literature.

To transcribers: Lynn Mathers, Marti Snyder, Lucia LaBarre, and L. Grace Kohan—who captured the recorded, spoken word of each spiritual reading in written form—my abundant thanks. Because of your genuine love for the subject matter, great commitment, highly focused, careful listening, and long hours of precise typing, the transcriptions of the 70 spiritual readings I did in Japan—October and November of 2003—came into visible form.

May all of you who participated in birthing **A Journey to the East** appreciate and enjoy the reading of the finished book—a work that is partially your doing and has your spiritual fingerprints on it.

Much love and gratitude,
Philip Burley

CONTENTS

INTRODUCTION

Welcome to my world, the world of a spiritual medium. I am Philip Burley, and my profession is being in touch and communicating with the afterlife, or as is classically called in my work, the spirit world.

As mediums or bridges between this world and the next—our job is to communicate with persons who have died and *initially* want and need to communicate to their loved ones on earth the reality that they are very much alive and existing in the spirit world with other souls who have also departed from the earth plane.

An estimated one hundred and fifty thousand people die and leave the earth each day. That comes to four million, five hundred thousand per month, adding up to fifty-four million souls per year going into the spirit world. We can't even begin to grasp or imagine the amount of sorrow and grief that emanates from our world because of the ongoing dying of loved ones among us.

Throughout human history, the grief over the death of parents, a spouse, beloved children, and dear, close friends abounds. Not only are minds unbelieving because a dear one has just died and only silence follows, but there is also unmitigated grief and longing that makes the heart ache beyond measure. Many who are grieving will say, "If only I could know that they are alive *somewhere* and could speak to them if only one more time, I would be so grateful, and a lot of the pain would go away!"

Spiritual Mediums Are Not Accidental

By way of the Creator's love, planning, and creation of human life, the existence of spiritual mediums is intentional, and they serve in varying and often hidden ways. But most significantly they serve to lessen ongoing grief and sorrow caused by the death of loved ones. Throughout human history there have been spiritual mediums, like me, who are born with an openness and sensitivity that allows us to discern the existence of the afterlife and share the same with those on earth who come to us for this purpose.

Historically, the masses of humanity have not clearly, absolutely known through empirical evidence whether there is life after death of the physical body. Many *believe and have faith* that there is life beyond the grave and that we do go *somewhere* but they are not sure exactly where. Mediums help to bring the spirit world alive, providing a glimpse of the afterlife and what is in store for all of us when we pass away.

Spirit World's Presence and Influence

Individuals who go to the spirit world will, in time, come back to the physical world. In doing so, they are invisible and silent to earthlings' physical senses. The departed and usually unperceived soul remains in spiritual relationships with individuals, based on what they have in common. Quietly and often undetected, spirits seek to teach and guide us in our daily lives and, where possible, awaken us to the afterlife so that we may be most prepared to go to the spirit world when it is our time.

Without exception, everyone on earth is attended by the spirit world. Night and day, 24/7, those in spirit go back and forth between the earthly plane and the spirit world. Spirits return again and again to guide humans lovingly and wisely through life on earth. The collective influence of their oversight of humanity is monumental.

Some are bound to ask about—or point out the reality of—a portion of those in the afterlife being unenlightened and, as a result, spiritually ignorant and unevolved. The citizens of the spirit world are arrayed, just as on earth, from the spiritually lowest to the highest and affect individuals on earth accordingly. There are good and evil spirits and all shades in between who influence our world. Many factors need to be considered to grasp and explain the existence of this reality not covered in this book. I did not encounter low or evil spirits while doing spiritual readings in Japan.

Until we go to the spirit world, we truly have no idea of the great love of God manifested by way of His spirit world, which also includes the angelic realm. Without the perpetual, most enlightened, loving, and noble spirit world guidance, humans on earth would have perished long ago. In multiple ways, the attending spirit world seeks to love and care for people on earth. It is an ever-ongoing reality hidden from the awareness of most of humanity throughout human history.

The Influence of Belief Systems

The belief system of an individual greatly influences the type of input and to what degree the spirit world can influence and guide that person. An important and vital factor for all human beings, whether they know it or not, is how influenced they can become by transcendent, loving spirits.

For me, as a bridge or link between this world and the spirit world, conveying information back and forth, via clairvoyance, clairaudience, and clairsentience is one thing—but to be a *full channel* for spirit and God to use, is an additional reality and an expansion of the gift of mediumship.

We are all channels for spirit—and by that I don't mean that each person is some kind of puppet always and easily taken over by spirit.

For the highest, most positive, most loving experiences, sometimes the most elevated spirit world intercedes by temporarily and directly entering into this physical world, through individuals like me—a spiritual medium—to bring about higher spiritual awareness and an awakening in those who observe such intercession from Heaven.

Saint Germain

The major subject matter of *A Journey to the East* was derived from the transcriptions of the spiritual readings of 21 precious individuals who came to me to discover what I discerned coming from the spirit world of each one, by means of my spiritual gifts.

This book portrays rich, unique experiences. The truths in the book revealed through the readings—from the subtle to the most obvious—will take you to deeper and higher levels of spirituality centered on gaining greater awareness of and involvement with the spirit world and its Creator.

Central to *A Journey to the East* is the presence of Saint Germain and the interactions with him. As you will experience through your reading, he is pivotal to the unfolding of this book and much of its most elevated content. For this purpose, Saint Germain, a great spiritual master, and legend, came into my life nearly forty years ago. He has used me to speak to thousands of people. My relationship with Saint Germain is a long story and will be covered in my upcoming memoir, *The Golden Path*.

In the Beginning: The Need for Validation

When I first began my career forty years ago, information written on mediumship, the afterlife, and the spirit world, was much less mainstream. At that time, I would go to great lengths to give enough background information about myself and my profession to validate, most emphatically, the authenticity of what I do, and the constructive end results that my work brings to the many people I have the privilege of serving.

The contents of this book speak for themselves and give ample examples and plentiful proof of the accuracy of what I do, and who and what I am—as a credible, long-standing, professional medium. You have only to notice my interactions with the persons who received these spiritual readings for this to be confirmed beyond doubt.

How I Came to Japan as A Medium

My coming to Japan as a medium, to give public lectures and to do spiritual readings, has a long backstory. However, here I will give highlights and only as much as is needed to provide an overview of the whole story from beginning to end.

In the fall of 2002, 6 months prior, out of nowhere, I got a call from the leadership of the Wesak Festival (the celebration of Buddha's birthday) to take place in April of 2003 at Mt. Shasta, California. This was the very place where in 1930 the mystic, spiritual master Saint Germain made his first, monumental appearance and through which began a New Age movement. That is a whole other story and unrelated to mine.

I immediately accepted the offer to attend as a guest speaker and was invited to speak for an hour to some 2,000 people from all over the United States and various other countries around the world. I received a warm welcome as I spoke and then channeled Saint Germain. A very long line of people formed to meet me afterward on the auditorium floor. It was obvious that the decision to take up this invitation was meant to be, and my work after that began to spread more and more across the country.

Overall, during the festival—to which I was invited back the next year to appear twice—I could not have felt more blessed or satisfied by what transpired for me while simply sharing who I am and what I do with an audience primed to readily understand and appreciate my spiritual offerings that year.

Would I Like to Come to Japan?

On the second day of the event, I was approached by a woman in her mid-thirties with a warm and welcoming smile and obviously someone who did public work, as was apparent from her overall approach to me. She introduced herself as *Gayle* and proceeded to say that she enjoyed my presentation and was impressed and asked if I would like to go to Japan and do my work.

I did not leap at the invitation. In the speaking business and especially when one is the age I was at the time, 63, I was hesitant to travel overseas with the possibility of becoming ill or that the expense to travel and live there would be more than I could earn. Gayle as a agent had brought two other mediums to Japan and according to her, they had done very well. She would be responsible for making all the arrangements, including lining up plenty of people to attend any of my public lectures and to have a spiritual reading with me.

The Journey Begins

Gayle spoke fluent Japanese. (Some native Japanese later told me that often she spoke their language better than they did.) After a thorough discussion sufficient to satisfy my initial questions and curiosity, we agreed to meet in Colorado where she lived. A bit later I visited her there and accepted her invitation to Japan and all that it entailed. The next time I saw her was as I came off a 12-hour flight, via San Francico, at the Narita International Airport in Japan, about 50 miles from what was to be my home for two months, a condominium in Shinjuku.

As we traveled by bus from the airport to my condo, Gayle filled me in on everything, including that I was fully booked for two months of spiritual readings and almost all the arrangements were complete.

Upon arrival, we went up to my new 4th floor home and I was shown around. I was tired but hungry. I would take two days off and then begin my 60-day mediumship work in Japan! After Gayle left, I went next door to a Japanese restaurant where I ate some of my favorite food on the planet and went back to my condo and crashed. I slept for many hours and did not get up until the afternoon of the next day to unpack and seek to get my mind and body adjusted to what was ahead. The two days went by fast, and on the morning that we began the readings, I was still a bit tired from jet lag and a bit anxious but ready and pleased to begin.

The Work Ahead

Prior to my arrival at my overseas destination, my coming there was advertised in popular media. I was quickly booked up to do 35 spiritual readings per month or a total of 70 readings for the months of October and November 2003.

Each person I read for was allowed to ask four questions—questions that, in my experience, always lead to further questions and answers. As a result, each reading that I gave was abundantly full of evidential and inspirational content, and no one went away unhappy or wanting.

At necessary and timely intervals, Saint Germain took over my vocal cords and channeled directly through me to answer certain questions and to give any other input that the client's spirit world knew that they needed.

To present the transcript of all 70 readings in a book would be impossible. The 21 spiritual readings selected for this book are a good representation of the whole and more than abundantly share, through personal interactions, human life as aligned with the spirit world in deeply meaningful, inspiring—if not entertaining—ways.

The Setting

And just where did all of this take place? The specific and beginning setting and backdrop for *A Journey to the East* was a nice-sized, very attractive, modern condominium unit of about 800 square feet that took up the entire 4th floor of the building. Additionally, the condo had its own individual elevator entrance.

As I entered it the first time, I was told that it was more of a luxury condo and above average in size. To me it was, upon first sight, a beautiful place because of its simplicity and a very pleasant, uncluttered, spiritual atmosphere. I was very humbled and exceedingly grateful to be able to work in a space of this quality. The condo consisted of a living room/dining room combined in one large room, a bedroom, a full bath, and a small but fully furnished kitchen with enough space for one person to cook.

There was little furniture except for a small television on a stand, a small sized, yellow colored, leather couch with a light blue 5' x 8' area rug in front of it. The place also had a small, rectangular shaped dining room table with two chairs and a large mirror on the wall beside the table. And finally, there was a twin bed usually kept behind a thin, wooden, foldable, hanging wall.

The front wall of the condo was taken up with one tall, wide window in the living room and one large window in the bedroom area, both looking out to the sky, the buildings across the street, and the street below. The large windows allowed for great views and let in a lot of light. They were hung with simple, white brocade curtains that were used sometimes in the daytime to close out the sun and at night for privacy.

The building had been only recently built and was eight individual condos high with each one taking up one whole floor. The building was located on a major street in Shinjuku, one of six wards or population centers surrounding Tokyo, Japan. The entire metropolitan area in 2003 consisted of a total population of approximately 31,350,000 residents.

Shinjuku is on the western side of Tokyo and much less busy and quieter than the central district. Within 20 minutes, however, I could walk to the center of Shinjuku which contains the busiest train and subway system in the world, with more than *3.5 million passengers* passing through the station every day.

I was present there several times during rush hour, walking with the masses of people hurrying here and there. I did not panic but it was both a sight to see and an experience remembered long after it was over. It was not unfamiliar, just more crowded, and much more tightly packed than I had experienced by walking through Grand Central Station in New York City, at rush hour, many years prior.

However, because I kept my wits about me, I did not get lost, and safely found my way to the world outside of endless streets and traffic and—quite literally—large store upon large store and shop upon shop, and restaurant upon restaurant. There were signs everywhere created from neon lights causing the night to appear almost like day.

While I appreciated taking in this reality of central Shinjuku, I was always happy to return to my condo and the extreme peace and quiet it afforded the entire time I was in the Land of the Rising Sun. Due to the lack of time and energy expended doing readings, I did not go out that often.

Most importantly, my condo was in a central location where individuals came from all directions throughout Japan to meet and sit with me for their spiritual reading. For some clients it was a two-to-three-hour train ride each way.

My Clientele

Most did not speak fluent English—if any English at all—and so a translator was needed. Usually, in the United States, my readings are an hour long or less, but in Japan they were extended to 90 minutes to accommodate the translation factor. My readings in the West are $300.00 per hour whereas in Japan they were double that price at a standard rate of $600.00 per hour. If greatly desired or needed, family members could help with the cost of a spiritual reading. Because the

Japanese are generally very thrifty, many have a sizable nest egg some-where to draw from.

The routine of doing spiritual readings was very predictable and enjoyable. Time went neither fast nor slow. Rather, I reserved the proper amount of time and kept my mind focused on each person so that I would be deeply and closely attuned to them and their spirit world. I became acutely aware of the variety of people coming before me and, in fact, how unique each one was—whether exhibiting traditional Japanese conformity or not.

I found the Japanese people easy to read spiritually. Among the 70 I read for were a wide variety of people from divergent working back-grounds and ages and, of course, both men and women. They believed in an afterlife, almost without exception, and did not question its exis-tence or struggle with its reality. Consequently, their universal, innate openness to the spirit world made my job far easier.

What is more, their ready acceptance of the concept of the spirit world made it easier and faster for their spirit world to manifest with them to my clairvoyant, spiritual eyes, and my clairaudient spiritual ears. Their spirit world generally appeared brighter and more clearly and vividly than spirits around clients I had read for in the West. Often many of their spiritual guides would appear, and clearly so, in significantly large numbers—meaning more than just the appearance of close, deceased loved ones alone. In cases where a client's family were descendants of the samurai, a whole clan would appear around the client and when I would mention what I saw, individuals would say, "Yes, my family belonged to the samurai."

While the translator did an outstanding job—mostly that of trans-lating Japanese into English and vice versa—she has not been included in the spiritual readings in this book. Rather, without changing the words greatly or their meaning, all dialog presented in the book was kept between myself as the medium or Saint Germain speaking through me, and the client sitting before me and their spirit world, directly or indirectly.

Without a translator, doing spiritual readings in Japan with a Western medium who does not speak Japanese would have been impossible. Much credit and appreciation are owed to the person who translated reading after reading during our sessions in such a precise, speedy, clear way. She was better than good, she was excellent! I am exceedingly grateful to her and all those who worked with her to make my time there both much easier than if I had been alone and much more profitable spiritually.

While these spiritual readings were done in Japan and with Japanese residents, many of the persons I read for—and also according to one person (an American) who helped edit this book—*found them to be profound and have universal appeal* and I, most objectively, wholeheartedly agree. While you may have your own experience while reading this book, I am confident that you will not go away disappointed.

As you may recall, I needed to do 35 readings in October and 35 readings in November. And since I usually did readings only during the week, I had only 20 days in which to do the first 35 readings. Consequently, on some days I had to do two or three readings per day. Sometimes, due to scheduling complications, I did readings on Saturday as well. However, I always had at least Sunday off for rest and to do nothing. In addition to doing the spiritual readings, I also gave four seminars, two hours each, to gathered audiences, usually averaging about 40 people in various settings; some were held in my condo, which could easily accommodate 40 people with most sitting, Japanese style, on the floor.

I spoke first on channeling and demonstrated the phenomenon while Saint Germain took over my vocal cords and spoke at length to the audience on various spiritual topics and answered their questions. I also spoke about the spiritual instrument of *the trumpet* and its use throughout the earlier evolution of spiritualism. It is always a fascinating topic and one that audiences in both the East and the West often find very meaningful.

The use of this instrument, the trumpet, is explained in context in Spiritual Reading Five, page 71 and will give the reader an explanation and the details of the use of a trumpet that the spirit world uses, as one means to speak from the spiritual plane of existence to our earthly plane.

My Stay in Japan

Because of the demand of doing readings and the inevitable taxing effect on my spirit and body, I never traveled to do any sightseeing the entire time I was in Japan. I did see Mount Fuji, the most iconic symbol of Japan, through a restaurant window located on the 30th floor of a high-rise building in Tokyo. Fuji was 70 miles away and looked more like a picture on a postage stamp from that distance. I laughed to myself at the time of the irony of being in a world-famous tourist spot but not sightseeing, but I was okay; it was good and sacred to devote my whole time to serving each client. I wouldn't have had it any other way. I would take a vacation or break from mediumship work when I returned to the United States.

I had a picture taken of me with each of the 70 clients and when I look at them now, it is with much affection, deep appreciation, and fond memories. All of that took place twenty years ago and I am sure much has happened and changed in the lives of these dear people who came to me—many with a most obvious, humble, open, and child-like heart. More than a few told me, during their reading, that they like life and themselves better in a foreign country—*for in Japan too many people know your business and one could not feel the same freedom to be oneself in Japan as outside of Japan.* They obviously felt free to share this sentiment and perhaps so for the first time in their lives.

While I greatly appreciated and personally enjoyed my time there—in fact, I thrived significantly—I could understand, from the point of view of some of my clients, their wanting more freedom from the Japanese culture. That is, freedom from the pressure of needing to always conform culturally and freedom, consequently, from the constant need to always make sure that one does not stand out.

Conducting the Readings

As you entered the living room of the condo, there was a two-seated couch to the left with its back against the outside wall. It stood about eight feet from the front window. The couch, built to Japanese specifications, was rather small compared to similar Western couches but it worked fine. It was here that I sat—often cross-legged with my eyes closed—while giving all the spiritual readings in Japan.

Each client sat directly in front of me on a chair about four feet from me. The translator, by her choice, sat on a cushion on the floor, about four feet to my right with her back against the wall, with alternately crossed legs or legs stretched to full length. During seminars and classes, she sat to my right, about four feet away and on a chair.

I had two tape recorders running during each reading so that I had a recording for each client and one for my own record-keeping and later to be able to type a transcription of each session so that I could share these readings with others, as I am doing now, though the names of all participants have been changed to retain anonymity and privacy.

Each tape was forty-five minutes to a side and the two recorders automatically reversed each tape at the forty-five-minute mark to capture each reading consisting of ninety minutes, including translation activities.

It was a complicated reality for me, having to be mindful of managing the recorders and tapes while being highly concentrated and engaged as a channel to be able to give each client a high-level spiritual reading. All of this included allowing Saint Germain to come through and take over my vocal cords to speak, when needed or desired. While it may sound like a juggling act, after getting into the swing of it, all went very smoothly. (Please note that sometimes a reading went beyond the capacity of the tape, accounting for a lack of a formal closing on some of the readings.)

We started each morning at 10 a.m. with the first client and from that moment to 60 days later I listened intently to person after person, poured my heart out and had tears in my eyes many times, hearing stories and feeling the life situation of each person. I adjusted quickly to the routine and remained diligently on time for every reading and convened each one exactly on time. Such discipline is vital to the seriousness of my profession, and I did not vary from a strict, but an obvious, semi-relaxed atmosphere and schedule as I went about the business of mediumship.

It was obvious to me that Heaven, by way of my agent Gayle, had planned this experience, I gave much, and I got much. Prior to this experience, I had already given thousands of spiritual readings, so nothing about the process of reading was new—except the experience of reading for one Japanese after another. I did not find the Japanese *inscrutable* as some from the West find people from the East. I encountered those of various ages, sizes, shapes, and degrees of spiritual awareness and enlightenment.

As the days passed and I looked at this one and that one, I saw in them people of a very similar look and personality to what I had seen in the West. After all, we all bleed, we all laugh and cry, we are all spirits spending some time on earth and we are all destined to return to the place, the spirit world, from which we came. At heart and human-wise, I found we are not so different.

Reality Dawns

On the last day of October, while sitting on the diminutive couch lengthwise with my longer Western legs hanging over and down the right arm, I suddenly realized that, while I had just finished one month, I still had another month to go! Though I was not suffering, I was very tired at the end of each day and needed plenty of sleep each night to get through the entire two months.

At that point, I immediately became depressed. "How will I do it; how will I get through another 30 days and 35 more people?!" It was not so much self-pity, as it was realizing the practical challenge of continuing on—I could not lessen my focus or decrease my dedication and determination while serving the remaining Japanese brothers and sisters—as I called them in my heart—who were already scheduled to have a spiritual reading with me.

I dwelled for 15 to 20 minutes in this depressed state and a vision of what was behind me and in front of me. I had never experienced anything like this degree of desperation before. I didn't want to cry, but I wanted to be relieved of the extreme heaviness that I felt about the work that lay ahead. Otherwise, how could I go on?

Saved by the Light

Suddenly I was overcome with a peace so deep and so profound that I knew my spirit world, the four spirit guides who had worked with me over many years, were present and energetically, mentally, emotionally, physically lifting me up into a spirit of "can do." The sensation of love pouring over me and through me caused all of the heaviness to be lifted completely, and closure came with the words coming from them of: "You will do it, you will get through it, just as you have the last thirty days and in the same way, one day at a time!"

In that moment, I experienced a great sense of relief followed by unbelievable elation and peace. The depression and dread had disappeared and instead I became mentally very clear and filled with the conviction that I would experience complete success with each reading ahead. And Heaven, over and above my own human frailty and weaknesses, would walk beside me and provide, when needed, spiritual support and inspiration in the hours and days ahead.

In the end, that is exactly what happened. On the final day, November 28, 2003, after doing the last reading, I felt immense gratitude, pride, and happiness. All had worked out. Seventy dear Japanese souls had been served with a spiritual reading and the overflowing blessings of their spirit world in attendance.

A Satisfying Conclusion

My feeling at the time was one of elation—it does not get any better than this! All my mediumship experiences up to this point told me that we had been successful and the spiritual seeds that were sown would continue to germinate and grow in the minds and hearts of those precious 70 souls in Japan.

My work was done. I could go home now and back to a world quite different in many ways but, nonetheless, a world also filled with countless other people who were searching. Some of them would find their way, through the guidance and direction of spirit, to my door, that I might be a channel to seek to bring Heaven down to Earth for them and, in turn, each one closer to their Real Self and the Source and Creator.

I was and still am grateful that Gayle approached me at the Wesak Festival, *Buddha's birthday,* no less, and that Heaven used her to bring me to Japan. Years later, as I went over each transcript of the taped readings preparing them for this publication, I was deeply touched while recalling person after person, remembering them and our time together. Just the sheer truth found in the words—and the sensation of spirit between the lines—spoke volumes as to the authenticity of the readings and their genuine, life-altering effect on each person. Reading these transcriptions many years later, was the first time I ever had a chance to recapture the beauty and lovely drama that unfolded in that 800 square foot condo in Shinjuku, Japan. I knew that I had to publish them not only for history but mostly because of the sacredness of each one who came before me seeking their spirit world's presence and guidance.

Did it make a difference? I'll let you answer that question as you read through one reading after another. Just don't be surprised at what you also learn about them and yourself. This is how and why I came to Japan and the contents of the book will tell you the rest of the story.

THE
SPIRITUAL
READINGS

THE PATH TO SELF-MASTERY

Itsuki W.—Male

Philip Burley (PB): First of all, welcome! When I do a reading, I go back and forth between trance and semi-trance, so unless I listen to the tape, I don't really know what was said. I work so closely with Saint Germain that I don't know when he will come in, because it always happens very spontaneously. I will hold your written questions in my hand so I can feel your vibration, but I will hand them back to you periodically so you can read the next one. Just be very relaxed.

Let's begin with a prayer.

Our Heavenly Father and Mother, descend at this time so this young man can receive from you all that he needs today. Lead him through this experience to reach the goals you intend for him in this life. I ask all of his guides and teachers to come very close to me to pass on the information he needs to receive. Thank you for this wonderful privilege to serve him today. May he receive healing energy from you and know that he has been visited by heaven. All this I pray with a grateful heart and mind in divine love. Amen.

You are in a period of transition right now, and by this we mean significant spiritual change. They show me your third eye, and it is very, very sensitive. As you get older, you are going to have the ability to experience significant clairvoyance. My guide Tiffany just said, "He has a good balance between his left brain and his right brain." And I see many, many books around you.

Balance of the Left and Right Brain

IW: I have many books.

PB: I don't know that, but that's what they are showing me. You have a very brilliant mind, and Albert Einstein works with you. He is standing behind you and a little bit to your right. His reason for being with you is your intelligence, but also the spiritual things he wants to bring through you, because you are going to write books. Do you like to write?

IW: No, I don't like it, though I do like to write little memos once in a while.

PB: I didn't like to write either, but I have now published three books. You never know what is going to happen. But that is one of the reasons he is working with you. You are not going to work on an atomic bomb or anything like that! I also see comic books. Do you read comic books?

IW: Yes.

PB: They are showing me comic books all around you.

IW: Comic books are huge in Japan.

PB: I don't know that, but I am just seeing a lot of comic books around you.

In terms of your spiritual growth, you are standing still right now. There is a gentleman wearing a Japanese costume from several hundred years ago who stands directly behind you. He is not a samurai. I don't know if scholars in Japan wore special costumes, but it feels that way. Did they?

IW: I think so, yes.

PB: He is a scholarly person, and also a Buddhist. He is telling me that he too had a very good balance between his left and right brain. He lived probably around two or three hundred years ago, and he achieved mastery through the martial arts. Have you taken martial arts?

IW: I took a little bit of Judo in school, but I am really bad at sports.

PB: That doesn't matter, as it's not the reason this person is with you. You are not going to become a sumo wrestler! In this gentleman's presence the feeling is that he was very devout. He is dedicated to higher spiritual things. He is telling me that he has been with you ever since you were born, and he shows me very clearly that he not only leads you on your path, but when you make mistakes, he helps straighten out your path. The energy around this gentleman is pure white.

Spiritual Sensitivity

Your energy has a lot of gold in it. And as I am becoming more attuned to you, there is electricity coming into my body that goes across my back, down my arms, and through my hands. I don't know how to describe it except to say that you are like an open vessel for spiritual energy. I don't know if you will ever do formal healing, but you have an innate receptivity to healing energies that you can pass on to others. I don't know if you have gone to channeling school or not, but spirit shows me your throat chakra. There is above-average sensitivity in this chakra. But deep inside you are still trying to decide who you are. Do you understand?

IW: Yes, and I want to make that decision.

PB: Yes. In the beginning, they showed me that this is a major question on your paper, so go ahead and read that question out loud.

IW: On the paper, it is written that you say you have to master yourself, and I don't understand what that means. What are you supposed to master? In order for me to master myself, what are the things inside of me that I am still lacking?

PB: Okay I am going to let Saint Germain come through and speak.

Saint Germain (SG): This is Saint Germain. Can you hear me?

IW: Yes.

SG: I am very pleased to be with you and in your energies today. First of all, you are a pure soul. Your motives are pure. And while we don't look upon you as a religious person, you are a spiritual person.

Path to Self-Mastery

I came on earth to teach about self-mastery. It has to do with learning to direct our thoughts and actions towards good outcomes—to think good thoughts and act accordingly. To think and act correctly is the way to self-mastery. Most people in the world today know what is right but don't know how to do it. They start out with good intentions and even a plan of action, but they fail to stay focused. They head in the direction of their goals and then get waylaid.

If we know what is right and good, then that is what we should do, but most of us cannot make ourselves do that. We imagine and daydream about what is good, but then we don't act. Sometimes we just become lazy, and sometimes we forget what we were going to do. At other times, we become distracted by something and lose our direction.

So to answer your question, self-mastery has to do with directing your thoughts and acting upon them to achieve the right ends.

Ultimately, self-mastery has to do with loving correctly—that is, loving all people as yourself, unconditionally. To the person who achieves self-mastery in this area, there are no strangers. When such a person sees another person, he sees himself. The reason Jesus Christ of Nazareth stands out among the greatest of masters is that he achieved that kind of love. He had it from childhood, you see. Even as a child, he was so concerned about others that he was at the temple talking to the priests about those things.

To sum up, to achieve self-mastery is to have right thinking, right action, and right results. And the most essential right thought, right action, and right results is loving others as yourself. To know in your mind what love is and act accordingly to bring about the right result is self-mastery. Does this help you?

IW: Okay.

SG: (Chuckle) Just okay? Isn't this answer better than okay?

IW: Very good.

SG: Very good; that's better. I, Saint Germain, work very hard to bring you the information about self-mastery. I know about self-mastery because I achieved it, and I want to make sure you don't take my words for granted because you are born for the same achievement. But first you must understand yourself and the concept of unconditional love.

In any case, let's go to your next question.

IW: I want you to teach me about the innermost part of my spirit or about my level of spiritual growth. What are the particular themes I need to focus on in order to reach the next step?

SG: The answer to that question was just given, but I will refine and add to what I've said. The first part of your question is about the level.

IW: Yes. Please tell me about my soul or about my spirit.

Stages of Spiritual Growth

SG: Yes. First of all, I have said that you are a pure soul. You have good teachers. The spirit of the Archangel Michael works with you, and if you don't know him, look him up. Learn about him because he is going to be with you throughout your life on earth. He is a protector and an educator, but, above all, he is an educator in angelic love.

Now about your soul or spirit: You came into this life to be who you are. Your parents named you, but it was God who gave you spiritual birth. You came directly out of God as all human beings do. The energy that brought you to the earth plane is God's love and God's light in a solidified form. That is your core energy and always shall be. By whatever name you give it, it is the core of yourself, and it is truly the only part of you that will live forever. Your physical body will grow old, as all human bodies do, and die one day and disappear back into the earth eventually. Only your spirit—your eternal Self—will remain and be rejoined with God from whom it came.

IW: Yes, I understand.

SG: Good, I know you do, but I need to hear that. Your true ultimate self is really from God. Your parents gave you your name, and your body came through the bodies of your parents, but everything else came from God. You did not decide the color of your eyes, the color or kind of skin you would have, or your birth in Japan or in any other country. All of this was decided for you. In truth, you are really not in control as much as you think you are; at least while you are in this body.

You came into this life as a soul in a body, like all human beings do. You did not come here, especially you, just to be preoccupied with a career or business. Fundamentally, essentially, you came here to work on your spirituality. There is no way that you would be sitting here before this channeler if it were not in your life's design to work primarily on the spiritual portion of yourself.

Your being here today to talk about these things can be a turning point for you. At the beginning of this reading we said that you are in a period of great transition. This does not mean something dramatic or traumatic, but there is an earthquake going on inside your soul. Your inner self is trying to come out, and that is why you have the kind of questions you have. Your inner self is asking those questions so it can be freed. What I am speaking of is the central purpose of your life. Don't stop searching, and don't stop asking questions.

As for where your spirit is, I told you that you are a pure soul. If there were three stages to life in terms of spiritual growth, you are in the second stage. And if the second stage had three stages within it, you would be in the second stage. You are, therefore, right in the middle between the lower world and the upper world. That is a good place to be in at your age, and you are on target. If you remain a pure soul, it will not take you many years to achieve the upper levels of spiritual growth. Just do not waste time on foolish pursuits because your life is precious. You need to move forward to discover in what capacity and in what form God wants to use you.

You are in a good place, so don't worry. Just keep on keeping on. I am going to leave Philip now to let him come back. If I think I need to speak again, I shall come back through. This is Saint Germain.

PB: Did you get your answer?

IW: Yes.

PB: Good, you may ask your next question.

Spiritual Perception

IW: I think Saint Germain answered this question the other day. When you look up at the sky, you know how you sometimes see little dots? I want to know if that is spirit.

PB: Was I in a trance when that was answered?

IW: Yes, and I remember the answer.

PB: Can you repeat what Saint Germain said?

IW: He said it is one of two things. Either you are seeing the very outer part of your eyeball or sometimes you are actually seeing energy in the air.

PB: Yes, you might be seeing microorganisms, but these are not spiritual beings.

IW: Does this have any spiritual meaning?

PB: It is universal phenomena, but some people are more observant than others. I can see it, too.

IW: I can too. I've seen it many times.

PB: And you have to be in a certain light.

IW: Sometimes when you are focusing intently on objects, all of a sudden you can see the energy of that object. I do this sometimes, and I am asking if I should continue with this type of training.

PB: Saint Germain is going to speak again.

SG: I am back, my son. Philip told you that he perceived energy at your third eye, and he mentioned that you had significant ability to ultimately open up in that area. I am coming back through to affirm that yes, you have that gift, and yes, you should work with it.

My driving ambition is to help as many people as possible to awaken to their own inner spiritual gifts, not necessarily to become a channeler, but to realize their own inner power. You can use your gifts to help yourself. For example, if people could read auras, they wouldn't make friends with certain people; and when some people just look at their car, they are sensitive enough to detect an engine problem. Even in outer space, United States astronauts tried to communicate mind to mind. Philip has done that with his students and has been very successful.

There are many, many practical applications for the use of spiritual perception: crime solving, discerning mechanical problems, quick communication in emergencies, and many other such uses demonstrate how important it can be to awaken one's spiritual power. Can you imagine a world in which telephones are not necessary? You will not find one telephone, cell phone or otherwise, in the spirit world except in a laboratory where they are trying to bring new inventions to the earth plane. If we want to communicate with someone and invite them to dinner, we just send out a thought and it reaches them in a nanosecond, and their answer comes back the same way. What a convenient gift! I am speaking at length about this because I want to inspire you to become inspired yourself to develop your own awareness. Have we answered your question on this point?

IW: Part of it, but I have more to ask about it.

SG: Yes?

IW: I would like to use this gift to make a living, but I do not know how to put this gift to such a practical use. Do you have any ideas about this?

Practical Application of Spirituality

SG: I am looking at the movie of your life. Why do you think all the information thus far is pointing in this direction? You may not know how to make your gift useful in a job, but God does. In order to be successful with any gift, you have to study everything you can about the particular field you are entering into. To develop this gift, you have to practice it. You must learn how to meditate and pray to communicate quite literally with God within and quite literally with your master teachers and guides in the spirit world. Then the door will open wide for you, and you will be most useful.

Philip did not particularly want to do this kind of work. But even at the age of four he had visions. He saw himself speaking before very large audiences, and he saw that he would become known for this work. He did not consciously pursue it, but it pursued him. He had no choice but to become a channeler because it was in his spiritual genes or DNA. You are the same kind of person, and that is why it is so easy for him to read for you. You are yet young, but he, too, looked very young at your age.

Set your sights upon your spiritual gifts and your desire to use them in your occupation. There is a very appropriate saying that what you think about all day long is what you become. Philip became what he is because all he thought about all day long was this work, and his work demonstrates that what you think about is what you become. If you truly feel called to work in this field, then focus, focus, and focus more on doing that. If you do this, you can't go wrong.

I, Saint Germain, am here in Japan to find people like you; not to do your work for you or to take over your life, but to help you help yourself. Call upon me. I am good at what I do, and I will help you. Perhaps in the future if Philip returns, we can meet again. Do your best; with or without his return.

Now I am going to leave Philip and let him come back, and we shall see what we shall hear. This is Saint Germain.

PB: Do you have another question?

Relationships and Appreciation of Self

IW: It's about relationships. As soon as I start to talk to people and want to ask a question so I can get to know them better, a lot of fear comes up inside, and I am not able to continue to ask the questions. How can I overcome this? Do I need to overcome this fear, or am I getting a message that I am not supposed to ask that question or get to know that person? Why do I feel this fear inside?

PB: How old are you?

IW: Thirty-seven years old.

PB: I have the same problem. Now this is me talking, but I am a spiritual being also, and the spirits around you will also be speaking about this. You struggle with self-acceptance, and that's the core problem. When you think of yourself or look at yourself, you can't see the fullness of who you are. Most pure souls are this way. If you could see your inner power, you might have misused it. It happens all the time.

There are people who love themselves or believe in themselves too much, thinking that the power to do things resides in them, and when they come across their own spiritual power, they misuse it. Those who do the highest and best work are very pure souls, and they give credit to God and others outside themselves. That's who you are, so until now God has hidden your power from you. You were given a sense of inadequacy on purpose, so you would be aware of your own sensitivity. But now, in this transition I talked about at the beginning, it is time for you to turn it all around and use your sensitivity for your good and not allow it to cause you to feel fear.

Aside from feeling inadequate, you also tend to put others higher than you, thinking "They are better than I am; they are higher than I am," or "They will be critical or laugh at me if I ask any questions." All of this is deep inside, from your childhood, and it's within you on a subconscious level. For example, to my eyes, you are very handsome, but you probably don't see yourself that way. Am I correct?

IW: Yes.

PB: Yes. You need to hear that—not to feel flattered, but to know that your appearance is a part of your power. God can use it for the good of others. Since childhood and as I grew up, I always thought I was ugly. I wore glasses beginning in the fifth grade, and I always felt inferior and inadequate. I was very thin, and all the other boys were big, so in my mind, I felt like an inferior human being. Does this sound familiar?

IW: Yes.

PB: It took me many years to make the transition from rejecting to accepting myself, and you can save many years of suffering by hearing this from someone like me. It's not because I'm special, but in this setting your energy is very open, and there are holy and high spirits here. In this environment, the information goes in quicker and deeper than in other situations, and there is healing energy all around you, right now.

From now on when you look in the mirror, I want you to really see your own handsomeness. Your features are very even, and there is a good contrast between your black hair and fair skin. Your ears and facial features are well balanced, so you need to start changing your thoughts about your appearance.

Also accept what Saint Germain has said about your own purity and goodness. Just accept it and start living that way. Yes, you have made mistakes and may continue to make them like every human being does, but essentially you are a good person. If you start living this way, then when you approach people to ask questions, there will be no fear. Watch and see what happens. Today is a big turning point for you. When you walk with spirit and God, most of these things just go away by themselves. Is all of this helpful?

IW: Yes.

PB: Please ask your next question.

IW: I already asked about my gift of clairvoyance, but I want to know if I have other spiritual gifts.

PB: Yes, you have the ability to channel healing energies.

IW: Can I ask a question about my physical body?

PB: Yes.

Physical Health

IW: I have several questions about my physical health. First, I have pressure in my head where it almost feels like something is holding my head and pushing on a certain area. Second, I have a very weak stomach and digestive system. I also know I have a hormone imbalance, and a doctor said it's from the pituitary gland. He said the pituitary gland is not producing enough life hormone. Very few of my sperm are living, so it would be very difficult, the doctor said, for me to produce life. Is there any way this problem can be resolved?

PB: The pressure that you feel in your head is related to your natural inclination towards clairvoyance. I do not know about your sperm, but they say there is modern medicine that can balance the pituitary gland.

With most physical problems, the root cause is spiritual and in the soul. Part of your reality in terms of imbalance has to do with your self-image or how you think about yourself. Many of the people I work with are healed by a change in the way they think about themselves because thought energy is constantly broadcast to every cell of our bodies. Consequently, if someone has in mind the thought that they are inadequate or unworthy, all of the cells get the same message. This doesn't mean that all human diseases are caused by the way people think or that you should ignore your doctor, but it's important to know what is happening on the spiritual or energetic level.

You should work with your doctor to strike a balance between working on the spiritual side and the practical, physical side to find remedies. In many cases, doctors can treat you, but if the spiritual understanding is missing, no matter what the doctor does, the solution doesn't come. I think you know this already.

They are not showing me whether your condition will be totally healed, but the most important thing about health issues and life itself is to always think positively. Everything is karmic in that it happens to teach us about us. We never know what heaven is doing or how heaven is working to teach us, so we have to be discerning and watch and listen.

Let's go to your next question.

IW: Since my head hurts, does that mean I should stop trying to use my clairvoyance?

PB: No. Some mediums or channelers have severe pain for a while because spirit is working with them, but as they fully open, the pain goes away. In your case I don't know, so you should work on opening and see if the pain diminishes. Don't ignore medical advice, but work on the spiritual side as well. Are you sitting with a circle of people, or a group that you are happy with?

IW: Yes I am. I am happy with part of it and not so happy with another part of it.

PB: Get what you can from the experience, because in spiritual work, there is seldom perfection. To get where I am, I worked with people some would call abnormal, but I learned a lot. The most important thing I learned is to love all people equally, whether or not I thought they were "normal." Has anyone done any healing work on you to try to ease your pain?

IW: Yes, many times.

PB: Keep working on opening your clairvoyance and on balancing medical and spiritual healing approaches.

Upbringing and Sense of Inadequacy

How is your relationship with your parents?

IW: My father has already passed away.

PB: How long ago?

IW: Six months ago, in March.

PB: What did he die of?

IW: Stomach cancer. My father never talked much, but he had a negative perspective on things. I respected him quite a bit, but I was afraid of him, so I wasn't able to talk to him.

PB: That is where your sense of inadequacy began. When I am working with Japanese people, in America or here, they often feel inadequate or inferior because their parents have been so critical of them. In your father's generation and to some extent in this generation, there is no tolerance for mistakes, but that is unrealistic and causes unnecessary emotional pain.

Just before you, I read for someone whose mother was so cruelly critical that she suffered from a sense of inferiority all of her life. Because she loves her mother, she believes what her mother says about her and thinks it is true. Right at the beginning of her reading I asked her if she had a question about her mother, and we spent the whole time talking about how she could overcome the negative influence that her mother had on her mind. I think it is a major problem in many Japanese families. Your generation will teach your children differently because you have the benefit of more education and understanding.

Let's go to your next question.

IW: There was one question I really wanted to ask, but now I have forgotten it. I am really worried about my spleen and my stomach. I have been worried about these two areas for years.

PB: Most of these problems are related to emotions. There is a Chinese doctor working with you in spirit, a chi gong master. I see this guide very clearly. The deeper we are getting into this, the more I realize that your nerves are affecting your physical body. You tend to have excessive worry about your health. This doesn't mean you don't have health problems, but you worry too much about them.

A part of the transition you are in will be a change in your whole thinking about your body and your spirit. I am not saying that you don't have any problems with your body, but you do not have problems to the extreme that you think you do. The reality is that, wherever our thought is, that's where energy goes. When you are worried about some part of your body, just send love there. Then you will gain the power to heal yourself.

Because I am a public speaker, I have to be careful of my throat. Sometimes I would get a sore throat before a speaking engagement, and I would then go into meditation and tell my throat to be well. I still practice that, exercising the power of the mind. This is related to what I said earlier about looking in the mirror and saying, "I am handsome," or "I love you." See yourself as being healthy and whole.

The Chinese doctor who works with you in spirit is Dr. Lee, and he wants to work through you with healing in the future. But right now, when you just sit quietly, call him in, and he will work on your whole body. Dr. Lee is very capable of working with you.

Okay, we just have two minutes left.

Fulfillment of Dreams

IW: Many times in my life I have had a dream of doing something but was not able to do it. I know I have created this tendency in myself, but I am just not sure what to do about it.

PB: There are no accidents. The important point is that you tried, and we don't have to accomplish everything we think we should. The reason you didn't accomplish some things was that you weren't supposed to. Most of us dream of all kinds of things and try many of them, but we don't accomplish most of them! Once you are in total attunement with heaven, however, what you dream of will always be fulfilled. The key to your life and the fulfillment of your dreams is to be in attunement with heaven. For such people miracles happen. Without their asking, what they want comes to them.

IW: I know the session is over, but I just remembered my really important question.

PB: It is only going to be one hundred dollars more, go ahead and ask. I'm *joking*! (Laughter)

IW: I haven't met a partner yet. When I am healed, will I meet my lifetime female partner?

PB: Yes, you will, but you must first go through the transition we have been talking about.

End of recording

LIFE EXPERIENCES AND SPIRITUAL GUIDANCE

Riko S.—Female

Philip Burley (PB): I like to open with a prayer.

> *Father, wherever we are, you are. We are the object of your love, and your energy is always a part of us, so as we turn even verbally toward you, you are here. Thank you so much for your presence.*
>
> *This woman has asked for this opportunity to communicate with her spirit world. Open the door very, very wide for her, please, to bring the answers to questions on this paper, but also to those in her heart and mind not written here. I ask, as always, for the teachers and guides to come very close to me and to coordinate with my guides. Thank you for this blessed opportunity to do this work for her. All this I pray in divine love.*

The first thing that is shown around you, going out a distance of many feet, is an energy—not an aura—that is hard to explain, but it is an all-white light. I haven't seen this before, and the light is like billowing clouds. There is also an angelic force with you. They appear very clearly, standing behind you. There are three of them, and they are talking to me, saying wherever you go, they go, and they are always there guarding.

You have a violet aura. On the outer edges, it is pearl white, but inside it is a beautiful violet color. Next to your body is violet, and the outer edge is pearl in color. Though I don't understand why exactly, Dr. Palmer who works with me is right behind you, pouring energy into you, particularly through the heart chakra. Have you been a bit tired or a little heavy in the heart?

RS: Yes.

Kwan Yin

PB: They are just giving this energy, and it is a green light that is coming into you. As the energy goes in, they are showing me that the green light is causing each atom to spin more. I have never seen this before.

Standing behind you is the spirit of Kwan Yin, just beautifully radiating pink light all around. She is talking to me about your speaking the truth of things. She says that you are in a period in your life involving major decisions, and now is not the time to pull back.

RS: What does "pull back" mean?

PB: They are saying you should speak the truth of things as they come up, and don't pull back from the truth. Also, while you may have some doubts about different things that have happened to you, there are no mistakes; there are no accidents. Everything that has happened is as it is supposed to be.

Do you have a question on your paper either about your husband or your marriage?

RS: I didn't ask about my husband because I know he's happy over there. I want to know who brought me the message about him.

PB: Well, first of all, he is standing here, just to your right, and he has tears on his cheeks. He says that he knows that you are okay, but he wanted to make an appearance. He says, "I am happy to be with you, and I just want you to know I am still climbing the ladder of life," meaning that he is doing his best to go higher and higher in spiritual understanding and growth.

The feeling with him is that you were more aware of and more sensitive towards spiritual things, inner things, than he was, and he is now catching up, as it were. He is crying and says that he never really leaves your side. He is sorry for things he didn't understand and for the times when things were difficult. I am waiting for him to tell me who it was that brought the message to you about him. (Pause) It was Kwan Yin. She is working with you, and she is even helping you with your finances.

Okay, I took a little time because I was scanning your energy field. You are very sensitive in the third eye, and you are sensitive in clairaudience. Saint Germain is right here, to my right. He just touched me, and a great amount of heat is coming over me. He said, "Don't doubt either the authenticity or the accuracy of your receiving from spirit." He is going to come through in a moment.

Saint Germain (SG): I am here. This is Saint Germain. Can you hear me all right?

RS: Yes, I can hear you.

Saint Germain and the Violet Light

SG: I am so pleased to be here through Philip. God bless you, dear one. I don't know if you can feel it, but I am radiating a tremendous amount of energy toward you right now. It is called by Philip "electric love."

I want you to know also, that I, Saint Germain, am more here today than I have ever been because of you. It is a special day for me because I am able to make a more specific appearance through Philip than at any other time. This morning I made an appearance to him also, in which I said I would be more penetrating of his energies than in the past. But I also felt your pull today and I came to you likewise. Don't ever doubt it.

I want to tell you the reason why Philip saw the violet light around you. It's because you are being guided by me. I have been waiting for some time to get your attention. I want you to find out as much as possible about me, so that I can draw closer to help guide you. I am creating, as I have told Philip, a circle of people around the world today. It is my responsibility in these latter days to do this. These are not just any people interested in the metaphysical field, but rather individuals who have a significant inclination towards the ability to channel or to be psychic. Here and there on my journey in Japan, I am meeting such people through Philip. You are one of those.

You are a more advanced soul than those I am used to meeting. You are truly interested in this phenomenon, not for the sake of phenomena alone, but because you want to spiritually understand and grow. That is the vital prerequisite for me to work with someone. There are many people, as you know, who channel, and often the channeling becomes an end in itself. But it doesn't matter one whit to me about channeling, it just happens to be a means by which I can work on earth to bring the truth. Because you and I will have connections in the future, I wanted to say this much to you on a personal level about me.

Your husband is a very willing student here in the spirit world. He loves to sing here, and he sits very patiently to learn all that he can from the masters. Happy is not a full enough word to describe his mood. He is indeed surprised and thrilled with his life here in spirit, and your prayers and your thoughts have contributed greatly to his elevation. So beloved one, you should take great comfort in the reality of his joy and the fact that you have helped him to experience it. I am going to stay here with Philip, and if I think it is necessary to return to speak, I shall do so. This is Saint Germain.

PB: Let's start with your questions. Saint Germain just told me he is coming back in.

SG: I am here again. This is Saint Germain. Can you hear me?

RS: Yes, I can hear you.

SG: Now state your question, please.

RS: You have said that I have the potential for being a medium who can channel spirit, correct?

SG: Yes.

RS: You said that you have been trying to connect with me for some time. I understand that. However, I just don't know exactly how to contact and connect with you.

Spiritual Sensitivity

SG: As far as contacting and connecting with me as you did prior to coming here today, I heard you. How did you make contact with me this morning? Think about it.

RS: I felt some energy, so I asked and sensed your presence.

SG: Yes. And so, dear one, you are already a medium. As I told you, you are an advanced soul. That doesn't mean that you can begin tomorrow to give readings for people, but it is not far off, if you should decide to do it.

You see, because of your spiritual life, you are very much attuned already. One does not necessarily have to be praying and meditating all the time to be sensitive. There are some mothers who are so busy with their children they have no time to meditate, pray, or even think about themselves. They are so busy serving others that they create within themselves a spiritual sensitivity. Many are looking for where they can go to serve God, but when you serve others with all your heart, you are already serving God who lives in them. One does not necessarily have to be religious in the classical sense in order to be used by us.

Philip happens to be one who does pray and meditate regularly. That is his path. This does not mean that you can't learn meaningful meditation methodologies and use them; you can. That will serve to enhance your already established spiritual openness. If you are at all interested in meditation, Philip will be giving a course next week in which he will give the basics of learning to become open to spirit and be used by spirit through meditation.

But I tell you, even if you do not have that meditation methodology, the method you used this morning will work well. The goal of meditation is to learn to come into attunement with spirit. Attunement is the end, and meditation, whether long or short, is the means unto that end. Very quickly this morning you attuned to me, and they told you, yes, it was me. What else could we want? You did very well. Do you have any further questions on this matter?

RS: No, I don't.

SG: Good. That means either you are afraid to ask more, or you really understand everything. I am just joking with you!

Study of the Physical Body

RS: I am studying about the physical body, kinesiology, polarity, and facial reflexology. Should I be studying more about that? Of course, I want to go deeper.

SG: As your soul is speaking to you in its desire, follow that desire. That is the voice of God within you, so don't hesitate. Learn to obey that inner voice.

RS: It is quite expensive, so I have to consider my finances. I am not sure which course to take . . .

SG: Step by step. Yes, you can take one, then another.

RS: Which one should be the first?

SG: We think the one on polarity, because it is the basis for much of all you are learning. But again, many people have the idea that spirit knows everything, but only God knows everything. I can discern various things when I look at you, and your guides and teachers around you are signaling me and helping me respond, but at the same time there are certain things which we leave up to you to discern, particularly a student like you, who is intended to use their spiritual senses to help others. You have to learn the path yourself in many ways.

That is what my medium did. He had teachers, but those teachers could not be inside of him—like he could be inside of himself, or God could be inside of him. For many of his questions he had to go deep inside and learn to listen and trust the answer. When he did that, everything always came out as it needed to. That is part of the talent, you see, and you have it, as you demonstrated with me this morning. When you felt my energy, you asked if it was me and you got the confirmation that yes, this is Saint Germain.

Life Experiences and Spiritual Guidance

Don't be afraid of making mistakes. You will, but more often you will be correct, and even mistakes teach us. Most people in this field are afraid to step out because they are afraid of making mistakes, but the analogy I use often is that the child who is afraid to fall down on his bicycle will never learn to ride. The child who falls down here and there will learn to stay up. You will make mistakes in this work, but the further you go in it, the fewer mistakes you will make.

RS: I understand.

SG: Very good. I want to just say one more thing. That is, more than the average person, you were born to go through struggles, particularly inner struggles. So it is with my medium, and most people who will aspire to, or be inspired to, go toward this direction. For if you are going to help other people, and help many of them, you must have a wide variety of experiences in order to empathize with them. If you have no such experiences, you have no basis upon which to help them. Through the experiences you have already had, you know how to overcome sorrow, you know how to save money, and you know how to do things that many people do not know. In this way, you will become an authority. Never take any difficulty or struggle negatively. Take it as an opportunity to learn from it and grow. We see that you already do that.

You may go on to your next question. I shall stay here.

Dreaming and Spiritual Awakening

RS: When my daughter was young, she had a dream that she went to Polaris, to the North Star. When she had the dream, she told me about it, but now she denies the dream, and says it is my imagination. When I talk about spiritualism, she hates it. Why?

SG: The dream has two meanings. One is that she went there, and the other is that the North Star represents God. It means that eventually she will turn to God. Right now she is rejecting all of this because of her peer group and because of her growing intellect that argues with the spiritual side. It happens to many young people.

Right now your daughter must be in denial because her intellect is wrestling with her spiritual side; but have complete faith that the day will come when she will reawaken, and before she passes into the spirit world, she will turn to God. She will awaken and accept the spiritual aspects of reality. It is her destiny, so don't worry. Just be at peace and let her be. Let her go through what she is going through. The less you talk about it, the less defensive she will be. Does that bring you comfort?

RS: Yes.

SG: Yes. She has to go her path. Often the path towards awakening is downward at first, because the soul must enter a place where it becomes a little lost before it seeks to find why it is lost and begins to find its way out. This is not atypical. But there is a gold star that appears above her head, so we know from this side that she is destined to succeed, and she is destined for a public life of some sort and a spiritual life.

May we have your next question, please?

Physical and Spiritual Sensitivity; Self-Protection

RS: I have a problem with my nose and throat, my sternum area, and my thymus; also my hip joint and my knee. Sometimes everything is okay except my nose, which is always a problem.

SG: Part of this is the climate you live in, and part of it has to do with a certain chemical imbalance within your body.

RS: When I tested myself using kinesiology, my brain refused connection. I was not able to be treated using kinesiology, because my eyes moved right and left at certain times, and my body did not accept the work that was done. Do you feel this is caused by the chemical imbalance?

SG: A chemical imbalance is part of your problem. But you are also ultra-sensitive, so what works for others may not always work for you. It is the same with my medium. You see, to do the kind of work that you are doing, your chemical makeup is altogether different from that of the average person; otherwise spirit could not use you. I am coming through Philip, overshadowing his mind and his vocal cords. This is not just taking him over like a puppet. It is also a chemical-electrical process. The chemicals within the physical body must be of a certain kind and must be very well balanced in order to do this work, so sometimes the body becomes depleted.

My medium is in a period like that now, having been used so much during this trip, and we are working to bring his chemistry back into balance. I tell him here and there what to do in order to help this happen. For example, to his right is a glass of orange juice. Normally he does not drink any liquid other than water with some vitamins in it during these sessions, but I told him before this session, "You need vitamin C." He also puts certain vitamins and minerals in the orange juice for this reason, because he knows his chemistry is low, or off balance. He is getting his balance back now, as you can see, because I am able to come through in a powerful way. This indicates that he is coming back into a higher level and a true balance that we can work through effectively.

You have the same problem as he has. Mediums, psychics, and channelers often are ignorant of this reality, and they use up their energy very quickly. Either they do not have longevity in this work, or they keep trying to do it, becoming less and less effective because the chemistry is off balance.

RS: When I meet somebody or even when I'm on the telephone with someone, I receive their aura or energy, and my body receives their exact condition sometimes for a couple of days or even months. How can I handle this better?

SG: My medium has the same problem, but actually it is a gift. When he was a child, he would feel the pain of other people's bodies, and this would affect him greatly. Periodically, people are healed in his presence, because there is the reality of his sensitivity and our ability to use him to heal others. You have the same gift, you see.

To protect yourself, don't listen too much to people's sad stories or their health problems. If someone is going to talk to you about their problems, simply put the white light around you and say to your soul, "We will not take this on. We will listen, but we will not take it on." Then it will not come into you. You can still help people, emphasize with them, and sense their situation, but you will not take on their symptoms.

Philip learned through his childhood to ask people, "How are you?" and they would tell him. And if they had a cold or sore throat or some other problem, he would pick it up, and it would take him sometimes days or weeks to throw it off. By putting the white light around himself and actively refusing to take conditions on, while still empathizing and treating others, he could be effective. But from time to time, he has taken on some of the illness or karma of others, even here, and he must take care to restore his strength and energy at times.

All of you who are called to the high level are called to be masters of taking on karma but also ridding yourself of karma. Sometimes, if you are doing healing work with your hands, run them under cold water, and that will kill the vibration so it will not attach itself to you. You can also just shake the etheric energy off your hands. I cannot do it through his body, but I can imagine shaking it off. If you do these things consistently, the problems of others will not become a part of you.

The worst part of the work of a medium is the same as the worst part of the work that Jesus of Nazareth did. Jesus loved people so much that he didn't discern. He had so much compassion that he brought difficulty into his own body. That is why he often went off alone, to throw the energy off. Sometimes he was so compassionate that it would take him a long time to get rid of the pain and infirmity in his own body. If you remember from scripture, as Jesus walked through a crowd of people, one woman touched the hem of his robe—his garment—and he said, "I felt power go from me." So he was saying, "I felt my power, based on empathy, go from me." His energy went to heal the woman who had touched his robe. It was drawn upon in that instance.

But the ultimate secret, dear one, is to make sure you connect with God above as the source so that you will be replenished, and also to allow that energy to stream through you to do the work instead of using up your own energies. That is the ultimate secret, and there is a technique or a methodology for that. That is part of all the things you are learning, is it not?

RS: I am not learning that yet.

SG: It will be a part of what you will learn. If not, you can ask Philip.

RS: Can I call somebody if I don't know how to feel my daughter's energy in my body or know whether it is really her energy or my imagination?

SG: Her core is high energy, so don't worry about that. That is what will ultimately bring her back to awaken and accept spirituality and the phenomena of receiving spirit again.

RS: But if I don't know about a person, should I call that energy to me to be able to help the person? Or doesn't it matter?

SG: You can do that in order to help them, but do not take the energy on to the point that you develop their symptoms. You see, when we care too much, and we don't have discernment to know just how to hold the energy but not to take it in and keep it, then we become victims of that energy.

RS: You are saying to protect our own body?

SG: That is correct, that is absolutely correct. You are not the savior of the world, and your job is not to take on other people's karma. If it happens to be your job to take it on in spite of yourself, you will take it on if necessary, no matter what else you do. Some masters do take it on, and I did that when I was on earth.

My medium does it periodically. He will purposely ask God to give him the pain, and then he will burn it up in prayer and meditation. But he does not do it these days so much. He did that more when he was younger. He was in the healing field, as well as doing spiritual readings, but he got out of it because it drained him too much. It was more than he could handle, and he understood then that his true focus should be the work of mediumship and channeling. You can burn yourself out if you are not careful, because as you interact with spirit, we are drawing on your energy.

Let us go to your next question, please.

Dreams, Apparitions and Atomic Movements

RS: In more than twenty years, I have never remembered my dreams—never. Why? Is there something wrong with me?

SG: You don't need to remember them, and that is why you are not remembering them. Philip very seldom remembers his dreams. That has nothing to do with whether you are spiritually attuned.

RS: Also, I see so many small, tiny, round things moving and gathering in the air. Is this an omen or something like that?

SG: Well, there are two kinds of phenomena. There is one in which there are certain kinds of microorganisms or microscopic things in the eyeball, and when looking in a certain direction, one can see them moving on the surface of the eye. That is one thing.

But those who are spiritually advanced can see various atomic movements. Anyone who is very advanced looking at this couch that I am sitting on through Philip's body would not see it necessarily as solid, but would rather see it as billions of atoms coalesced or gathered together into this configuration to make a couch. That may be part of what you see.

But why does it concern you? It's not important from our perspective. Just know it is a phenomenon taking place and don't place too much importance upon it. And forget omens, because life is what you make it, and that is what mastery is all about. In this world there are many people who are mastered by forces, fear, superstition—all kinds of things. But a true master is one not bothered by any of those things who can master life in the face of all situations. That is a true master. Do you understand?

RS: Yes.

SG: That is what I keep trying to teach Philip—to have no fear and no superstition. Don't attach to any of those ideas or those stories. Be confident that as you live positively, God lives through you. God is in charge of all life, all energy. When you release that God presence within you, through God's presence you become in charge of all things. That is self-mastery.

We will take your next question, please.

RS: You said not to be afraid, but my daughter always has fear. Why and how can I take away her fear?

SG: It depends on what she is afraid of.

RS: Everything—everything. She does not want to be alone.

SG: She is very open spiritually. People like this often have this problem, and they draw other entities to them. We draw to us what we are. Somewhere in her life as a child, she had a situation in which she became fearful and then she built her thought forms upon—

The Earthquake Interrupts

I feel an earthquake.

PB: I am coming out of trance.

RS: It is okay. Oh, it is really rattling over there, wow. (Laughter) I knew there was an earthquake coming.

PB: I did too. I knew today.

RS: We have a lot of these. They come all the time. Maybe in a few more minutes we will have another one like this, because often you have one, then another and another, so it may go on but not for a few minutes.

PB: (Laughter.) (Pause in session)

SG: I am back, did you enjoy the rumble? God was just having fun, shaking the ball of life.

Let us resume the energy we were in before. I remember your question. I am now reviewing what we have said about it. Give me a few moments and I will continue.

Daughter's Fear

I was saying that your daughter's fear can draw an entity to her. These energies can appear from childhood. The opposite of fear is security, and security comes from feeling and knowing one is loved by someone.

The only way to ultimately grow out of such fear is to have enough experiences in which one can feel fear and at the same time watch one's own mind and watch one's own thinking. Just as when the earthquake took place here a few minutes ago, if one examines one's mind, one thought the worst of that event, or of the possibility of the worst, and therefore one's fear grew out of that thought. But if your thought was, "I am protected, because God is with me, I will not be harmed," then no fear can come upon you. As you can see, thought precedes fear.

Therefore, it is the way that your daughter thinks about life; the stories and ideas that she has surrounding her when she is in a room by herself, or in any other circumstances in which she feels fear. The root of that record in her mind goes back to childhood. The best thing you can do, dear one, is to pray for her. Pray for her, and just ask that the root of this problem, whatever that is, be removed.

Ultimately, it will be your daughter who will have to overcome her own fear by exposing herself enough times to things she fears and realizing there is nothing to fear but fear itself. Let's go on to your next question.

RS: I love my daughter. Just when you said my daughter has no security in her mind, I was thinking about attachment. How can she grow in security? Also, I know that she likes one person in particular. Is that person the one for her?

SG: We don't think so, no. She is shopping around. Her soul is shopping around. That special person will come along, so don't be too concerned. Follow the path of affirming. God—and we in spirit—work best in positive energy.

When you are working on healing someone, in your mind's eye you see them getting well, do you not? In other words, if someone has a disease, in your mind, your imagination, you view them as not having the disease, correct? Because if you look at them and imagine them with the disease while trying to heal them, that is contradictory energy.

Therefore, whenever you think of your daughter, no matter what her infirmities are, no matter how difficult, no matter how negative the situation may look around her, do not accept that. Do not push her and tell her that she should be different, because she is what she is. From the standpoint of your helping her, it is important for you to keep the most positive frame of mind.

That energy can have a great effect upon her, just like prayer, affirmations, and mantras. They are all energy and can have a great effect. Hold her in your mind, your imagination, your prayers, your meditations, all of your thoughts, with only positive attitudes. Know that she will become whole. She will be successful. She will find happiness in her life. Just hold those ideas. Then you can rain favorable energy down upon her. Have I made myself clear?

RS: Yes.

SG: Yes. We all have this tendency to worry, but worry does not solve anything. Worry is the projection of the mind visualizing the worst outcome, consciously or unconsciously. It is a disease. The masters imagine only the best outcome and then make it happen. When an earthquake comes, we can't really do anything about it. We can't stop it, can we? If we retain our objectivity, we can put ourselves in a situation to protect ourselves, whereas, if we become overwhelmed and paralyzed, we can't even do the minimum amount of self-protecting.

You have been very interested in spirituality. You're in a final cycle of spirituality at this time which will lead you higher than you have ever gone. You are on the right path, whatever you study, wherever you go. The most important thing to remember is your own spirit. It is unique and all of your relationships are for a purpose—to learn from each other. But again, we come into this life and leave it as individuals, so it is very important to know self, because it is in self that God is contained.

Now do you have a final question?

Sibling Relationship and Growth

RS: While my older sister and I are both close to my mother, who is very spiritual, we argue in relation to anything about her.

SG: You are together as souls to learn from each other. If you always think that you are the one that is right, then you cannot hear in order to learn what God is trying to teach you through each other.

RS: My mother doesn't like this kind of conflict. She believes, you know, in spiritual things, so she doesn't want to see us argue.

SG: Mothers are sometimes like that with their daughters. She is working out her own karma also. Even though she is an old woman, she has not yet arrived, and she is still working on her soul. She makes mistakes, and she is not perfect, but all of you are learning from each other. That is the important point: It is the one who listens to what God is teaching them about themselves who will grow fastest, because who else can learn for you but you? It is in learning that we gain truth, and through truth and its application, we grow spiritually.

Rather than to go into a relationship thinking you are right, go into a relationship humbly, and listen to what it is that you need to hear to find out what you need to change in you. After all, you will leave this earth plane one day, and you want to make sure when you do, that you have worked out all the imperfections in your own character. You cannot work them out for someone else, so it is best to stay in your own business as you move along your path. Leave the business of your family, your sister, or your mother up to God and to them. Focus on *your* business.

Develop Full Potential

RS: I'm very interested in art. Is that part of my spirituality?

SG: Spirit gives what it is supposed to give and tries to give the fundamentals. But sometimes we allow you to work out the details because you are destined to be a certain type of master. That is what you want, and it is why you are studying. If you are studying just to accumulate knowledge, that is one thing, but that is not your interest. You want to develop your full spiritual potential to do God's work, to be used by spirit, like Philip is used. Yes, we know that, we see that, and that is why this reading began as it did. This medium could see the outstanding character, the potential, and the past, not all at one time, but as the reading unfolded, we zeroed in on the fullness of your life and came up with all the details to give them back to you.

Now I am going to leave Philip. I am so very, very pleased that I could be with you today. Please call on me. I am going to be working with you. Just know that. This is Saint Germain. God bless you.

PB: He just whispered in my ear as he left, he said, "She is going to be okay," meaning don't worry about your daughter.

RS: Thank you.

PB: You can thank them, and you are very welcome. The master Jesus also works very closely with you. Just now as I was looking and closing my energy, I saw him behind you.

RS: Thank you.

PB: You are very welcome. This is a very exciting reading that you will never forget because of the earthquake. (Laughter)

End of recording

FINDING PURPOSE
THROUGH DIFFICULTY

Ryuto Y.—Male

Philip Burley (PB): I hold this paper with your questions on it to feel the vibration, and this is the basis for me to work with you and your spirit world. I go between full trance and semi-trance when I'm reading for you, and I will hand your paper back to you from time to time so you can read your questions. If I may hold it now, I would like to open with a prayer:

> *Our Heavenly Father, we greet you and the holy spirit world this morning. I ask for the outpouring of your presence here, that you can bring all the information that this gentleman needs and is looking for today. First, I ask for healing for him and for his family. Please use this opportunity to bring that energy in now.*
>
> *Father, we are all born with a purpose and certain goals to be reached in a lifetime. May this reading contribute meaningfully to his seeking and reaching those goals. As always, help me to step out of the way that you can come through completely. All this I pray and ask in divine love.*

First of all, as I was praying for you, I felt a tremendous amount of prayer energy in you and all around you, and I was aware of a master who is with you. This man was a master both of the martial arts and spiritual self-mastery. I don't think you have ever known this master in life.

RY: Are you talking about the entity standing behind me?

PB: Yes. He was a martial arts master and a spiritual or religious master. He is Buddhist, and behind you is another very high master from a Shintoism background. This master is totally surrounded by gold light, and this pours into you.

I see much healing energy with you, particularly in your hands, with a lot of blue light in your solar plexus. You already have the power to heal, and I see this has been with you for a long time. Spirit says that wherever you walk, you leave an element of healing energy, and I see this happening everywhere. You don't have to say anything; if people just sit in front of you, there will be healing energy coming to them.

Life Balance

Saint Germain (SG): This is Saint Germain. I wanted to step in here to congratulate you on all of your efforts towards spiritual unfolding. Both in character and in practice you are a tribute to your work. As I look at you, I see a good balance of left and right brain functioning together, as you are both logical in your approach to life and spiritually intuitive. You have what you need to live a well-rounded life.

Some people believe anything and everything said about spiritual things and just flow with it, without using their brain to think about it. I, Saint Germain, teach people to develop a proper balance between the yang and yin, and I want to encourage you to trust your own inner voice, the inner awareness that you have.

You may wonder how I came through so quickly to speak to you. Your very beautiful energy pulled me through, and I did not even need to announce myself. I had been watching you in the classes, and Philip and I both noticed the energy around you. Be very greatly encouraged in your walk—and keep going!

Now I am going to step back from Philip and let him return. I may come again later. This is Saint Germain.

PB: Okay, I am back. Let's get to your questions.

Healing Originates in Spirit

RY: I have a lump in my abdomen in the right side, and I have been to different healers as well as to chiropractors and other Japanese doctors, but nothing has helped.

PB: That's because this originates on the spiritual plane. Something happened, my guide says, in childhood, a kind of emotional trauma. You were doing something, and you were chastised by your mother. Because you are a sensitive soul, you took it so personally and so deeply that the thought energy from this experience was locked away in that area of your body. My guide, Dr. Palmer, is working on you and just asked you to breathe deeply and not hold your breath. Breathe in and out one more time.

The life force of your whole body is broken up, so I am going to touch your head because I want to take away this fear, this insecurity. The energy is pouring in, and I've never received this much of an anointing. It's coming from my guide, Kathryn Kuhlman. Take another deep breath. Okay. There's enough energy here to fill all of Tokyo! You should feel much better now.

Please read your next question.

RY: I have trouble with the mucous membrane of my nose and throat.

PB: It is all connected, and the healing I did on your head was partly for that purpose. I was listening to my guide tell me where to put my hands.

Are you one of these people who is afraid to speak up for yourself?

43

RY: Yes, and I also have a number of other issues written here on my paper. I have problems with my left wrist and with detachment of the retina on the left side. I have hoarseness of my voice and stammering, and I have pent up anger. I want peace of mind—here and now! All of this is part of my first question, so I wanted you to hear it all together as one question.

PB: Two things have happened: one is the trauma from childhood with your mother, and the second is that you have negative energy because you have never felt free to say how you feel or to show anyone else your real inner pain. Fundamentally, the two things that are blocking you are the thought energy from your experience with your mother in early childhood and the fact that you are holding back your own negative energy, anger, or bitterness. But you can get beyond this.

Your aura is very open. When you are around other people, do you sometimes feel that you pick up their energies?

RY: I look at other people's eyes and focus there.

PB: Because . . . ?

RY: My heart starts to beat fast.

Love of Self and Unconditional Love

PB: Yes, you are very psychic. You are very open, so you experience both the higher energies and the lower energies. The major way to change what is happening is for you to engage in ultra positive thinking and action. I had the same problem, and that is why I read you so easily. The way I transformed my life was by forcing myself to think positively. I learned how to master my thoughts so I could draw upon the cosmic positive energy of God and spirit all around me. It has taken me a lifetime to develop this ability, but that was my karma. Now, very little negative energy comes into me. I don't have bitterness, anger, or resentment. I changed everything by really loving myself just as I am, with all my strengths and weaknesses and all my abilities and mistakes. Many times, my mantra in prayer was to speak down into my heart and say, "I love you, Philip; I love you, Philip."

Most human beings don't like themselves, and this is a major problem within humanity. Even those who seem to like themselves really don't, and there are two reasons for this. The first is that we are cut off from the spirit world and our essential spiritual self, so we don't really know the fullness of life and don't know ourselves completely. This is a problem for all of humanity, because if we could see and experience the spirit world, we would know ourselves as we truly are.

The second reason is that we do not realize that God's love is unconditional. In society at large, and even in the relationship between parents and children, we are accepted only if we fit in, and even our parents may not love us except when we do exactly what they want us to do. We live in a world where love is very conditional. If you do this or you don't do that, I will or I won't love you. This is true everywhere, not just with you, and not just in Japan; however, that's not how God created human beings to be. The solution is to give ourselves unconditional love, forgive ourselves of all our mistakes, and love ourselves under all conditions. We can't let anyone rob us of that. Am I making sense?

RY: I have a question: You forgive yourself, but do you also forgive your spirit guides?

PB: Forgive everyone. In other words, unconditional love must be universal, so you must give it to yourself and to everyone else. Jesus is held up so high spiritually because he forgave everyone. He is standing right behind you now, surrounded by blue light. He even forgave those who were trying to kill him. He knew the heart of God, and he knew that God loved all people equally and unconditionally. It's because of the unconditional love of Jesus that many people are healed through him.

I have met Jesus many times in dreams, and he actually works on the inner core of my soul more than Saint Germain does. Among all the masters I have ever experienced, Jesus has more of that core element of deep compassion and unconditional love than anyone else, and that's the major secret to his attaining perfection or oneness with God. I am now listening to Jesus. The information coming to you is timely, and it's essential for your healing.

RY: I went to a missionary school for eleven years.

PB: A Christian missionary school?

RY: Yes.

PB: Jesus came in at the beginning with you, but I didn't say anything. That connection is there.

RY: The problems in my body occurred when I first went to that school.

PB: The energy or element at that school allowed what was already there to surface. Do you remember the day you were first aware of it?

RY: Kindergarten. I don't remember the exact day.

PB: Do you remember what happened?

RY: Before I left for school, I had to eat breakfast, but I was running late, so I would eat really, really fast and then walk fast to school. Halfway to school I'd feel great pain inside and I doubled over.

PB: The thought energy from childhood is the cause. It stayed there, because I can see it. Saying the mantra "I love you," will clear out all conditions that need healing. When we focus on loving ourselves correctly and forget about the problem, then the energy that comes through loving ourselves does the healing. Try to forget about the problem and just repeatedly say down into your heart, "I love you," even calling yourself by your name. The more intimate and personal we make it, the deeper the healing goes. In your case, spirit says, it may be better for you to lie down while you do this. Even if you make a tape of your own voice saying, "I love you" over and over, and listen to it as you go to sleep, this too will bring healing.

Like you, I went to many people for healing, but I couldn't find anyone who could heal me. Last year, I had a dream in which I saw myself die, and the parent within me was so worried about me as a child that I woke up crying.

RY: Your inner parent was afraid for your inner child; is that what you wanted to say?

PB: Yes. In the dream I was actually drowning, which means I was drowning in my problems. But the dream showed me that I had the power, as symbolized by the parent, to save myself. In the dream, I just barely saved the drowning child. I was holding the child and crying and crying with relief because I saved it. I had saved myself. When I woke up, there were tears on my pillow and tears in my eyes, and I couldn't stop crying for about twenty minutes. This same dynamic applies to you, and you can bring much healing to yourself in the same way. What I am telling you about saying "I love you" into your heart is not coming from me. I do practice it, but I was told by spirit to do it, and spirit is saying the same thing to you.

People who have continuous health problems often have them because they keep building negative energy within themselves. Their thought energy of worry goes to the problem, and it just keeps building. Our own thought energy can block us from healing. By focusing only on "I love you," the energy that has built up over the years can begin to melt away or dissipate.

There is no mistake that you have these problems, because this is your karmic path. But as I told you in the beginning, I see many very positive spiritual things around you, and the purpose of your karma is for you to achieve self-mastery. If you turn it around and around in your mind, you'll see that you're very lucky. You have the opportunity to heal yourself and move forward rapidly on your spiritual path. As quickly as possible, start practicing saying the mantra into your heart, "I love you," and through that experience, you'll come to know what the word "love" really means. Love is not manifested only through serving someone; it is also expressed through human warmth and affection.

My own suffering taught me a great deal, and that is the core reality of how most people achieve self-mastery—through suffering and overcoming. You are well on your way. You and I needed to meet so you can go to the next plateau. As you know, there are no accidents, so our meeting is no accident. I don't have all the answers, but you absolutely needed the information given to you today to go to the next level.

Let's go on to your next question.

RY: I am confused about what to say because saying "I love you," makes it seem that you are outside of yourself. Isn't it better to say "I love me"?

PB: Whatever you feel most comfortable with. Just use common sense.

Finding Purpose through Difficulty

RY: My next question is this: When I have been walking my path, every once in a while I will wander off to the side, and when this happens, I have become very poor and have no money at all. You are telling me that my guides are bringing nice bright lights, but when I have become poor, my guides have done nothing for me. How on earth am I supposed to ever forgive them for not helping me? There is no way I can forgive them, because they weren't there for me at all.

PB: Let me let Saint Germain come through and speak to you.

SG: I am back. I am laughing with you. Don't you think we all went through this? In his lowest of times, this medium I am speaking through would shake his fist at God and say, "You love nature and other people more than you love me." But God didn't create you as a puppet. You must be allowed to experience joy and sorrow, prosperity, and poverty. When you are in the valley of life, you want to be at the top of the mountain, and when you are at the top of the mountain, it's very lonely, so you want to be down in the valley where most people are.

The soul that does not know its purpose is never satisfied. It zigzags its way to God like a woman who goes into a department store looking for some lipstick. She comes into the women's department and goes here and there before she ever gets to the place where she buys her lipstick. She stops to look at purses, at earrings, at coats, and all kinds of things, wandering about before she actually gets to the lipstick counter. Little does she realize that she could save time and energy by just going directly to the lipstick counter without being pulled away from her goal. On some level, she may even be aware that she is being distracted, but she may still choose distraction over accomplishing her goal sooner. This may seem to be a silly example, but it's really not so silly from our point of view.

The anthill, where ants live, is highly, highly organized, and so is the beehive. But if some human being comes and puts a stick in it, the workers scatter in different directions. The perfect order and thus the harmony is broken up, and the individual ant or bee seems to be lost until they reorganize and get back to their purpose—the purpose of being an ant or a bee.

As we look at earth, we see that human beings are much like the stirred-up anthill. They are running in many directions. If they ever knew it, few remember their purpose; so, like the woman in the department store, they go this way and that, back and forth, and up and down. Then they wonder why they are confused. They wonder why, at age 65, they have not reached their goals. To tell you the truth, more people are like that than not. Those who achieve self-mastery do not allow themselves to deviate; they go directly to their purpose. I had problems with my medium because he wanted to go here and there, but through joy and suffering, he learned to be obedient to his purpose. So that he could achieve self-mastery, we let him experience what he experienced. Otherwise, it is not self-mastery.

RY: Is it because you are his spirit guide that you allowed him to do this?

SG: Yes. Gradually, little by little, he learned to stay on the path because he found there were more rewards from maintaining consistency towards purpose than from zigzagging. We stood by him like the parent of a child who was learning to walk. We did help him here and there, as much as we could, but we were not allowed to do his work for him. We were not allowed to stop him from zigzagging because it is *his* self-mastery, not ours. All of us who are masters went through the same thing. So you see, as we say in spirit, life teaches us. That's what this life is about. Eventually the soul learns not to zigzag, and that awakening is a part of self-mastery.

And so, my son, your spirit guides, like parents standing by to watch you learn to walk, have been there to protect you, but they could not keep you from falling down. In order for a child to learn to walk, it must fall down from time to time to strengthen its legs by getting up. God created the phenomena of walking but also allowed for the phenomena of falling down. Because walking, falling down, and getting up are all a part of the whole experience of learning to walk.

You see, you were never alone, and your spirit guides did not cause you to do the things you have done. It has been your karmic path, and you had to learn to overcome on your own. Then you will have the credit in heaven to have mastered self. Your guides and teachers never abandoned you once. They never stopped praying for you or meditating on you. You had the idea that, somehow, they misled you or did not protect you enough, but this is because you have misunderstood the role of spirit guides and teachers.

What happens to those individuals who drink a lot of alcohol and become drunk? Did their holy, reverent spirit guides lead them to drink?

And when they were drinking and became drunk, could the spirit guides knock the bottle out of their hands? Of course, the answer is no. You are far, far more responsible for your soul than you realize, so don't be naïve. Rather, awaken to a new awareness of self, and awaken to the understanding of the actual role and responsibility of spirit guides and teachers. This life is about self-mastery, not my mastery, her mastery, or anyone else's mastery, but your *own* self-mastery. Then in heaven, you can stand tall and say, "I did it. I was victorious over self. This gold crown that I am now wearing in spirit—I won this crown."

When Jesus was hanging from the cross, no one saved him. He said he could call upon many thousands and thousands of angels, but he did not do that. He had magnificent spiritual powers, but he did not use them on the cross. For him, the cross was both death and a victorious entrance into a new life. On the cross, Jesus said to God, "My God, my God, why hast thou forsaken me?" In the last moment, he hoped that God would do something to stop the pain and stop the crucifixion. But, because God wanted his son to be totally and completely victorious over self, he did nothing to stop it. Rather, God and all the holy spirits surrounding Jesus prayed for him and urged him on, weeping as they watched him suffer. Because he was victorious over self under those circumstances, he stands tall, crowned as the son of God in spirit.

So, my son, you are here today to learn all this, to grow up spiritually and learn to take full responsibility for self and blame no one else for error. If and when you do that, you will become a fully mature man before God and a true son of God. I smile through my medium because I know these words are not easy to hear, and I know that they challenge you to think bigger, outside of the box which you have built around yourself. But because I do love you, and I am the bearer of truth, I say all of this out of the deepest kindness and for the sake of your own success.

Now I am going to leave Philip and let him come back. Perhaps I will come back here again. This is Saint Germain.

PB: I am back. Where are we?

RY: I have two more questions.

PB: Ok. Do you want to ask the next question?

RY: I have not had a chance in this lifetime to have a lot of money or a lot of joy. What do I need to do now in my life in order to get those things? What should I do in order to be able to live abundantly?

PB: Jesus is standing behind you, surrounded by blue and gold light. He is saying that when he was on earth, he told people to seek the kingdom of heaven first. What is the kingdom of heaven? It has to do, he says, with what Saint Germain just talked about—achieving victory over self.

Achieving Self-Mastery

RY: Can you explain, using other words, what it is to master self? I can say self-mastery, but in this case, I'm not sure how to say what it is to be a master over yourself.

PB: You have to direct your energies towards the right ends through self-discipline. In other words, the path to God is a specific path. Jesus is saying that we have to learn to stay on that path by doing the things that keep us on that path—that keep us heading towards God. When we do that, we find lasting peace, and that peace is the kingdom of heaven. When he was on earth, Jesus said to seek first the kingdom of heaven, and this means to first seek God within you, and you will find the peace that you want. That is heaven. And then everything will be given to you.

Jesus is saying, "This channel before you went through the same struggles as you, and like you, he suffered when he didn't stay on the path; but when he was on the path, he had significant peace. Now, after many years, he has achieved a certain level of ability to stay on the path; the ability to be consistent and obey God first. Having come to this level, the things he needs come to him—people, money, and opportunities. He did not seek to come to Japan, and he wasn't even thinking of it, but because he was obedient to God, God sent someone to bring him here. And the more he is obedient, the more money, people, and opportunities will be given to him. In other words, Philip and people like him who achieve a certain level of self-mastery do not seek money, opportunity, and people first. They seek God first. Such people try to stay completely one with God. Having achieved that level, God takes care of everything else. They don't even have to ask for things to come, they just come.

RY: Does this mean I should just obey my spirit guides?

PB: I am now listening to Jesus. . . . What it means is to know and understand your own path and follow it. Come to know your purpose, why you came to this earth, and follow that purpose. It doesn't mean you shouldn't work, you shouldn't do worldly things, or you shouldn't use your own judgment. It means to make following your spiritual path your number one priority. Focus all your heart and mind on this, and gradually you will come into that place of self-mastery where things will just come to you.

Jesus says, "This is a universal experience among masters, meaning because they follow the spiritual path, things just come to them, and this is based upon science. If you follow the path, in the end, it's not God who blesses you, it's you who blesses you!"

Let's go to the next question.

Persevere and God Will Provide

RY: I need to leave where I am living very soon. I am trying to find a new place, but I am having a terrible time finding a place to live right now, and I am not sure what to do.

PB: Saint Germain said, if someone came to you with the same question, what would you tell them? Keep looking. It's a simple answer, but keep on looking! Spirit has prepared a place for you, and spirit always prepares a place for everyone—always—and there are no exceptions. They prepared who would be your parents, where you would be born, what color your eyes would be, and what nation you would live in; so your job is to keep looking and to trust God. There is a certain karmic aspect to all of this for you.

There have been many times when I was financially down to zero, but God always provided. He always, always, always, provided. I have had many miracles take place regarding money. A friend of mine offered me his house, but I had no money to buy it. In a few days, a very wealthy student called me and said, "I had a dream of you last night, and God and the spirit world told me that I should give you money right now, so I am obeying." She sent me a check for fifty thousand dollars, and I was able to buy the house.

When I say to stay on the path and really pursue the spiritual part of your life, it's because by doing that, you gain merit. Then more and more things will come to you automatically. It's not easy, and it requires patience. I know that. But it is a divine principle, a divine law, and it is as absolute as the law of gravity. According to the law of gravity, whatever goes up must come down, and if you are obedient, gain God's trust, and accumulate merit, you must get blessings. It's not something you have to guess about or something that you have to beg God for. Just demand of yourself consistency towards your spiritual goals, and the rest follows by spiritual law. It's not a case of reward or punishment on some subjective level, but a case of divine law.

How old are you?

RY: Fifty-six.

PB: You are very young. You may not think so, but you are still very young, so you have time.

RY: I just want to make sure I have asked all my questions.

PB: Yes. Did you get them all answered?

RY: Instead of just living on the brink, which I am really tired of doing, I would like to have more abundance. Is strengthening my connection with God the way to have this?

PB: That is the way, primarily. It's divine law, and it's a law of divine love. You can't expect someone to love you without your investing love in them, because a person who just takes and takes love from another person is a thief. After a while, if you don't give something back, you lose that love. It's like having money in the bank. If you keep taking it out and spending it, after a while there is nothing left. But if you keep putting money in, you will have more and more money and receive more and more interest, to the point where you can take money out without losing all of your money. In the same way, if you trust God and invest in God over and over upon your path, you not only invest something, but you gain interest, and that's your merit. When you have invested enough in God, according to divine law, you will receive things from God.

End of recording

LIFE STORY OF SAINT GERMAIN

Haruto K.—Male

Philip Burley (PB): I was born with this gift. Spirits began appearing at my bedside when I was four years old, and I have had many such experiences throughout my life. While I worked at various occupations, the gift of spiritual sight did not go away. I eventually stopped all other work and with sufficient training, I took up full-time mediumship. However, even though I was gifted, I had to work at it.

When working with new clients, sometimes I like to share both the process I go through and the messages their spirit guides bring in: I can see clairvoyantly with my eyes both open and closed. I begin with prayer to experience the presence of God and Heavenly spirits. That is, practically speaking, the prayer raises my vibration and attunes me most directly to the spirit world surrounding me, both my spirit guides and those of my clients.

During my prayer I begin to see many things about a client's life. First, I usually see their aura, in other words, the spiritual light coming from them and surrounding them. Its colors and level of brightness convey certain things about the client, and I share that information.

Next, I begin seeing and hearing spirits and usually the first to appear is a close relative and/or a master teacher or guide. After I share this information, more spirits usually appear and they tell me who they are and why they are here. Often, they will say something that is an answer to one of the questions the client has written on the paper that they hold, or it is a question in the client's heart that they have not written down. In this way I seek to serve the client. The amount of information and/ or spirits that come through is case by case; it depends on the needs of the person and what their calling is in life.

The average reading (when no translator is involved) will run from 50 minutes to an hour, and it takes that long to convey what I, as a medium, see, hear, and feel pertaining to the client. For most clients, the highlight of the reading is when Saint Germain comes in and takes over my vocal cords and speaks to the client directly. Usually, his appearance is in response to one or more of the questions that the client has written on their paper. Saint Germain may elaborate on certain points and emphasize them—especially if the person has an important, or above average, calling in life. It is case by case. He has been known to speak for 20 to 30 minutes or more.

I bring the reading to a close at the right time with a prayer. I wish I could convey the entirety of what I experience but some is just not possible, and this is enough for this setting.

Fire Energy

With all this said, in tuning in with you, I see a great amount of energy coming from above through you. You have a very great force working with you, and this energy comes down through you and goes out to many people. You are more influential than you realize.

Also, you have a lot of actual fire energy around you, as I can see flames around you. This has two meanings: One is that you are essentially a very strong person, and when you have an idea that you want to do something, you do it. The second is that you're very protected. My guides say this fire has been around you from the time you were born. As I'm touching this paper, my hands are getting very, very hot. Though you're not a practicing healer, you have natural healing energy. As I look at your hands clairvoyantly, I can see healing energy coming from your palms.

Your guides are telling me that you're very much on a spiritual search. You're curious and you want to do something with your inner life, but you're not sure what to do. Is that true? That's what they're telling me.

They show me stair steps, and as far as earthly accomplishment goes, you're very far up on the steps. In terms of your goodness and your intelligence, you're also very high on the steps. All the energy around you coming outside of the fire is pure white light, which shows you to be a very highly evolved soul.

HK: The energy that's coming from around me?

PB: You have, first of all, the energy of the fire around you, but outside or beyond the fire is this white light. It shows that you're a very pure soul. You have very good motives in what you do in life. In terms of your spiritual evolution on the inside, very deep inside, you are about one-third of the way up the stairs. But you're exactly where you should be. You were not supposed to begin working on your spiritual life until now. Everything else had to happen before this time so you could know that no matter how successful you are in life, there's still some empty feeling—something else needed.

In any case, your present condition of feeling empty, was necessary to make you begin to search. Do you understand what I was saying when I use the word "empty"?

HK: No.

PB: I see. Try "dissatisfied condition." You had to be in this dissatisfied condition so you would begin to search. That's why everything else had to come first. The more dissatisfied we are, the more seriously do we look. The greater the pain we have, the more we want to get rid of the pain.

They tell me that on your paper you have a number of spiritual questions. So let's begin. First, Saint Germain, my master teacher, greets you. Later he will come in and use my vocal cords to speak to you. You know about channeling, right?

HK: No, this is the first time. Everything is for the first time.

PB: Okay. Please read your first question.

Spiritual Guides

HK: What spirits are working with me?

PB: I'm listening to Saint Germain. That's why I turned my head. I nodded to let him know I heard him. You have some kind of hidden inner power, probably hidden even from you. Saint Germain is going to come to you, through me, and talk about this whole reality later.

I'm seeing Confucius standing right behind you. I've seen Buddha and other spirits here with people, and I've seen Confucius in the background, but never directly behind someone. He is helping to guide you in this life. Your path to spiritual enlightenment is not so much through experiencing spiritual phenomena but through learning by reading, studying, and talking. That was the path of Confucius, too. This doesn't mean that you won't have spiritual experiences, but predominantly, you will learn by studying.

Let's go on to your next question.

HK: How am I going to die, and what will be the reason?

PB: You're going to die a natural death without any suffering, cancer, or anything like that. Probably you'll go in your sleep. From now on, you will live a more internally peaceful life. You see, it's not you who has guided you to this point; it's God and spirit world. It was planned this way so that you would find the answers and pass out of this world peacefully, meaning all the major questions of your life are resolved. Those were questions such as, "What is the purpose of my life? Is there a God? Who is God? Where is God? What do I need to do to raise myself up spiritually? What is meditation?"

As you find the answers to all these questions and live them out, peacefulness will come automatically. Your mind will be centered away from the earth plane toward spiritual things, and you'll be less and less attached to this world. Then you'll be able to leave freely. That's what they show me. When you die, there are going to be lots and lots of people coming to your funeral. Are you into sports?

HK: Golf.

PB: Golf. Good, because I very much feel sports around you.

HK: Not golf only, but in business also.

PB: Really? I feel sports around you, and it is very good energy. Yes, that is very good for you, and you should continue doing what you're doing. It's very good for your health.

Let's go to your next question.

HK: I'd like to ask a question or two about the things you've already talked about. Is that okay?

PB: I'm going to let Saint Germain speak directly to you.

The Life Story of Saint Germain

Saint Germain (SG): Yes, I am here. This is Saint Germain. I am so very, very pleased to be able to be with you.

Much like Philip, I, Saint Germain, had the gifts of seeing and experiencing the spirit world when I was a small child, and this is one of the reasons why I have a rapport with Philip. I knew my mission in life because of my direct relationship with the spirit world. They informed me, as I grew up, what I would be doing in life.

I was born of royal blood, but the people of my country rebelled against my family, and I had to escape to save my life. I first went to Italy from Transylvania, where my family was located. You can research that and find the location. My brother, sister, and I escaped to Rome, and I stayed with the very wealthy and famous Medici family. With the help of the spiritual world and my own intelligence, it was there that I prepared for my mission. The Medici family had some idea of who I was, but not entirely. Their great mansion still exists in Rome, and if you go there, you can see it with your own eyes.

When the time was right, I began to travel incognito across the continent of Europe. God had prepared many people, years in advance, for me to meet over time. To protect myself, I used different names. Saint Germain was not my real name; it was Prince Rakoczy. I chose the name Saint Germain, which was taken from an area in France. If you look up the meaning of my name, Saint Germain, or *Jer mahn*, as they pronounce it in French, you will find that it has a deep meaning.

As I traveled, I built a network of friends around the continent. These were individuals like you who were searching for answers and tired of life as it was. Either they had deep spiritual experiences or were inclined towards spiritual seeking. In some cases, I formed groups of people, and together we searched for God in literature, meditation, and discussion. We all had in common our belief or knowledge that God lived in each of us.

In contrast, the Catholic Church taught people that they could come to God only through the Church; but we knew experientially and logically that this was not true. My mission was to free people from such ignorance by teaching them that God emphatically lives in each of them as the temple of God. As long as people were dominated by the wealthy class and by the church, they could not think for themselves, and without such freedom, one cannot pursue the idea of God living inside of them. You see, it was even dangerous to teach such a thing in those days, so we did our work secretly.

To continue with my story . . . It was necessary for me to work with the royal families of Europe who, along with the Church, were dominating the hearts and minds of the people. It was not so different from your samurai period of the 1100s. In Japan, as well as in Europe, individuals could not think for themselves. They had to absolutely obey the leaders, or their lives would be in jeopardy. My greatest effort was to meet the royal families and try to get them to bring democracy into the world. It was very similar to what General Douglas MacArthur did in bringing democracy to Japan.

I have not said anything about this before, but I was behind MacArthur when all that happened. That is my grand revelation here in Japan, and this is the first time I have told anyone in Japan. Through MacArthur, the position of emperor lost its power, and democracy was established, bringing more freedom for the people. If that had not happened, modern day Japan could not have emerged.

I was behind the establishment of democracy in America first and then I tried to work through the royal family of France, Louis XVI and Marie Antoinette. But Louis XVI was often a weak leader and king, and democracy could not come there without the revolution. I warned both of them that if they did not follow what I told them, they would indeed die on the guillotine.

I've taken a long time to answer your question. You were inspired by me to ask that question so that I might give all of this information. Even Philip has wondered why—why did Saint Germain bring me to Japan? It was for this very moment—to reveal how I influenced Japan through General MacArthur. Our meeting here today is no accident. When this session is over, I very much want you to tell Philip that he must listen to this tape.

HK: Okay, I certainly will.

SG: God chose you to reveal this information about my coming here to Japan and why. You see, General MacArthur was a great spiritual master, far, far more spiritually advanced than President Harry Truman. Truman was a simple country man and knew little about the kind of things that General MacArthur knew. In Korea, it was a great, great political and spiritual error to stop MacArthur. If Truman had not stopped MacArthur, Korea would not be divided today. Given enough men, money, time, and political support, MacArthur would have driven the Chinese out of North Korea, and there would be one solid democratic Korea today. What happened in Korea at that time is not dissimilar to what I told you happened in France.

Now you know the whole story. I worked with MacArthur here in Japan and in Korea. When he was in the army, Philip was also just ten miles below the 38th parallel in Korea. Until he hears this tape, he will have no idea of the full picture. When he was in Korea, he came here to Japan for eighteen days. Through his friends, he was invited to speak at a Lions Club with fifty or sixty people in attendance. He spoke on the necessity of good relationships between the East and West, and though he did not know it, I was already working with him and through him. Is this not all fascinating?

HK: I'm really surprised that Saint Germain is connected more to Europe than Japan.

SG: Yes, but I did things here as well. What is important is *what* we do on earth, not *where* we work. Having been alerted, you will find yourself very much pursuing answers to questions regarding spirituality, God within and how to reach God. Until now, it has been like living under a 100-watt light bulb, and now it will be like living under a light bulb with 500 to 1,000 watts. You're coming into true enlightenment.

Now because of time constraints, let's move on to your next question. I am going to leave Philip, and if I think I need to come back, I shall.

HK: Before I forget, Philip, you have to listen to this tape. Saint Germain told me to tell you to listen to it. You have to listen to it today.

PB: Really?

HK: Yeah. You'll really like it.

PB: Okay. Let's go to your next question.

HK: I want to thank you very much for all this information.

PB: Okay. I don't know anything about it, but I assume that you're telling me that it was very helpful?

HK: Yes.

PB: Good.

HK: What is my mission now?

PB: How old are you?

HK: Fifty-four.

PB: Well, I don't think you are close to retirement, so you'll keep doing what you're doing in terms of work. But now, you need to seriously look into your inner life and begin to practice meditation. You're very bright and very capable, so these things should come to you pretty fast.

The Practice of Meditation; I AM

I'm listening to Saint Germain now because I don't know anything he told you, and I'm just repeating what he's saying. It's very important for you to establish a regular pattern of meditating. The method is not what's important. You just have a place that you go to where you sit every day to reflect and think. He's saying to watch your breath and slow your breath way down. And in English, use the words, "I Am." He identifies with those words. After you slow your breath down and you become very calm and peaceful, focus on the third eye. Just turn your eyes upward a little bit with your eyes closed. And then, on the "in" breath, you think "I," and as you breathe out, think "Am." "I am." What would that be in Japanese?

HK: There is no similar language.

PB: I didn't think so.

HK: You have to say something like, "I exist."

PB: No. Use the English words, "I Am." The reason, Saint Germain says, is because using the "I Am" words means that you are present now. You always were, and always have been, and always will be. There is no beginning and there's no end to you. It is the most fundamental statement about self: "I Am."

Secondly, he says, the "m" sound will bring the right and left brain together, and then your whole being will be in greater harmony. He's going to work with you. He may appear in dreams or come to your bedside, but he's going to work with you somehow.

In the beginning, he says to do about fifteen or twenty minutes of breathing as you say, "I Am." You can say in your mind: "I Am." Then, as you go deeper and deeper into this, you can do it for a longer time. Keep a journal of your experience, for your own sake, so you can record your progress.

Saint Germain says, in your daily life, as you feel moved to do different things spiritually, do the things you are inspired to do. For example, if you find a book in the library or in a bookstore, and you feel very attracted to it, then spirit is pushing you to read it. If there's some kind of meeting of a spiritual nature that you hear about or you read in the newspaper, if you feel very attracted, go to it. He says, "This is the way I have been guiding Philip for the past twenty years."

He and Confucius and others, but those two mostly, will bring your attention to different things and will guide you to them. They will use your natural curiosity and interest to draw your attention to things. They do this with all people, but you have the privilege of hearing about it directly from us.

Saint Germain is laughing. He says, "Most people have no idea how much we are guiding them. We are watching all the time. We are aware of everything, so we know how to guide the individual person. There are even times when people are about to hurt themselves, and we stop them."

He says our biggest problem here in Japan has to do with alcohol. Some alcohol is okay, but when someone uses too much, it blocks spirit's ability to direct that person. Even if a person just had two or three drinks but was not dead drunk.

HK: I don't drink.

PB: I didn't say you—he's just giving you general information. No, I don't see that vibration with you at all. You're a pure soul. And pure doesn't mean that people who drink are sinful. I just mean you don't take that kind of thing into your body. Okay, that's basically the answer to your question.

Do you have a dog? Or did you have a dog at one time? There's a little dog right here on the other side. Are you married? Does your wife want a dog or something? Did you talk about it? Or did she have a dog when she was younger?

HK: I've never had a dog.

PB: Never?

HK: Forty years ago, maybe.

PB: Well, you see, in spirit, they never die. And when we love them, the energy of our love really gives them a soul. The soul is there, but the love is what causes the soul to become more obvious.

We have time for one more question.

HK: When will I die?

PB: When? You see, when I began this work, I told my guides I didn't want to know those kinds of things. But because you asked, then I'm free to tell you. You'll probably pass over in your mid-eighties. But you have plenty of time, so live joyfully. Use these years to really raise your spirit.

Next question.

HK: I am married. But in the mid-1980s, I had a child with another woman in America. The child, a son, is now eighteen years old, and I want to know if I will ever meet him. I am not in contact with the boy or his mother.

PB: That's up to you. It's not like someday suddenly you will meet, or he will call you. But if you pursue it, you will meet him. However, your having this son was no mistake because that's how his soul had to come into the earth plane. By your relationship with that woman, you provided his soul with a body. So deep inside of him, he's very grateful that you provided the body. It's up to you if you want to pursue meeting him—it's up to you.

Your overall energies are very good. You have a very good life, and you're a very good person.

HK: You said that you could see fire around me. What is that about?

PB: It's energy, and it's of a nature that it looks like fire. It's really an icon, or an image, for protection. Spirit world put it around you.

Please, please study about Confucius and about Saint Germain, because they're the two people that appeared behind you. There are others, but they didn't identify themselves.

When I first started in this work, the only person I knew about was Saint Germain because he's the foundation of my work. Later, I learned about all the other guides. It can be a big ego trip for us to know about our guides in some ways. It's better sometimes not to even know. But please study Confucius and Saint Germain.

HK: Thank you very much.

End of recording

WHAT IS LOVE?

Hayate R.—Male

Philip Burley (PB): While I'm working with you, I may go in and out of trance very rapidly. Sometimes I'll be talking, and Saint Germain will suddenly come in. When he first started working through me and spoke through the trumpet, he told me that if I loved people as myself, regardless of who they were or what they did in life, that would draw him close to me. He would become permanently cemented into my energy field or aura, and we would move together at all times. He's here right now, touching me, and I can see him smiling. He says he is very happy to be here for you.

The Trumpet and Spiritual Communication

The first time Saint Germain spoke to me was through an instrument called a *trumpet*. Spirits build a spiritual voice box inside this earthly object, belonging to the medium, and speak through it, and the trumpet's megaphone-like shape and size amplify the speaking spirit's voice.

Trumpets are usually about 3 feet long with a diameter of 5 inches at the large end and ¾ of an inch, in diameter, at the smaller end. At each end is a hole of the same dimension. The trumpets I have owned are made of very thin aluminum. When in use, a trumpet usually floats in the air as if free floating, though directly and invisibly supported and guided by the spirit world. I've seen as many as four of them floating in the air at the same time.

The second time I spoke with Saint Germain, he brought *the object described below* (which, at the moment I was showing to the client) through the trumpet to me. It just passed through the small hole at one end of the trumpet and out the larger hole at the other end.

Such an object from spirit is something found on earth, belonging to no one, and is not from the spirit world. To bring it from where it is found, on earth, to the trumpet spirit transforms it from a solid object to a form of invisible energy and then places it in this form through the small hole into the trumpet. It is then instantly transformed back into a solid object. The object—in this case a beautiful, green malachite stone—became very hot as it was transformed back into its original, solid earthly form.

A moment before the stone's arrival I was told to hold out my two hands to receive the object coming out of the large end of the trumpet. I immediately heard the object tumble down the trumpet (being held by spirit in a downward angle) to and through the 5-inch opening. It was almost too hot to hold when it fell into my waiting hands. To say that I was amazed and touched very deeply is a great understatement. It is my most treasured gift from Saint Germain and I always keep it near me and guard it carefully.

After I received the stone, Saint Germain said, "This stone being green represents life, your life. On one side it is perfectly smooth and on the other it is rough. The rough side represents your present life, with the need to master it. The smooth side represents your life once you have mastered it."

This precious gift from the Master is a constant reminder of that first communication with him and a living symbol of what I am living and striving for, human self-mastery. As you can imagine, there are not enough words to express my ongoing gratitude to Saint Germain—as my master spirit guide and teacher—and his ongoing protection, most loving care, and unending guidance.

About a year and a half later, Saint Germain began speaking to people directly through me. I wanted to give you this introduction to help you understand the phenomenon of Saint Germain and his working through me and what will happen in your reading today.

The Crystal

Just for your personal interest, I am holding your paper because it contains your vibration. Like tuning into a radio or television station, I tune in with my third eye, clairaudience, and feeling. These three things combined enable me to tune into you spiritually and the spirit world surrounding you. My guides have told me to use this crystal (which I was then holding), because in the early part of my work I was getting very tired when I channeled and had to rest a lot. When Saint Germain comes through me, I project my energy toward this crystal, and he vibrates off of it because crystals send, receive, and retain energy. It is why crystals are used in radios, for example. When he comes in, he attaches to me through the crystal, and I don't get as tired.

I'm going to open with a prayer. As you will read in my literature, that's when spirit will start bringing things through for you.

Our Heavenly Father, what pleases me most is we do not have to go anywhere to meet you. You are all that is. There is one energy, and we are all extensions of you, radiations of eternal light. All the characteristics that are yours are ours. We are all facets of the great diamond that you are. What you are, we are also. We are the thought of your thought, the feeling of your feeling, and the heart of your heart.

You are here now for this man. Bless him today through this experience. Surround him with the mighty force that you are and fill him with eternal healing energy. Father, you know how much I depend on you. You know that I know it's you who speaks through me, and that without you, there is no life. Please use me to bring through the information that this man is seeking. May all of those lovely, caring spirits that work with him come very close to us today to give the answers he is seeking: those written on this paper, and those in his heart and mind. Father, please open the door wide for him.

I thank you ahead of time for all that you have done for this man, all that you are doing, and all that you will do. He is a good man, and I can feel that in my heart. I thank you for the privilege of being a bridge between the two worlds for him. All of this I ask in divine love.

Presence of a Holy Man

As I'm looking at you, right from the center of your heart there is something like the sun. It is a brilliant gold light. It shines up into your mind and down into the lower part of your body. Spirit says this is a symbol of the fact that you were born to do divine work.

There is a holy man present with you in spirit. He is like a samurai warrior, but he never killed anyone. He says he only used the samurai lifestyle to discipline himself. He was born a spiritual person, and he says that in his day, the samurai lifestyle was the closest thing he could find to having a spiritual structure and discipline. He has much healing power, not because he practiced healing, but because he loved people very deeply. As his heart developed, his healing ability just came out of that.

He says he has been with you since you were around the age of ten to twelve, and he came when you were alone somewhere in nature. You may not remember this. He stands to your right, and he appears all in blue and white. It's a deep blue. He is like a master, and he helps to guide you. He just said in my left ear that he's also a protector, and with him you can't go wrong. Your physical and spiritual life are totally protected. If there were times you wanted to do something bad and couldn't, that's why. If your conscience bothered you, that's why. He is there as a force to help direct you on the right path. Do you welcome him, he asks?

HR: Yes.

The Way of Buddha

PB: When I was praying for you this morning, Buddha came to me and said not to worry about the future. He will help you and work with you. He said that your nature and his are very similar. When he was on earth, he was actually closer to your size than the big round Buddha image. He is standing right here talking to me now and I can see him spiritually.

He says that he especially notices your ability to concentrate. Do you know what I mean by this? He says that ability or power within you is the secret to your own spiritual ascension. He says not to worry about all the details or try to understand all the spiritual or religious theology. It misleads and confuses. Rather, through the power of concentration, particularly in meditation, you can raise your spirit and awareness, your self-realization, higher and higher in this lifetime.

He also says that sometimes you have a strong intuition or feeling about something you should do, but you don't do it. Later you find out you were exactly right, and that you should have done it. You know exactly what I'm talking about, right? He says, learn to listen to the inner voice because sometimes God will speak that way. Even if you make a mistake, the important thing is to learn to listen to the voice.

HR: I'm not sure I understand exactly what you're saying . . .

PB: Let me listen to what he says again. Just stand by.

HR: Okay.

PB: He says that sometimes God appears to lead us in the wrong direction, even making us feel foolish, but the most important point is to listen to the inner voice and be obedient. Ask yourself about obedience, not about rightness or wrongness. And he says, "As you know, as a young man, my father wanted me to do one thing, but the inner voice told me to do something else."

HR: This is what Buddha is saying?

PB: Yes. He was afraid of his father, but he was more afraid of God. From the point of view of his father and the world, it looked like he was going the wrong way. He says, "But, as history shows, I went exactly the right way." He also says, "I want very much to work with you." It's not just his desire, but something like the will of heaven. In your meditation, in your third eye, seek to see Buddha. He's going to help with two things: deeper concentration and opening up spiritually.

HR: The first thing was to go deeper? And the other was to open the third eye?

PB: Yes, to open up spiritually. Always imagine that he is the one who is touching your forehead and helping to open the third eye. Also imagine him as the one in your heart and as the one sitting at the top of your head. God is using Buddha to lead you because his vibration and yours are similar. He says, "Do not worship me. But worship God within you." Just think of Buddha as a symbol of God.

Because God is invisible and infinite, we need a symbol that we can focus on. Buddha says it's something like an icon on a computer screen: You click on it, and it opens up a vast number of options. Buddha is your icon, and he will open the door to a vast number of worlds. "Good example!" That's what he just said. He says this puts it in the proper scientific perspective. Saint Germain said that for me, Jesus was the icon. God uses these "icons" around the world to lead mankind to God within each person. After you click on the icon on a computer, you ignore the original icon and go into what you were looking for. He says, "It's just a symbol and a doorway. And if you follow this pattern, it's the secret to ascending faster spiritually. Following this pattern, you will grow quickly in the next three years."

(Chuckling) Saint Germain is laughing, and he says, "How do you feel about all this?"

HR: Sounds pretty easy.

PB: Do you feel good, he says?

HR: Yes.

PB: As I'm looking at you, you have a bright blue light in the area of the third eye, indicating great potential to open up spiritually. When I prayed for you, I saw a lot of blue light, and I see it now. In your aura you also have a lot of white light, indicating a very pure spirit. Right next to your body there is white light, and then there is blue light. Then there is a small band of gold. The white light means you were born in purity, and the blue light means that your path is the path of truth. That truth, in the latter part of your life, will lead you to perfection or self-mastery, represented by the gold. This is the spiritual map of your life. I'd like you to take your paper and ask the first question.

Finding One's Partner

HR: I'd like to know about my partner.

PB: What do you mean? The person you are to meet and marry? Or someone you're with now?

77

HR: I'm with someone now, and we are getting along very well, yet my friends are always introducing me to new women. I think this is very strange and am not sure what to do about it. I'm confused.

PB: Saint Germain is laughing and leaned forward and whispered in my ear, "It's the history of man!"

HR: "Man" meaning all people, or meaning just men?

PB: Men. He says pure souls think of one mate because they want to build an eternal relationship. The other person is like your other half. I'm going to let Saint Germain come through. He wants to speak to you directly.

Saint Germain (SG): (Laughs.) I am here. I love your question. When you find your other half, that is heaven. Are you in heaven?

HR: Yes, pretty much so.

SG: Then why look in hell? Yes, it's the nature of men who are not pure hearted, or who do not know themselves well, to fish among women. They like to catch this one and throw it back, and then catch that one and throw it back. They love the sport of fishing for women more than they love women. Do you know what I mean?

HR: Yes, I understand.

SG: Yes, so do you want to fish, or do you want to love the woman that you have caught?

HR: I don't feel like I want to continue fishing.

SG: (Laughing) Exactly. Therefore, be pure hearted and cherish the one you have. To let her know how much you cherish her is to bring heaven to her. The husband is like the roof, the woman is like the walls, and together they are the foundation for their whole home. The roof protects and covers, and at the same time, the walls hold the roof up. As a man, you need to let her know how much you appreciate her, to cover her insecurities.

Both are needed. Often in marriage it is the wife who carries the emotional load. The husband protects, but the wife holds the family up and together. As the roof and the walls lean on each other, the foundation becomes solidified between you. Therefore, when your friends come with another girl, just say (laughing), "I'm done fishing." Do you like my answer?

HR: Actually, I very much like it.

SG: Yes, because we chose it for you. Spiritually, the roundedness of your face is ideal because it spells balance. It is the Buddha face; therefore, when you look in the mirror, thank God for *you*. Most important, however, is to have a rounded and balanced heart of love. If you and your beloved do that for each other, you see, this will be a very successful match. Part of you has already been listening to the voice within quite closely. Remember this one final thing, my son. There is no ideal man or ideal woman that is complete unto themselves. That is why God put the two sexes together; that as they go through life together, they will round each other out.

In a marriage, accept your wife and yourself just where you are. Don't try to change her but try to change yourself. In a true, ideal spiritual marriage, the two do not marry to change the other, but to change themselves, and true love will do that. Marriage is more than just the joy of sexual union. It is the result of a day-to-day united investment towards an ideal. You are a more advanced soul, so marriage, for you, is not just about sex. If you know the world I know, then you know that sex is the least of the concerns. When you reach the level where I am and experience the love of God inwardly, there is no parallel. No other love can exceed the love of God within. That is why, when people truly seek the inner path, they forget about the body and pursue only God.

Now I'm going to remove myself from Philip. We will move on to your next question, and if he is not able to receive the answer from spirit, I will step back in again. This is Saint Germain.

PB: Next question?

Healing Ability

HR: I am doing healing sessions for people. I'd like to hear more about my own healing energy; more information about that.

PB: Yes. Remember the man I mentioned in the beginning? The one who practiced a samurai lifestyle? Your healing work is the major reason he's with you. I'm listening to Saint Germain. In the intertwining of your marriage with your mate and your spiritual path together, it's very important that you keep a pure heart and mind. You have to be pure hearted in order to be used at the level God wants to use you.

The gentleman I spoke of at the beginning has the last name beginning with a T. He was a very pure soul. He said to you that he became a healer through loving others. Do you remember he said that? So that is also the foundation for your healing work. I did not know you were a healer, but now I understand why he came.

Now let me tune in and let's see what they have to say about your work. At this level, while you're doing healing for other people, much of what you are doing is for you. My guide Tiffany, whose real name is Kathryn Kuhlman, was a great healer. She just walked up beside me to speak about you and said, "Tell him I really love him!" She says that, in the beginning of her work, when she was young like you, God used her to heal people. But the biggest healing was her own personal healing. That's the level of your healing work now—on the inner level of yourself.

She says that your response to your friends who keep bringing women for you to meet is part of your becoming healed and integrated enough to be able to humorously say, "No thank you." She said God already planned the person you have now. "Your mate is like the salt, and you're the pepper," she says. Together you flavor life in a balanced way. Stick with the salt you have.

Next year there will be some significant change in your awareness of your own healing ability. The gentleman who came at the beginning and other things that are coming together now, are vitally important because of the change coming for you next year.

I can feel the heart of spirit here, so I'm close to tears. I feel so much love for you in this room that it is almost overpowering. The master Buddha is still standing here. Everything unfolding here that I've been telling you is being coordinated by Buddha. It's very important that you know the specific information that's been given today so you can move forward with confidence. This is not an accident. Do you understand? Everything that you don't need is being pushed out of the way, and everything you need is being brought to you. Tiffany just said that in the future you will definitely work with a team of people.

Have you studied Reiki?

HR: No, I've never done Reiki before.

PB: You are a natural healer. You know that, right? Just follow this gentleman, Mr. T., we'll call him, or follow what Buddha said and what Tiffany has said, and you can't go wrong. Tiffany is a channel for you also. As she touches in, they're going to use her to guide your work because she loves you very much. This is what they're telling me. In your ministry, love is the key, not technique. Love is the core of it.

HR: For the healing work, correct?

PB: Yes. The core of Tiffany's healing power was love. She has come to me in dreams in which she wrapped her arms around me with so much love that I passed out. In one dream, she and I were doing healings before 60,000 people. The core, the center of healing, is love. I advise you not to talk about this with anyone. Keep it as your secret treasure. Then the energy will build.

I became an effective medium by not talking about it. To the world, I just look like a normal person without that ability, even to people closest to me. But I went to one medium who came to me as the first one in an audience of many people, looked at me and said, "First of all, you are an old, old soul, and secondly, you have many hidden secrets." What that means is yes, I've read for thousands of people, but I never talk casually about that. To me, it's a very sacred work.

As far as your future is concerned, don't worry about it. I'm focusing on you right now. I'm not worrying about anyone else. I could become very overwhelmed if I think of all the work that lies ahead for me—that I will read for many people and that my work will be successful and effective. I could be anxious, but I have great faith in God's use of me. It comes by being extremely focused, so when I'm working, I don't take my eye off what I'm doing. I do not say this to impress you, but to say you can do likewise.

I'm listening to my guide. Finally, she says, the best thing is to keep a good journal. Write all of your secrets there. Write all of your heart's longing there. Write your communications with spirit there. I have kept journals for forty years and that is what has helped me in large part to be successful.

Let's move on to your next question.

HR: I have a question about what we're talking about.

PB: Yes, please.

What is Love?

HR: I read about love and understand logically what I read, but I really don't know what love is yet, at all. I don't feel love and can't really understand the whole concept yet.

PB: I'm listening to Saint Germain. He wants to come through.

SG: Only you and about a billion other people are asking the same question! It is the favorite question of all that we are asked in spirit. "I understand love, but I can't feel love." Even as healing is a science, so is love. We begin to feel love according to natural spiritual law. When you put money in a bank, if you keep investing at a good rate, you will make great interest off that money. But if you don't invest, there's no interest. If you put your money in and take it out quickly, you'll make very little interest.

The secret is this, my son: *invest in yourself first*, with all of your heart. Love your uniqueness. In your country, love is a major issue. Your people know how to follow the right order of things, but still they feel significant emptiness when it comes to loving and being loved.

You are the literal temple of the living God. Worship God within you by appreciating your own beauty and uniqueness. Say to yourself while in meditation, "I am so happy to be me. I celebrate my own uniqueness. I am not an accident, but a divine, unique manifestation of God." Spend time in meditation getting to know your inner self. I did that. I found I fell deeply, deeply in love with myself, because I invested in myself.

From that storehouse of personal love, I was able to give love and invest love in others. We cannot properly love others until we properly love ourselves. But in a culture where there's such great conformity and sometimes blind following, people often miss taking care of themselves.

HR: Can you repeat the last part of that sentence?

SG: Yes. In a culture where there is such great conformity and sacrifice of oneself for the culture, people often don't know themselves. Some people think one bouquet of red roses is outstanding beauty. But a bouquet of flowers with a lot of variety is another kind of beauty. Gradually your culture is becoming like a mixed bouquet, rather than just red roses, because more and more people want to know themselves and be independent. You are one of them. This can lead to greater universality in consciousness within this culture. Are you following me?

HR: Pretty much.

SG: Yes. Where I'm leading you is this: after you have invested in yourself, or as you invest in yourself, invest equally in the ones you love. The more you invest in others, the more you will fall in love with them. It is the universal law of sowing and reaping. Even giving a small kiss on the cheek or a small gift will cause your own heart to begin to expand in affection. Love is born of action. Love is more of a verb than a noun. Therefore, if you want to love, you must act in a loving way. Invest, invest, invest in yourself and in others. Then you will have something in the person of yourself to draw on.

If you place your investment in another by giving, serving, and taking care of that person, that's where your love will be. Then you can receive love back from another. That is the secret. Don't just wait to feel love, act on the ideal of love. Invest, starting with yourself. My advice tonight, when you finish this session, is to go out and buy yourself something that you've been wanting. A new billfold, a keychain—it doesn't have to be expensive. Invest more in yourself and see how that feels. Do it with the purpose and intent of investing in yourself. Then you will find a smile appearing on your face because you will find how easy it is to love self and others. Jesus and Buddha and others like them are great lovers of humanity because they invested their whole life in others.

HR: Not in themselves, but in others?

SG: We saw clearly their love for others, but they could not love others without having discovered God's love within themselves first. God has loved humanity by giving all of himself to humanity. We become able to love others as God does by investing in ourselves enough to discover God's love within.

Preparing for Success

We want to make sure before the time is up that we answer all of your questions. I will step back and . . . better still, please read your next question, and I shall stay here with Philip.

HR: Even though you or Philip has said I should not worry too much about my future, my third question is about that. I'd like to know if there's anything that I should be doing right now to prepare myself for the future.

SG: In order to be successful in the future, learn to know yourself better and better. The law is that blessings come as you gain understanding of yourself. Spend enough time in meditation so that you understand through experience that you are not this body, you are not your thoughts, you are not your feelings, but the observer of all of these things. The observer is the true you, which many have come to call the God-self or higher self. When you learn more and more to live with objectivity and detachment, and heaven sees this, heaven will automatically open the doors for you.

Success is not the result of wishful thinking, nor is it mere luck. It comes from applying divine law to all situations. Gaining self-mastery is a science. In religion, God has been obscured, and the simple divine law has been lost. But in order to go home to our true self and to God, we must apply ourselves to gain self-understanding. Consistency toward purpose is part of the science of self-mastery. After a period of days, months, or years, the door will open. That is science. Therefore, do not think about yesterday or tomorrow but about today and about applying the science of consistency toward purpose. Apply yourself each day with consistency toward purpose, forgetting about the outcome, and the right results will come. We will see to that.

Now, I'm going to remove myself from Philip and let him come back, and we will conclude this wonderful session together.

PB: I have to get reoriented. He was here a long time.

HR: Yes. At one point he was going to leave, and then he decided to stay.

PB: That's okay.

Do you have other questions that you haven't been able to ask? Do you have more questions on your paper?

A Teacher Who Passed

HR: I have written the name of somebody I would like to have come today, and want to know about that person.

PB: What do you want to know about this person? You see, the more specific your questions are, the more specific the answers from spirit will be. Was this a very good friend of yours?

HR: He's somebody who taught me a lot of things, especially about healing.

PB: Well then, he was a good friend. Not necessarily a personal friend, but he was friendly to you, and you learned from him. Did he die of cancer? Yes, he's here. I just heard his voice saying he died of cancer. Apparently, he had some confusion when he died. On the outside, he may have appeared peaceful, but inside there was some conflict between what he taught and how he lived. Do you understand?

HR: I understand.

PB: He didn't go into as high a place as his students thought he would. He's not in a low realm, but he's not as high as he could have been if he'd practiced what he preached more. Did he have some kind of difficulty in a marriage?

HR: He did.

PB: Well, that's what he's telling me. He was a healer, but he didn't master personal love; therefore, he couldn't go as high. As I'm seeing him, he has tears in his eyes. He wants to say he thanks you for calling him in, and he says not to do what he did. Don't become well known and have everyone applaud you and look up to you, but not live what you teach. He said he was listening very intently to the point that Saint

Germain made about love. He said, "I understood that concept on earth, but I didn't live it."

He's going to continue to work with you. I see him standing behind you and to your left, and he helps bring energy down through your shoulders, your arms, your hands; but he's not the only one. He's like a secondary helper, not a primary one. Partly he is helping you out of obligation or duty because he didn't do everything for his students he should have done. Do you understand? That's what he just said, and that's why he's crying. He's very sorry that he didn't do better. But he's very grateful to you, he says, that you remember him, and he would like you to pray for him.

That's it. How do you feel after this session?

HR: Kind of relaxed, I guess.

PB: Did this reading bring you peace?

HR: Yes.

PB: What surprised you the most?

HR: I was able to get a lot of confirmations from what was said today.

PB: Yes, that's very important. Phenomena don't mean much, but to get the truth is what's important. You've seen other channelers. The true ones are interested in your soul and in your spiritual growth and happiness. That's the difference between the genuine and the non-genuine medium.

End of recording

Spiritual Reading Six

EXPERIENCE GOD WITHIN

Yuito E.—Male

Philip Burley (PB): I would like to begin with a prayer.

Our Heavenly Father, this gentleman has come today to listen to the spirit world and be guided. I thank all the guides and teachers who are here now helping him. Please bring through the information as clearly as possible. May he receive an abundance of love and information in his reading. May he go from here aware that he has been visited by spirit. Thank you for this privilege, Father. All this I pray in divine love.

You have a lot of blue energy around you. Spirit brings the energy very close to my spiritual sight. I can see it in detail, and it contains very fine, fine lines. It shows that you were born in peace, you live in peace, and you will die in peace.

The first thing that spirit wants to say to you, and this is coming in from Saint Germain, is that you have to feel more secure and more confident in yourself. You have a tendency to put a kind of mental protective covering over yourself most of the time. The master Jesus comes directly up behind you and puts his hands on your shoulders, showing that he is very much guiding you.

As I'm in your energies, I'm almost going into trance, because you also have that ability. Just know that. Of all the people I've met here, you are closest to approximating who I am and what I do. Your energies are very much like mine. I can tell from being in your energies that you have the ability to channel. Whether you think that or not, is not important. I'm just telling you that you have this ability.

Buddha also comes very, very close to you, and there's a large golden temple behind you.

Practicing Channeling

PB: You also have healing ability. As I went deeper into your auric field, my guide Tiffany was showing me that it is very warm healing energy. I don't know how she did it, but I was taken into your energy field, and all of a sudden, I was very warm, feeling the same kind of energy that I recognize as healing energy. You may think that you have to go to more classes or get more education if you're going to do spiritual work, but I want to tell you that much of what you need is already in you. It's more a matter of just practicing what you already know, particularly about channeling, and letting it happen.

Jesus keeps referring to your wife, saying that there are many reasons your souls are together. Your situation is very similar to that of my wife and me. First, there is deep friendship, but the ultimate purpose has to do with your spiritual path. If you and she would sit with each other, even a half an hour to an hour, two or three times a week, both of you would develop at a very high level. When I say sit together, I mean in a darkened room, with no candles. You may put on a little music in the beginning, but basically just sit very quietly across from each other, maybe no further than two or three feet apart. This is coming in from

Saint Germain: Just sit very quietly with your eyes closed, in a meditative state. Call out to your guides and tell them, "We are doing this now, please come and assist us." Once you get into a significantly altered state, let them speak through you. Your wife will be used like a battery for you. Jesus says you should have a tape recorder there and once you start channeling, let her turn it on to record your words.

Saint Germain is speaking. He is not coming through, but he's talking behind me, saying not to worry about what's going to be said when you channel. Just let it come through. Don't have any kind of idea that you have to be a special person or meet a special condition. Anyone can be a channel for spirit. And no matter how short the message, or how unimportant it may seem, the purpose of this practice is to get used to the process.

Saint Germain and Jesus are both going to be working with your couple. Mother Mary helps also. She is standing right here, to your right, and she's talking about those nights that you will practice channeling. She will be there because there will be a lot of healing energy. They're saying to sit this way for a minimum of three months, always on the same two or three nights each week, at the same time and in the same place. If you channel, say, for ten or fifteen minutes to start with, and sit in silence for ten to fifteen minutes before you start, that's about a half hour. Then for the practice, you should be the battery for your wife and let her channel.

They are saying that the purpose of channeling at this level is just for the two of you to learn how to do it, and also to get information for the two of you. If you prefer, and they're okay with this, you can invite a few people in to make the circle a little bit bigger. Invite new students or people who are not channelers. The purpose of those people coming is to increase the energy, but also so that you can give messages.

The most important thing, in your case, is not to be self-conscious. I didn't want to say it in the beginning, but Jesus was showing that it's as though you have a black umbrella you hold over yourself. This is a symbol of being insecure. Just be yourself and have confidence.

The two of you are going to travel overseas at some point. Are you planning a trip?

YE: Not at all. Are you talking about a trip for fun?

PB: I don't know. I'm just telling you there is travel coming up. Quite often I'll tell people they're going to travel, and they say they have no plans. I told one man I read for in America that he would be going to Japan and then China, and he looked at me cross-eyed. He said, "I have absolutely no plan for that. Your reading is inaccurate." He called me the next day and said, "You're not going to believe this, but my boss just came in and threw an airplane ticket on my desk. He said you must go and do research in Japan and in China." So, you never know!

Always, with spiritual readings or channeling there is the possibility that the prophecy won't come true, because human beings may do something to change things, or because of other circumstances. But I see this, so I'm just telling you what I see.

Grandmother in Spirit

Is your mother in spirit? I keep seeing a woman standing here.

YE: She's still alive.

PB: Was your grandmother, your mother's mother, very close to you?

YE: My mother's mother lived far away and I never really knew her at all, but when I was little, I lived with my father's mother.

PB: She may be here, but I'm not seeing her. I'm listening.

YE: My mother had two mothers, the mother that gave her birth, and the mother that raised her. The mother that bore my mother has already passed away.

PB: And she lived at a distance from you?

YE: My two grandmothers from my mother's side are dead.

PB: Again, I come back to your mother's side. This woman is very, very close to you. She is your mother's mother, and she appears as a mother to you because she's working very closely with you and has been for quite a long time. She says that she works on the inner band, which has to do with inner, personal things—not spiritual things, but practical things—and she's very happy with your relationship. She just said that.

Before I hand your paper with your questions back to you, I want to say that you're born with a lot of luck. You may not think so, but it shows. Your life will always be . . . I don't want to use the word, "easy," but your life will always be okay.

PB: Now please take your paper and ask your first question.

The Inner Life

YE: First of all, I want to know if there's anything that I'm supposed to be doing.

PB: I'm going to let Saint Germain come through and speak.

Saint Germain (SG): I am here. This is Saint Germain. I'm very pleased to be with you.

Now as to the question you are asking regarding whether or not there is anything you should do for yourself, my answer is, "Of course." My son, the greatest truth is to know yourself. From the answers that you receive about yourself, you can know God. But most people spend their time focusing on the external aspects of their lives. When we are speaking of things that have to do with knowing self, we are not talking primarily about external talents, abilities or activities—the external realities of life. The truths that you need to know about yourself are eternal truths about eternal life, and these answers are obtained only by going inside.

In the deep meditation experience, God speaks to us through us. The deeper and higher you go in meditation, the more you know that God lives in you. This is a universal truth. Not one soul who has ever lived on earth is an exception to the reality of God living within them. Therefore, my son, move as quickly as possible away from too much concern about the external world and focus your attention on your inner life. As you do so, much needed guidance will be given to you for your life.

Now I'm going to remove myself from Philip and if I think it's necessary to come back again, I shall do so. This is Saint Germain.

PB: Okay, you may ask another question.

Spiritual Guides

YE: I'd like to hear information about my guides.

PB: What do you want to know? Thus far, you have been told that Jesus, Buddha, Saint Germain, and your grandmother work with you.

YE: For example, how many guides do I have?

PB: About twelve, and they're working at different levels. Some are like relatives, working very close to you, and there are those on the deeper level who work with you on your spiritual growth. Some are just protectors, and others have to do with helping you go deep enough to learn of God within.

They're not all Japanese. There's a Western guide who works with you in the financial area. He was in the military and lived here, doing advisory work in finance in Japan after World War II. He is working with you. I don't know his full name, but his first name is Kenneth. He's a very handsome man. There's also one who is a ritual guide. He works with you with rituals.

YE: So about twelve people, is that right?

PB: When I asked Tiffany, she said, "Tell him about a dozen," but there are more than that. I can see, just right over here on your father's side of the family, your father's ancestry, six or seven generations, with many people standing here. Where they're standing, I can see very clearly that it's all blue. I wish you could see it. I couldn't possibly name all those people. But they're not as important as the people close to you, your master teachers.

Now, why your ancestors on your mother's side of the family didn't appear at this point, I don't have a clue. I don't pretend to always understand. I just say what I see, and that's it.

Okay, you may ask your next question.

Self-Mastery

YE: What is my soul's destiny in this lifetime?

PB: I already heard that. Saint Germain said, "He's going to ask that question." If Saint Germain is working with you, the plan is self-mastery. Some people come into the earth plane and their realization is to raise a good family. Some people's realization is to be the head of a country, and that's all they do. But very few come into life with the specific purpose of obtaining self-mastery. It's the highest of high callings. There is no calling higher and there's no calling more difficult. Saint Germain says it's the ultimate goal of every human being, every life that comes on earth. He says you have the makings of one who can achieve self-mastery, and he will guide you regarding all of this, but you must ask yourself the question, what does self-mastery mean? Saint Germain says, "It's our job to help you along the path, but not do the work for you. Otherwise, you cannot achieve "*self*-mastery."

Saint Germain is laughing. He says self-mastery is sometimes like playing a game of chess with yourself. Sometimes you have to lose in order to win, and sometimes you have to win in order to lose. Self-mastery is not about perfection. There is nothing perfect on the earth plane. That's a naïve point of view, he says. The only thing that one should worry about in terms of perfection is perfecting one's love. Another word for perfect love is unconditional love—loving all people at all times as you love yourself. You have a good beginning, because you have your wife, and you know that the two of you have gone through struggles, but you continue to love. That is unconditional love—to love as God loves, under all conditions.

Since your purpose in this life is to master yourself, direct yourself toward being free from all misunderstandings and all self-centered love. And Saint Germain laughed and said, "When someone like Jesus is working with you—as he himself works with me—you've got to know that the major feature or the major concern on your path is love, love, love. To achieve self-mastery, it is more important to love oneself properly than it is to love another person."

It's not an easy task to walk that fine line—the line between proper self-love and proper love of others, but the secret is to remain humble. Then the answers will always be there. Focus more on listening to the voice within than on listening to other people. God and spirit world are not at all concerned about mistakes. From God's point of view there are no mistakes. The idea of mistakes is of man's making, not God's.

The Importance of a Balanced Life

YE: Okay, I think I've got it now. For example, in society, there are certain things you're supposed to do in a certain way, and people bring guilt upon themselves for not doing something the way they're supposed to do it. But the way you're supposed to do things is often the common-sense way, so does that mean I should ignore common sense?

PB: I'm listening to Saint Germain. The common-sense way is usually God's way. God placed you between two worlds. Common sense requires you to live with your feet on the ground, but living a spiritual life requires you to have your head in the clouds. Live each day on earth responsibly, toward the practical reality of existence.

YE: You are saying that I should live with my two feet on the ground?

PB: And with your head in the clouds, Saint Germain says, which means to have a vision of your spiritual life. You have to satisfy or fulfill both responsibilities. You could go live in a cave somewhere and just meditate, but that's not very realistic, because you have to take care of your body. This means you have to have money, which means you have to have a job. And he says that applying oneself to the practical or commonsense reality of everyday life helps balance the spiritual life as well.

Did you have more on that? Obviously, you are struggling between living on earth and aspiring towards a spiritual life. Is that true?

YE: Yes.

PB: Yes, I've been there. How old are you?

YE: Thirty-four.

PB: When I was that age, I was exactly where you are right now. My experience is that it's a matter of striking a balance between the two, not focusing on either one to the exclusion of the other.

YE: You are saying don't think only about spiritual things or only about three-dimensional things, and try to find a balance between the two, is that correct?

PB: Your understanding is exactly right. That's it. Saint Germain is here, but this is Philip talking. From my experience, the person most useful to God and the spirit world is the one who is balanced. God calls such people to be an example to other people. Most people cannot afford to live only a spiritual life, going into a monastery or giving up the three-dimensional life.

YE: So you would have to become a little bit of a strange person, or different from everybody else to be able to do that?

PB: Yes, and there aren't many people who do that, except in India or Tibet where there's a strong tradition that embraces the eccentric person.

YE: What does that mean, exactly?

PB: For example, society in those countries embraces the reality of people living in caves or devoting one hundred percent of their lives to the fourth or spiritual dimension to the exclusion of the third dimension. In modern society, I am probably an extreme example of devoting most of my time to the fourth dimension. My spiritual work is full time, here and in the United States. But I am very aware of money, of keeping bank accounts, and paying my bills, so I work to strike a balance between my earthly life and the spiritual work I do. Is this answering your question?

YE: Yes.

PB: I understand. Again, I've been where you are, and I understand very well what you're going through. What kind of work do you do now?

YE: I'm a computer engineer.

PB: That's what I thought. Are you bored with it?

YE: That's actually one of the questions I wanted to ask you today. There's a part of me that feels being a computer engineer is just right for me, but there's another part that feels being in computers is absolutely not right for me. I want to know what that feeling is that this work is not right for me.

PB: It's not about that work being wrong for you. Your talents, education, and your natural abilities all go in that direction, and that's why you wound up in that field. This is Philip speaking, backed by my experience in spirit. Many hundreds of people have asked me this same kind of question, over and over. What I have found is that most people don't need to change their job. Number one, they need to change the way they look at their job, and number two, almost all human beings have the element of spirituality missing in their lives, and they need to realize that God lives in them.

God lives in you. Do you know that? Do you know that experientially?

Experience God Within

YE: Not really, though maybe I have . . .

PB: . . . the idea as an intellectual concept?

YE: Yes, exactly, and I understand it.

PB: What is yet to happen is for you to be born into that experience. I don't say this immodestly, but because I have had that experience from childhood until this very day, I work sacrificially to do whatever I can to assist other people to experience it.

Once you make that contact with God within yourself, everything changes, because it puts everything in proper perspective, and I mean everything. Your priorities change, your energy literally changes, the way you look at other people and at yourself changes, and experience at work changes. As I am looking at you spiritually, I don't see the necessity of changing your occupation. All I see is the need to change the way you look at it—or the way you experience it.

I started working on a certain level in spiritual work when I was twenty-three, and I'm sixty-three this year. After forty years of great devotion to spiritual matters, full time for many years, I've found that the majority of humanity is not happy. This has nothing to do with the third dimension, ultimately. It's because people have not met their real self and God within.

YE: It makes no difference whether they're very rich or they're very poor?

PB: Exactly. Once you meet God face to face, once you know God as a living, breathing reality within you, you're still responsible and able to live on the practical level, but you are in a state of bliss. As I said earlier, everything is placed in a proper perspective, and you see everything more clearly. To such people, there are no strangers, and they are at home anywhere. Whatever appears on their path, they totally accept. Once they discover God inside, they also discover, almost at the same time, that everything is contained in God, including themselves, and they realize that they are not different from God. That's why I said their whole perspective changes.

In that state of mind with God, you see this world as really, truly an illusion, and though you can't just change the dream, you know you are in the dream. Once you have the experience of God within, you stop fighting external reality. You just flow with it and you're happy in it. Nothing can depress you, and nothing can turn you negative or pull you down. That is what I want to give to other people. That's what bliss is, and that's where you're headed—both you and your wife.

Your questions are among the best that have been asked here in this room or in other readings, because some people who come to me for readings around the world, ask almost exclusively about the practical world. Sometimes their questions are centered around their expectations of life and sometimes they border on fantasy. You're the kind of person who's very valuable to God, and the questions you ask indicate to me that you will find balance in your life. You will find God within.

After all, what else is there? You know what love is like between man and woman, but that's not the be-all and end-all. Even though you love each other one hundred fifty percent, you're still alone, even living in the same house. When you finally find God within, all the loneliness leaves. You're never, ever, ever alone again.

I have a very dear Japanese friend who lives in San Francisco. His wife, also a dear friend, died while I was here in Japan. He is a very highly developed soul, more advanced than a number of gurus I've met in India. When I asked him about his wife's approaching death before she died, he said, "Of course I'm very sad that she's going to have to leave, and I will miss her. But I totally accept all of this as part of life. I will not grieve her. It's her time to go. This is the way her soul decided to go. So why should I resist reality?" I happen to know that since she's passed on, he is completely at peace. He's neither sad nor happy, nor grieving, because he's a man who found God inside.

Mohammed and Muslim Religion

You have a Middle Eastern guide who is standing with you, all in light. He's coming from the Arab nations, and he is Muslim. I didn't discern this until just now, but it's Mohammad! I'm pausing a moment, because I haven't beheld him in a long time, but the atmosphere with him is very, very beautiful.

RY: I was working with him and Maitreya last night, so I'm not surprised.

PB: Oh, really?

YE: Yes. Not directly with Mohammad, but with Maitreya. All the Arab energies came.

PB: That's interesting.

YE: I'm not surprised. I started feeling the energy before you said there's a Middle Eastern man, and I said to myself, well it's either Mohammad or Maitreya. Normally I don't say those things during a session, but I just wanted to mention it.

PB: Yes. He's standing right near you. He's talking about why he came in. He works with you, and there's a good example he wants to talk about in the Muslim religion. The country of Iran, he says, has had a terrible time because there are those who want to live one hundred percent for the spiritual life, they think I (Mohammad) taught. In the process, they failed in the area of the human heart, and they failed to live in reality. They created a big mess, and I feel responsible. The people who will finally save Iran will be those who are moderate—those who really know and love God, but also know how to bring God to earth.

Mohammad says, "Go to some poor country and teach about God. They will not be able to hear you until you literally fill their stomachs with bread. There must be a balance struck between high-mindedness and naturalness. As Philip says, God works best through the man that's most balanced. Please pray for my people." He's crying, and he's very, very troubled. He is really asking you to pray for his people.

Now, did you have another question?

Spirit and Mother Earth

YE: I have another question about a spiritual matter. I would like to know where I have come from.

PB: "You came from God," is what Saint Germain said. The universe is inside of God. I was watching to see if they were going to show me a certain place, but no, you came directly from God to the earth plane. You haven't been elsewhere. Unlike what some people might think, Mother Earth is the most privileged planet to be born on. It's the hardest planet to be on, but because of that it's the place where you can learn the most and grow the highest. Jesus was born here. All the great masters that we know were born here. So, you're literally not "far out." (Laughter)

YE: My wife wants to know if I will go into full trance at some point.

PB: Yes, you can. You already work together very closely. When my wife sat with me, I had the most profound experiences. But like everything, you have to really apply yourself. Genuine, genuine channeling is a very rare thing. There are people who channel energy, and there are people who channel thoughts, but to actually have a spiritual entity come into you and take over your vocal cords is a very rare thing. The biggest and most difficult thing is to not have any concepts about how it should happen, and how you will be used. In learning trance, I was initiated into it through an advanced medium who spontaneously anointed me with spirit energy coming through his hands and out of my mouth came the voice and words of Saint Germain, originally, but more things came to me as I continued my work.

For example, today, there was an outstanding breakthrough in which Saint Germain came through me—for another person *and* also for you—more than he has at any other time. They never told me they were going to do that. But it comes because I have been consistently dedicated and serving in relation to spirit and other people. Sometimes I want to stop, but over and over, I just re-commit myself and surrender by saying, "Not my will, but your will."

I can't give you any more today. That's it. I'd just like to close with a prayer.

Beloved Father, thank you for this precious young man's desire. I love the fact that he searches for truth in a balanced way. Use him and his wife for your glory. Teach them your way and bring them to full success. All of this I pray, Father, in divine love. Amen.

End of recording

LOVE AND THE SEARCH FOR TRUTH

Hina K.—Female

Philip Burley (PB): I hold the paper with your questions to pick up the vibration. Then, as I pray out loud, spirit comes and a white light comes around us. I may hand the paper back to you, especially when it's time for you to ask your questions. During the session, I go in and out of trance. One of the gifts I have is to go in and out quickly. When I had a radio show, I had to go back and forth quickly, and I have been well trained to do that.

In addition to Saint Germain, I have three other major guides, all master teachers. A young woman stands here, who is all in white, and my teacher who is a medical doctor stands here. I have a Native American teacher called Black Hawk who is present and protects the atmosphere to keep low spirits away. I just wanted to share this information with you.

Prayer: Our Heavenly Father, thank you for this young lady who has come to seek truth. Guide this session to answer all of her questions, and may she realize clearly that she has been visited by spirit. Father, I ask especially for your healing touch, that whatever it is that she needs healing for may be healed. All of us come into this life with a life map—things we are to accomplish and goals we are to reach. Father, may this reading give her the information she needs to guide her on her path. May all of her guides and teachers work with my guides and teachers clearly, and we thank them for coming. Father, bless her with all this information, that she may go forth in great joy and peace. All this I ask in divine love. Amen.

When I shook your hand and looked at your face, a great amount of gold and purple light exploded around you. Your life is indeed touched by God, and you are a pure soul. I saw many, many ancestors. Even now as I am speaking, spirit is touching me with great electricity. It is called electric love, and it's for you.

Also, I see three or four angelic forms around you, all in blue. They want you to know two things: First, you're to live a long life, and secondly, you're always protected. You will die a natural death. You are also to achieve self-mastery in this life. You have healing power in your hands, and as I look at you clairvoyantly, I can see light coming from your hands at the end of your fingers. My whole body is now covered with perspiration because of the great spiritual power coming through. I'm experiencing this, but it's for you.

Your path may appear very narrow at times, but that is because God and spirit are being very precise with what you are to accomplish in this life. They want you to reach specific self-mastery in this lifetime. Kwan Yin is with you very strongly, and I see her directly behind you. She has a most beautiful smile on her face that shines on you. She has her hands on your shoulders, so I know she's directly guiding you.

I'm going to let Saint Germain come through now and speak because he wants to introduce himself, and he wants to give an opening message, too.

Saint Germain (SG): I am here. Can you hear me all right?

HK: Yes, I can hear you.

SG: Good morning. I am so very pleased.

HK: I'm pleased, too. I've wanted to meet you.

Love and the Search for Truth

SG: Yes. I'm very pleased to meet you, but I already know you. The smile on Philip's face is my smile, not his, because you see, dear one, we belong to a universal circle of spiritual beings, you and I. You are not ultimately Japanese, nor am I ultimately French or anything else. We are all children of the same God. When you stepped through that door, you came into a new world.

Many are searching for truth, and there are different levels of truth, so we cannot know absolutely what is always true. One person proclaims the truth, another person proclaims the truth, and the messages are in conflict with each other. But the highest truth is love. When someone loves us, we know it, and when we love someone, we know it, and there is no argument. Therefore, love, as such, is truth itself and validates itself. I come to earth not so much to give truth in words, as to give love.

Yes, love is a verb, an action word. If we love ourselves or love someone else, we serve them. We take care of them. But even deeper than that is a feeling of affection. This affection is the gem of love. In simple terms, there is warmth, deep abiding warmth in our heart toward that individual.

You are born already in love. You could not be who you are without that fact. But now you are ready to go to the higher plane of the full realization of first mastering love for self. You are in that process now. Therefore, when you leave here, you will be enveloped by an energy called love that will stay with you. From now on, dear one, when you look into the mirror, greet yourself as love.

HK: Look into a mirror and greet myself this way?

SG: Yes. The more that we live this way, the more we become what we think and say. Doing this will affect your whole life. Allow that reality that is already present in you to come forth. One who uses this mantra, "I am love," reaches the high planes very quickly. All the rituals in the world cannot get you to that place unless you obtain love. In your country, you manifest this affection through honoring tradition.

Many people are searching for God. Who is God? Where is God? What is God? From our side, there is the obvious awareness that God lives in you. This affection I speak of as the gem of life is God. Therefore, if you dwell upon this love, and say, "I am love itself" over and over, then you will bring love out of both you and God. It will come forth from you. Do you find my message strange or different? (Chuckle)

HK: I've actually written this down as a question for you today. As I've been listening to you, I've received a lot of the answers that I wanted to hear.

SG: Yes. I know that! We know your questions already. Sometimes we inspire such questions. I did not look at your paper. But from your heart, I knew your question. This is why, in Philip's literature, he says we often answer questions before they are asked.

Now I'm going to step back from Philip for a few minutes and let him come back to himself. I shall come back and be with you again. Are you finding this meaningful?

HK: Yes, of course.

SG: Of course, because you see, dear one, thousands and thousands and thousands of years have been spent to come to this moment, so we could meet. This is your divine destiny, not so you remember Saint Germain, but that you remember that you are love. It is the most important fact of all of your life, and out of it will be born a new you. Now I'm going to take my leave and let Philip come back. This is Saint Germain.

PB: He's chuckling. He said he answered one of your questions.

HK: Yes.

PB: I would like you to read the question that he answered.

HK: He answered two questions, really.

PB: So we're finished! (Laughter)

What is Love?

HK: I've been really wondering what love is. I've been in a lot of emotional pain about that. It's not a very easy time for me right now.

PB: Yes.

HK: Saint Germain taught me to say, "I am love. I am love." That's one of the things he taught me to say. It is very difficult for me to remember to keep saying to myself, "I am love. I am love." I know it's important to receive healing from other people and myself during the difficult periods of my life. When I signed up for this session today, I had not one thought in my mind. I didn't even think. I just picked up the phone and called immediately, without even thinking, as soon as I saw the ad. Saint Germain said it took thousands and thousands of years for us to be able to come together at this point in time. I understand that, too. I really understand the reason I'm seeing you right now.

PB: Yes. If you read your first question, or the two questions he answered, you'll have that on the tape, so read your questions out loud.

HK: I asked for a clear message for this time in my life, right now. There is fear and anger inside of me, and I want to know the exact reason that these feelings are here. I haven't been able to create in my life what I want to create in my life, and I want to know why I can't create those things in my life, and how to clear up these problems. Those are the two questions.

PB: I always pray for people a number of days before they come to me. I've been praying for all the Japanese people I meet. I've been praying since June. This morning as I was preparing to meet you, Saint Germain came to me and said, "Her need is love, so when you speak to her, I will talk through you about love. She needs to understand the fullness of what love means for herself."

Let me have your paper, please.

HK: I haven't read the third question out loud, though.

PB: That's all right. I only wanted you to read the questions that had already been answered. I don't want to know the questions that haven't been answered, so I'm going to hold your paper now.

Ancestral Guide and the "Love of your Life"

As I'm looking at you, I'm looking to the East. I see you in the Far East, so your life is to be lived here. Some people want to go to other countries and travel. You can do that, but your quest is here. Your goals will be met or fulfilled on the soil of your own land. You have a very straight, very pure vertical line toward the Japanese spirit world. And that very straight line that goes up is all blue. Within your ancestry there were many noble people, meaning they were good-hearted and pure-hearted.

As I'm looking to your right, there is a gentleman standing all in blue, and he's rather scholarly looking. He is gesturing with his hand. He is part of your ancestry, and I just heard my guide say he is six generations back.

HK: Does he have a beard?

PB: Yes.

HK: On my father's or mother's side?

PB: Father's side. In my work, the right side is father, and the left side is mother. You don't know this gentleman, but he works with you. He is six generations back, a very, very wise man. He was a scholarly man who was very good in calligraphy. He's now touching me, and he said in my ear, "Thank you," just like that. He wants you to know that the questions that you have been asking could not be answered until now. It had to be in this setting. You are crossing a river, he says. This is the river of life, and you are in the middle of the bridge. But in the next three months, your life will speed up spiritually. He says you will feel something like a rebirth.

Have you been looking for the love of your life?

HK: I'm not sure what you mean. I have a husband right now and, of course, I love my husband. But there is a part of me that is looking for love.

PB: The love of your life means your love for *you*. This man said he already understood many spiritual things when he went into spirit, but he did not understand that God lives in us. As he says this, he's crying very much. I can hear him crying. He's saying that what he wants to bring to you is the awareness of why the answer to your question is on this soil. It is because the answer lies within you. A part of your education for self-mastery is learning how to go inside and awaken to God within. That's what he means by looking for the love of your life. He has been pushing you, but we needed this link to get through specifically.

In this lifetime, you will find the happiness and peace you're looking for. He's showing me his life, and he says, "When I was on earth, I was so hungry for love." He says his parents didn't love him, and his friends didn't love him. "I was looking everywhere for love. Only after I came here to the spirit world did I realize that I was looking in the wrong place. Our mother and father, our husband, our wife, our children, our brothers and sisters, cannot give us this love. Only God within can bring forth this love. I'm going to work with you, and as you grow, I will grow."

He's dressed all in blue. His costume is of six generations back, but I don't know what it is. It's not samurai, and not that of a wealthy person, but spiritually he is a very uncommon man. Very nice.

HK: I have all of the names of all of my ancestors written down going all the way back. Is there any way you could find the name of this gentleman?

PB: Yes, if you trace it back, you'll find him. He's not considered a major ancestor. Not from the direct line, but more indirect. The same blood.

I see you getting more education. Are you planning on going to school for something? I see you with many books, gaining earthly learning.

HK: Right now, no, there is nothing clearly planned. But I know I need to study something.

PB: Yes, it's coming, and the funds will be there, too. I don't know what it is, but there will be something like a scholarship or grant, and that's going to help you. Usually when I see these things, people call me up later and say, what you said happened. You don't have to worry about it at this point. Just forget it, and it will come.

The Female Guide

Did you have on your paper the name of a woman who you were very, very close to that you asked to come? There's a female who keeps coming, trying to get my attention.

HK: Yes.

PB: One particular woman.

HK: I've written her name down here.

PB: Yes. She keeps coming to me, and from the moment I started praying, she was there. She is talking to me and saying, "I've got to get through, I've got to get through, I've got to get through." She is here.

She said in spirit, "I walked a long way to get here." She comes from a very high level. Did you know that about her when she was on earth?

HK: I had no idea.

PB: She didn't necessarily have an active religious life, but she was a good person.

HK: It is not somebody that I ever knew on the earth. I never met this woman on earth, so didn't know if she was from a very high level or not.

PB: Well, this is the same person, and she's almost angelic. She seems to have lived almost like a nun on earth. And as I look at her—I can see her with my eyes open—she has a lot of sparkling gold light all around her, and that light comes into your light. She tells me she has to do with the healing part of you. May I touch your hand? Are you studying healing?

HK: I studied a little bit.

PB: Yes, and you need to study more because it's a part of your path. If you will be diligent in meditation, you will open up psychically very, very strongly. It's very pure, and it's innately in you. You shouldn't even question it.

Buddha and Kwan Yin

Buddha just walked up behind you. In America, I can't see him so clearly because the spiritual atmosphere is not this strong, but here I can see him very clearly with my eyes open. He wants to personally help you in your going inward, but not the way that he learned. He said that his path was too complicated, and you don't need it. If you just spend even twenty minutes a day with a technique or method that you like and repeat the words, "I am love," you will have many profound experiences. I can hear him laughing. He says, "I am telling you what I wish someone had told me." What took him many years to accomplish, you can accomplish in a much shorter time, and he is going to help you.

You have Kwan Yin and Buddha with you, and you have the gentleman who is your ancestor I have spoken about. You also have three or four angelic beings so you have plenty of people working with you. Saint Germain is going to help you too. I'm going to let him come through. Please stand by.

SG: (Chuckle) I am so pleased to come back through again and speak to you. Today you have indeed been visited by us, so your feet should fly as you leave here, like walking on air, because this is a rare experience, you see.

We do honor you. We jest and we joke to lift up the atmosphere, but it is for a serious reason. When you come here, you are transformed, and you *know* you have been visited by us. I will help watch over you in the coming months, and you will find your sacrifice to make this reading possible will be worth every yen you have spent.

In this setting we are not speaking of spaceships, UFOs, or outer galactic people. We are not speaking of specific religious traditions or practices. These may be good and necessary, but the top of the mountain is where God lives—not on Mount Olympus in Greece where they believe the gods lived. In truth, God is at the top of the mountain, and I come from the top. I do not mean to say that others you have spoken to do not also come from the mountaintop, but as you walk around the mountain, there are many different views, all from one mountain. They are all true, from a certain perspective or location on the mountain. But the highest truth is love. Therefore, it is important that you have received this blessing. This capstone of information for you personally will help you complete your climb to the top.

HK: Can you explain that in other words?

SG: It is important, in order for you to go higher, that you understand *how* to go higher. Where our spirit is, we are. Where love is, that's where our spirit is. If you love God above all, then you will be with God. But the top of the mountain exists within us so we must meet God here. Now I do not want to dwell on this topic longer because we want to make sure that if there are any other tributary questions you would like to ask, that you have enough time. I am going to stay here with Philip, and I will step back in if necessary. Please stand by.

PB: Okay, let's go to your next question.

Interpretation of Dreams

HK: My third question is quite different from my first two, and I have one more after that one. I have many dreams. In my dreams, when I'm sleeping or waking up, I see animals all the time, and many times I see crows. I'm sure that all these crows have a message for me, and I want to know more clearly what those messages are.

PB: I know the answer. Spirit just said it.

HK: I also have other questions. Should I read those now?

PB: No. There will be time. Let's go to the question about the crows. I'm listening to my guide Tiffany who said that the colors in the dream have two interpretations. Black can represent evil, fears, or humility. Humility is like dark brown. If you see spirit in dark brown, it can be a low spirit, or if it's a higher spirit like St. Francis who comes in brown, it means humility.

HK: I don't know St. Francis.

PB: It doesn't matter. St. Francis was a humble man, so he appears in brown. He's a monk and he is extremely humble. But a low earthly spirit could appear in brown also and be filled with pride or ignorance.

The crows represent two things in your dreams. The first message is this: If you walk your path obedient to the call to search for God within, that path to God is humility. In this case, the many crows mean to just keep having humility. As you practice that, the crows will disappear.

The other interpretation is that the crows represent your fears. As you practice loving yourself, the fears will disappear, and the crows will disappear. They will stop coming. It's a complicated answer. Okay, let's go to your next question.

The Role of the Female Guide

HK: A minute ago, I said that I was positive that the woman I spoke of is the one who brought me here today. I know I have many guides, and I also understand that today the most important message for me is to understand about love, learning about internal love. But I have been dealing for a long time now with the woman who is my main guide in life, and I can really feel her and I know that she's there. I would like to have more messages from her.

PB: Do you know the name of the woman?

HK: "Mary" or "Mari" or something like that. It sounds like Mother Mary, but I couldn't pronounce the name properly. It is "Maddi," or something like that.

PB: When I'm doing a reading, I become the spirit, or I become you. Because I'm becoming her, I know that this woman sacrificed a lot of her life to serve God. (Loud sound from a picture on the wall falling down.) Oops.

HK: What happened?

PB: The picture just fell off the wall. It's the damp weather. Anyway, yes, this woman did help bring you here, but she's part of a team. You have many guides around you. Because your destiny is to become a master of self, then you have master teachers working with you. The term "master teacher" does not always mean the highest. There are masters at different levels. These are people who mastered their life at a certain level. We may master the first grade in school, but we have to master the second, the third, and the fourth, all the way through. If there are ten levels, she's between eight and nine. She's very close to the top of the mountain, and I'm listening to her.

When she lived on earth, she placed God outside of herself, and she could not find God. She says the reason she came to you is because she knows your destiny is to find God within. She brought you here to hear the first part of the message from Saint Germain. As she works with you and you find God within, from the spirit side *she* will grow, too. Much like when teachers are teaching, they also learn, as parents learn from their children.

She watches you in your practices such as meditation, prayer, and so on, and she sometimes pushes you, but all of them do the same. That's why this narrow path was given to you. You have to truly understand you're not average. In the Japanese culture they say, "Don't stand out," but you must—not to the world, but to God, before God.

Speaking with God

God speaks to you, you know. Have you not heard the voice?

HK: Maybe, a long time ago.

PB: It's going to come back.

HK: I heard it, but I was very scared. I thought it was something other than God.

PB: No, it's God.

HK: If I'm able to release my fears, I'll be able to speak with God again?

PB: You don't have to release your fears. Just repeat the mantra, "I am love." If you have a bucket full of dirty water, there are two ways to remove the dirty water. One is to pick it up and pour it out, and the other is to drop diamonds in and as the diamonds fill up the bucket, the water flows over. Put the diamonds of "I am love" in yourself, and all the problems will disappear.

SG: I must come back through as Philip speaks. I have to come back through because my heart is so moved at this moment by the energy here. Beloved one, you have all that you need right within you, and so all of us who are here today surrounding you come to say one thing: You can do it! You can do it! You *can* do it. Don't look back.

I said to you, when you stepped through that door, you came into a new world. There is a reason you came here. If there is anything we all need, it's more love. But the most important love is the love we can give to ourselves by doing the right thing in life, and by going inside and uncovering the presence of God already there. We do not have to earn God. That is a terrible and false teaching. We don't have to go out among the stars to find God. That, too, is a wrong teaching. God is with you as much now as he ever will be. You have only to overcome or get rid of ignorance and increase your understanding. Practice that understanding. Then, God will come forth.

God has never stopped speaking to you. He knew of your fear. In the latter years he has been speaking to you through you, but not with a separate sound. Rather, he uses the tone of your own conscience, so you will not be afraid, or he speaks through spirits, but it is all one voice. The voice of divine spirit is no different than the voice of God. This lovely woman you spoke of, whose name in English means Maria, knows this for sure. It is why she prompted you to come here. God inspired her to inspire you.

Here in spirit, where I am, we know God lives in us. We know there is truly only *one* energy, and God uses us all to inspire others. Now I do not want to preach too much. I simply want to inspire you. You know, the word inspiration comes from the root "in spirit." Literally it means that I as a spirit here in the spirit world speak to you to move your heart. It is the true meaning of inspiration, you see. You were greatly inspired by us all to come here.

Now this lovely woman whose name you wrote down is like a mother and sister to you. She works with you in the same way as Philip's guide

Tiffany works with him. She works intimately with your inner personal life in your relationships with husband, children, parents, grandparents, and friends. In the core, at the center, she does all of this out of the motive of leading you higher and higher. When you tune into her, learn more and more to hear and feel her. Work with what you sense with her. Learning how to attune to spirit is the means to how to attune to God. Now let's ask your other questions.

HK: I have another question, but it's not a personal question.

SG: It does not matter.

HK: It's a question about Saint Germain.

SG: Yes, you may ask me. If I know, I will tell you. I should know about me, shouldn't I?

More about Saint Germain

HK: There is not very much information in Japan right now about Saint Germain.

SG: Just wait. I came here to let people know of me. I told Philip, because I come in the name of love, true love, that more and more people will come to listen to me, and then I will become very well known. You are just the tip of the iceberg of those people, and you will inevitably pull others through.

I looked for many years for someone like Philip to work with, and it's very rare to find someone who is as dedicated as he is. He loves this work more than anything. It's a great sacrifice, but his joy is to help you find joy. That is all he is living for, to see the smile on your face. In that sense, he and I are very much as one.

Now, what do you want to know about me? Do you want my address in spirit? (Laughter) Or maybe you want to know my bank account in spirit? If you have that number, you will find it is filled with nothing but love, the bank account of love. Yes. It's true that I've given you some of what I own, but there's plenty more where that came from. Now, go ahead.

HK: I feel that I have received the answer to the question I had. What I knew about Saint Germain, about you, before I came, was that you are a master of ascension and transformation, and I thought that meant transformation in terms of earthquakes and big changes in that respect. Now I understand that's not what it means. It means that you are a master of love.

SG: That is correct.

HK: Now I understand that, so I feel I received the answer to my question already.

SG: You are very wise. This is because you are already somewhat a master of truth. It's easy for you to deduce the truth if you talk to me. But you see, many people have the wrong idea about me. When Jesus was on earth, some people thought he was here for this purpose, and some for that purpose. Those who were threatened by the truth he brought wanted to kill him. This happened to me, also.

Christians today interpret Jesus' life in different ways. Some emphasize the crucifixion and others the resurrection—what happened to Jesus after he died. What Jesus actually came to teach is the same thing I taught you today. He wanted each one to realize God lives in each one. But when they tried to kill him, he could not bring this awareness to the earth plane as planned.

In the West the literature about my life emphasizes my dying without having to have my body die—that I made transition into spirit without the body dying. But from my point of view, what I came for then and what I come for now is the very thing I taught you this morning. Spiritual phenomena are spiritual phenomena. All of it is open to interpretation— a wide variety of interpretations. Think about this picture falling from the wall. Those who are gullible will say spirit did that, but the truth is what Philip said. The tape holding the picture did not hold. That was it—pure and simple.

I came to teach about love, and I will continue to teach about love. I do not care one whit if you remember my name. I know who I am, and I'm totally secure in who I am. I do not need human praise. Why should I? I already have God within me, and he and I communicate at all times.

But what I do want you to remember is that you are love itself. That's all. If parents are wise, they will teach their children that from birth. Could you imagine what kind of a world it would be if every parent, from the moment of birth, would teach each child that he or she is love? Then God would exist everywhere, in all human relationships, all societies and all cultures. That's the important point. Did I answer your question?

HK: All of my questions have been answered. From now on, I will try to receive most of the important information by myself.

Keeping a Journal

SG: That's true. I taught Philip from the beginning to keep a journal. His second book on the table to your right has a representative picture of me on the cover. The book was based on his conversations with me in his journal for one year. As I dictated to him, he listened and he wrote, and that book is the result. You do not have to make a public book, but do keep a journal. For where you are going, dear one, you need to do that. Every Sunday morning, for 52 weeks, Philip got up at 4:30 a.m. and prayed, and then got in place with pen and paper, called me in, and I began dictating to him. Much was given, and it's not all in that book. That way, he developed his ability in a refined way. He came to differentiate between his inner voice and my voice, and from that, we began the ministry we are doing right now for you. That's it. God is a practical being. He is often obscured or hidden by very intricate teachings. God is also obscured by people who cover up the truth. In this way, God has been lost in complexity. You will find God in you through simplicity. It is so.

I'm going to take my leave now, but I shall walk with you. Please know our love follows you, everywhere, always. And if I could reach out through these arms, I would hug you tight and pass on God's love to you. But, instead, hug yourself, because God is in you. This is Saint Germain. God bless you.

HK: Thank you very much.

PB: I'd like to close with a prayer.

> *Father, I know this work is not my work, but the work of a great number of souls in spirit. What was delivered here today, the world at large needs to hear. But since that cannot happen, let us go forth into the world to show the world your love by just being loving, so that people can see you. Amen.*

End of recording

Spiritual Reading Eight

SEEING PROBLEMS AS OPPORTUNITIES

Akiko U.—Female

Philip Burley (PB): I've come to think I'm the normal one and everyone else is peculiar, because what I do is just human nature, and everyone should be able to do it. It's only because man is ignorant of his ability that he doesn't use it.

The cushion that I'm sitting on is not because I think I'm special. This fabric is wool and silk. It cuts off the earthly vibration and the earthly pull. Tibetan or Indian gurus used this. That is why I have it. Also, when I'm reading for you, you'll see me pick up this crystal when I channel Saint Germain. The spirit world has taught me that if I don't use this, my energies become drained. They told me to project my thought here, and Saint Germain and spirit will vibrate off of this. It provides the energy for them. It's because crystals send and receive energy that they are used in radios. You'll see me pick this up when I channel Saint Germain, and it makes a big difference.

The Voice of Saint Germain

I had just begun studying Saint Germain when he came to me. He told me that I had the right kind of energies for channeling, and I had certain dimensions and levels within me that I didn't know about. He said that he and I would meet each other halfway—in that I'd raise my vibration, and he'd lower his so we could work together. I can't tell where Saint Germain begins and where I end, or vice versa. When he comes in, my voice goes lower. I just wanted to give you an introduction. It helps.

AU: Yes, I'm glad I heard it.

PB: I don't think I work like any other channel who has come to Japan before. I'm not saying what I do is better, just different. I'm going to begin with a prayer, and then the information will start coming.

Almighty God, our Heavenly Father and Mother, we thank you that we can be together here for this high purpose today. This woman has come for this purpose, and she has a deep longing in her heart to learn the truth of things and know how you are working with her. Our meeting is timely in that you have been planning all of our lives that whoever is to cross our path, is to cross it at a certain time. This was our time to meet.

In this holy work today, please pour out your spirit upon her. In any way that she needs your healing love and energy, please let her receive it. May the content of this experience bring to her greater awareness of her own value, her eternal qualities, and her inner spiritual beauty. May she go from this experience knowing how loved she is by spirit. Please reveal to her clearly and succinctly the answers to her questions. Thank you for the privilege of serving her in this way. I pray this in divine love. Amen.

As I'm looking at you, a very large rainbow appears over your head. I can see way, way back—as far back as about 4,000 years behind you—and a dove appears over your head. This is the spirit of God descending upon you. There are many noble women behind you. You are very clearly a child of God, and your approach to life, spirit says, is simple, but pure and elevated. While you have struggled with life, and they show you struggling, God still keeps his hand on your life.

The next three months are very, very important for you. You are at a turning point. I'm looking at a compass, and you are being redirected in your spiritual endeavors. Since childhood, you have been a very caring person.

Do you have a question on your paper about marriage?

AU: Yes.

PB: Because they show me a ring on your finger with a question mark above it. Your question will be answered later. This is coming from my guide, Tiffany. She's laughing, and she's so happy to help you.

Living with a Heavy Heart

AU: I've always felt Buddha's heart.

PB: Yes.

AU: This is a term the Japanese use when we always have the feeling that we need to help or save somebody.

PB: Before I came to Japan, Buddha appeared to me in a vision, and said he would help me. If you could see him, he's right behind me now. But he's here for you today and says he's helping to turn your life around because you have not realized deep, inner happiness yet, though you're sincerely searching. Sometimes your heart hurts very much, and sometimes you feel very lonely. It's because God is calling, Buddha says. You are crossing a bridge, meaning you're in transition. I see this often with people.

The weight I feel here in your energy is very, very heavy. There are certain things that you have not told other people that have hurt you.

But that's going to change. I see a lot of prayer around you. You have been asking, so the energy around you is all gold. This is the color of the energy of a saint. Also, you vibrate with blue, like I do, and you have a lot of green right next to your body. That green energy is healing energy, so you have a lot of healing power. Do you do healing work, or plan to in the future?

You also have a small guide. You have a joy guide. You have a little boy with you—Tomo. When he was on earth, he was an old, old man and he was a master. He's in charge of your clairvoyance, your clairaudience, and opening the psychic senses. I would like to work with you, because you have significant mediumship or psychic ability. You may not think that, but I can see it. When you're alone, do you sometimes cry?

AU: Yes.

PB: Because that's how I'm feeling. I just want to cry. That's going to pass. God had his hand on you before you were born. All the ups and downs are on purpose because God has been training you. Even your difficulty with finding a man is God's work, so that you will be single-minded about spiritual things.

You're going to travel to the West in the future, particularly to South America; probably Brazil, but also other places. Do you know people in Brazil? You will travel to the West. When you work with your development, it would be very good to work with crystals. You're the kind of channel who could look into a crystal ball, and with training, see the future.

Your guide Tomo was a very powerful, mediumistic person when he was on earth. You also have with you an Egyptian woman, and part of what you're carrying in your own heart is from her life. She was a very pure soul like you, and she was a priestess, but she was murdered—stabbed to death. She was stabbed in the heart by another priest who was taken over by low spirits. He was jealous of her. Part of the heartache you feel is from her, so in part, you're helping her get rid of her karma. In this case, I have to say it would be better if you told her not to come around. For the next three months, just tell her not to come around, because she's taxing your energies. Do you understand?

AU: Yes.

PB: This is very important. You'll start feeling better. In your energy, I feel that you sometimes have a hard time breathing. It's a heavy feeling. Is it true?

AU: My heart beats very fast, very quickly.

PB: Yes, I'm picking that up too. You're easy to read because you're very innocent. Your aura is much larger than that of most people. Your aura is also very open, and that's what makes you suffer, but it also makes you easy to read.

Dr. Palmer, who works with me, is talking to me about your feet. You need to work on the bottom of your feet, particularly your right foot, around this area. Put pressure on the whole foot, and work on both of them so it's balanced. This will help with some of the heart problems. Also, particularly on the left little finger, just press like this—watch me—with this rhythm. This will help balance your heart chakra. There is some kind of emotional imbalance in the spirit level which is causing a physical imbalance.

Why do I keep seeing a child with you? Do you want to marry and have a child? Are you longing for children?

AU: Well, if I have a child, that would be nice.

PB: I keep seeing a child with you. There is a very handsome little boy in spirit with you. I've seen him twice now. But something is still being worked out for you, so don't push anything. As the river of life flows, just float upon it. It will be easier that way for you.

Do you go to a temple to pray? I see you at a temple praying.

AU: No, not at all.

PB: Is there a temple near you?

AU: No.

PB: Okay, do you have a place in your home where you have an altar?

AU: I have a Buddhist altar in my house like every household has.

PB: How often do you pray there?

AU: Twice a day, every day.

Preparation for Change

PB: For the next thirty days, starting tonight, spirit wants you to just sit and focus only on your breathing. They're making big spiritual adjustments with you.

Do you sometimes struggle with feeling that you're not very loving? Yes. It's a major issue with you, and that's what they're trying to change. That's the central problem. But I can see you in spirit, and I want you to know the light energy coming from you is brilliant. It's very, very bright and very elevated. You *must* hear this because it's time for a change.

You have two angels who serve you at all times. I see them right behind you on both sides. Eventually you will become a trance medium. Not now, but maybe in five to seven years. You have that ability, and it's part of your destiny. What is being decided in terms of your destiny is whether or not you should be single and completely devoted to God or marry and have a family. Fundamentally, you're the kind of person who, if you devoted yourself to God, you could go very far in your spiritual advancement. That does not mean you should not marry, but you have to think about what your real priorities are.

Do you pray for many other people also?

AU: Yes.

PB: I see long lists of people being prayed for with energy coming from you.

AU: When I sit in front of the altar, that's what I do.

PB: To go back to what I was talking about; you have a lot of healing power and prayer power. Without flattering you, just giving you what is coming in from spirit, I want to say that you're very rare. I've read for thousands of people, but you are one of the more gifted ones. Would you like to do this kind of work? Forget about whether you feel confident or not, but in your heart of hearts?

AU: Yes.

PB: Yes. That's what you're born for. You just have to trust more and believe more in yourself. For these next thirty days, focus on your breathing only. Don't pray. This is for you, and spirit is going to work with you to open you more. This is very important. Okay?

AU: Okay.

PB: There appears a symbol above your head indicating that you have natural fortune or good luck. You are coming more and more into that good fortune. But don't think of it in terms of money. Think of it in terms of spiritual fortune. And if you do the correct thing, both spiritual fortune and material fortune will come.

Okay, I would like you to start asking your questions.

AU: My number one question was about my reason for coming into this life.

PB: I don't know your questions, but my guides do. I just finished talking about your destiny. Almost everything that we've been talking about has been about your number one question. I don't tell people this, but when I'm talking, if Saint Germain is not channeling, I'm listening to spirit and translating from spirit world. I just speak it out to you. I don't say he said, she said.

What is your next question?

AU: I would like to know about my relationship with Saint Germain.

PB: He's going to come through and speak. He told me that he wants to talk in a concentrated way with you. Though you don't know anything about him, he'll draw closer and closer. He knows you love him very much, and you have spoken with him in the spirit world many times. Go on to the next question.

Leaving the Family

AU: This is another typical question. My family members all live in a small town. They have all stayed there, and I'm the only one who left to come to Tokyo and work. I want to know about my relationship with my family. Why did I come into this family?

PB: My guide Tiffany said, "You came into this family to leave it." Don't you know that already?

AU: Even though my mother got sick, I didn't go back.

PB: Yes. We're born into families to learn from that family. Some of us are more advanced, so we get what we get and then move on. I left my family at the age of eighteen. I never had a deep relationship with them. After that, from the age of eighteen until now, I had to be very independent. God can't use people who have deep attachments—deep connections—to family. Buddha left his home. Jesus left his family. All sincere religious people belong to God, and not to their families. Even in childhood they usually appear peculiar to the rest of the family, and often feel separate. They may ask, "What am I doing in this family?" There's affection or love, but it's not binding. That's your situation.

You didn't move yourself to Tokyo. God did that with your spirit guides and teachers, including Saint Germain. If you hadn't moved here, I couldn't have met you. These are spiritual steps you have taken. You have mostly received all that you need from your family. Love them, but without attachment. It's very important, and you are already doing that.

Now is your question about money or a job?

Earthly Work and Spirituality

AU: I have a question about my job. What work should I be doing?

PB: It's very hard for you because you're a spiritual person. If there was a school for people like you and me, we would be in that school which is a school for prophets. You will never be satisfied in an earthly job. You have always said, as you've watched people work, "What am I doing here? They enjoy going to work. They enjoy this work. I don't enjoy it. What's wrong with me?" You can't fit in. Don't worry about it. You're not supposed to.

Whatever work you can do to make an income where you feel relatively happy, that's what you should do. As a psychic person, it's not easy for you to be in the vibrations of the workaday world. You're very open here. Do you work on your chakras?

AU: Yes.

PB: You're very, very sensitive. When I was looking at your aura, I could see a lot of sensitivity. That makes you feel uncomfortable in many earthly situations. But as you know, if you stay focused here in the third eye and just keep returning to that in your meditations, your prayers, and your daily thinking, you'll become more and more balanced.

I live in that place. I've meditated for seventeen years, and I have been tested by those who study the brain using special equipment. The test showed that I stay at the alpha level of consciousness most of the time. Because of this, I don't fit in with this world easily. You're the same kind of person. You need to hear this. It's important information for you. Otherwise, you're likely to feel guilty and blame yourself, because you think you're not ambitious or successful. You have to get beyond that.

Presence of Grandmother

PB: Do you have a grandmother on your mother's side of the family you're very close to?

AU: Alive or dead?

PB: I don't know. It could be an aunt, grandmother, or great grandmother.

AU: My grandmother is dead.

PB: Okay, that's who I'm seeing then. Her image is not clear, and sometimes living people are sleeping and they're out of their body. I see them, but they're not so clear. Then I can't tell if they are alive or in spirit. That has happened a number of times.

She's standing right here and stroking your hair. She's an inner, personal guide who works with you, and she said you were her favorite.

AU: When I was very little, I lived with her.

PB: Yes, she is crying. See, what happens is that when they start crying, I want to cry. So mediumship is the use of clairvoyance, clairaudience, clairsentience, and intuition. A good medium uses all of them in a well-rounded way. That's what happens to me. Therefore, when I'm reading you, I see, hear, feel, and sometimes even taste and smell. When I taste or smell, regarding a visiting spirit, I am picking up from their vibration which includes from their memory bank which may include the unconscious inclusion of past experiences while on earth. Everything that happens to us on earth is registered in us, in our memory in the spirit world.

Anyway, she's standing there. She says that when you pray, she prays beside you. She sits on the floor. She helps carry your prayers to heaven, and you can call on her any time. She's going with you on a journey. And your little joy guide Tomo is going too.

AU: Oh, Tomo and the joy guide are the same person?

PB: Yes.

AU: Oh, because you said, joy guide and then you said Tomo, so I thought . . .

PB: No, it's the same person. Tomo is the little boy who is your joy guide.

AU: Okay, I thought you were talking about two different ones.

PB: No. As I was talking about your grandmother, Tomo walked up here beside you because he wanted to make sure that you knew he was going too. He walked in, and in that little boy's voice, said, "Be sure and tell her I'm going too!"

I hear a lot of music around you. What do you have to do with music?

AU: I love listening to music.

PB: Yes, that's what I thought, because I just hear a lot of music around you.

AU: Even when I go to sleep, I like to keep the music on.

PB: Yes, a lot of music. Sure, a lot of people have that, but your grandmother is the one who is sitting in front of me, and the music is what comes out.

Okay, please ask your next question. Saint Germain is going to come through in a few minutes and he's going to speak to you for a long time, but I want you to get any personal questions out of the way.

AU: I'm finished with all of them.

PB: Okay. Just sit for a minute with your eyes closed and think if there's any other personal question you want to ask. This is the chance of a lifetime. Take your time. (Pause.)

Bulimia and Loneliness

AU: I have something I have talked about in the past. I eat too much. I just eat and eat and eat, and I have been working really hard on stopping it. Finally, I am eating less than I did before, but I want to know more about that.

PB: But you don't look overweight at all.

AU: Now I'm better, but it's been a struggle. It has been difficult. I'm wondering what causes this.

PB: Is it a particular kind of food?

AU: Anything.

PB: I have to touch in. I need to hold your paper for the vibration. (Pause) Food is your friend. I would like to see you move into circles where you can find friends in this kind of work that you could be with more, because right now, food is your friend. You are a very lonely person.

AU: Every time I'm lonely, I turn to eating?

PB: That's right. It's a replacement for friendship.

AU: But when I eat, I throw up, and eat and throw up again.

PB: So, you are bulimic?

AU: Yes, I'm pretty sure I am bulimic.

PB: Again, it's loneliness. But I am also trying to see if there is a spirit. I worked with a woman in America who had bulimia. She was anorexic, and she got so thin she eventually died from it. Whether there is a spirit influence or not doesn't really matter. In order for you to do the right thing, you have to strengthen your own will. Some people who have an overshadowing spirit fight the spirit, but this just gives more power to the spirit. I'm talking about an entity that comes into the auric field. They don't possess, they obsess. They overshadow the mind and create the craving. On earth they may have starved to death or something. This is what often happens.

AU: That's what I thought you meant. Have you found a spirit with me that is causing this?

PB: No, I haven't.

AU: I thought maybe there was one.

PB: I haven't seen one today.

AU: Really, it's just me?

PB: I don't know yet. Many years ago I used to teach people to fight the spirit. But when you resist by trying to push anything away from you, you're focusing on it and pulling it to you. So, it's better to ignore the spirit, or any idea of spirit, and look into yourself and discover the weakness that you need to work on. It's that weakness that draws any spirit. To get rid of the spirit don't fight the spirit, but rather gain the understanding to strengthen your will in the area of that weakness.

Saint Germain is going to come through.

See Problems as Opportunities

Saint Germain (SG): I am here. This is Saint Germain. Can you hear me all right?

AU: Yes.

SG: Because I am coming from spirit through a human body, I cannot always know if my connection is sound. When I hear your voice coming back saying you can hear me, then I know I've made the connection.

Beloved one, I am here exclusively for you today. Nothing is more important to me this moment than you. As I look at you, I see great beauty. I see God shining in you. You and I are not different. The only difference is that I know that God lives in me, and you have yet to understand that completely.

Do you not find it very, very interesting that today this gentleman I am speaking through is able to discern your life at this point? Isn't it interesting? But it is no accident. We were intended to meet each other because it is time. You have met many people, and they have each helped you one more step, one more step, and one more step up the ladder of life. Through this instrument, we are taking one step higher.

Many people fight problems through worry, but worrying never solves problems. Only understanding solves problems. Therefore, rather than spend long periods of time worrying about self, spend that same energy in seeking to understand yourself. Your questions today are all about that point. They are courageous and noble questions.

We come to this earth plane for the purpose of solving problems. As you well know, this is a place of learning. If you did not have the problems you have, then you would have other problems. Of the thirty-eight million plus people living here in Tokyo, there is not one that does not have problems. Some are just better at hiding them than others. The richest man, the most educated man, the stupidest man, they all have problems. Some admit it and some don't. The prideful man who does not understand how to get understanding will deny his problems, but when you understand that this life is for learning about self, you become humble and seek to find all the answers to self.

Who decides what problems one shall have? You do. In each grade, from the first grade to the twelfth grade and beyond, we do two things: we study and we take tests to see if we have learned. Therefore, the most important thing in life is to study self and learn from the answers we find. With those answers, we can solve the problems of our life. You have your own particular problems in order to gain from them whatever it is that your soul needs to gain. In this way, all human beings are going through the same process but just don't know it.

Do you think I don't have problems? Self-mastery goes on throughout eternity, but we do not use the term *problem* here. Problem means opportunity: the opportunity to learn and to grow. If you learn and overcome your problem, then you do not need to recycle through that problem. The ideal pattern of life is not to go in circles, but to spiral ever upward. Consequently, when we are grateful for our problems, it is the beginning of solving them. Most essentially, from our problems, we gain wisdom, and the more problems we solve, the wiser we become.

From now on, beloved one, do not look at your problems as negative things, but rather look at them as opportunities. Turn the energy around and learn to go higher and higher spiritually. The ultimate reason they call us masters is because we mastered life in the very way I am speaking of. We went step by step, day by day, year by year, little by little, sometimes by tiny amounts, sometimes large amounts, until we reached the higher level of self-realization. Putting all of this in perspective, you have a principle by which to work. Be grateful for your problems and learn what you can from them. Again, I say if it was not for this set of problems, it would be another set of problems. There are no exceptions to this fact.

Spiritual Development

Now because of time, I want to speak about your relationship with me. Beloved one, the most important thing is to live right now. My relationship with you today has to do with the very things that Philip was telling you about your development. We want to work with you in your spiritual development, for we are looking for individuals like you to train and develop.

The longing you feel about me and your interest in me is placed there by your own soul and by me. It was placed there so that you would answer the call. Yes, we take you out of your body at night, and we meet in convocation in spirit, many thousands of us. What is important in your development is not whether you become a professional channeler or not. The reason for developing your own spiritual openness is to solve your own problems more easily. Because Philip is spiritually open, rather than struggling for a long time with problems, he comes directly to us and gets answers. The process we are using to work with you has a two-fold purpose: one, that you may learn the process for self-discipline, and two, that you may open up more and more specifically, safely, and broadly in being able to use your spiritual gifts.

Now, if you have any specific questions you want to ask me, we have enough time for one or two.

AU: I can't think of any questions right now.

SG: Yes. When you listen to this tape, you will discover many, many things you did not hear the first time. You have gained a tremendous amount of information and knowledge here. Ninety-nine percent of it is about you, and that is our intention. This is our way of loving you personally. Wherever you go, know that we are very, very near. Saint Germain and other guides and teachers will always protect you. Depend upon this protection. Call upon this protection. Demand this protection, and we will dutifully, lovingly serve you.

The greater your hunger for self-knowledge and the greater your faith to receive such, the easier it is for us to help you. This is the path to self-mastery. Even as many spirits are serving you, so they serve me. The masters are all one long line of servants. We are not glorified in some extravagant way as many people think. We are humble servants, or try to be humble servants, among you. We follow the great directive of Jesus the Christ in saying that those who are greatest among you are servants of all. That is the key and the secret to self-mastery. Find someone who is suffering more than you suffer, or as much as you suffer, and serve that person, even if it's only to pray for them.

Now you have your directives, and you have heard and spoken with Saint Germain. We are overjoyed in being able to do this with you. Go in peace and know our love follows you always. This is Saint Germain.

End of recording

Spiritual Reading Nine

HONOR THE GOD WITHIN

Kiyoshi T.—Male

Philip Burley (PB): As I work with you, I will go back and forth between being in trance and semi-trance. From time to time, I will ask you for your paper, as I like to hold it when I do the reading. I don't know when Saint Germain will come in, because he comes in spontaneously. If I may have your paper, I will open with prayer.

> *Heavenly Father, thank you for this time together. Lead this experience, that this gentleman may go away with new and confirmed knowledge. He has come such a long, long way physically to be here. And he has come a long, long way spiritually to be here. Please bless him through this experience for all his efforts and use the gift of channeling to serve him. I ask all his guides and teachers to come very close to us. On the vibration of this beginning prayer, may they bring in the information. All this I pray and ask in divine love.*

Saint Germain shows me, as a symbol, a deep, deep well, meaning that you have spent a lifetime plumbing the depths of your spirituality.

You have come to a time in your life where there is a significant transition into higher spirituality.

As you walk the road of life—that's how they are saying it, and how I am seeing it—you have many, many people serving you in spirit. You also have the potential for channeling. This is seen in the area of your throat.

You have Archangel Michael with you, who stands directly behind you. Michael is laughing and says, "I am neither Eastern nor Western. I have one foot in one side and one foot in the other, and I serve both."

I also see samurai, arrayed around on horses and standing. These samurai were very righteous and good men. They are all in blue and white gowns. These men used samurai principles to make their life better and not to make other people's lives miserable. As I look at you more, there is a ray of light that comes down, a blue-white light that comes right around your head. It is like the presence of God coming in, and spirit says that the longing you have for spiritual realization will be fulfilled.

Jesus and the Spirit World

You also have the master Jesus who comes to you, but Jesus in this case appears as a pine tree. Jesus' birthday is celebrated by the evergreen, the pine tree. Jesus says that you have qualities like himself, and that is why he has come to you. The reason he used the pine tree is because the pine tree exists everywhere in the world. It's a universal symbol; whereas, if he came simply as Jesus, it might look like pure Christianity. But you are universal.

The energy that you vibrate with has a lot of deep blue, and this is a color that vibrates with the third eye. I see spirit touching that color. They are touching your aura like this, many of them, so I know you have the ability ultimately to open up the third eye and be able to see the spirit world. You have a lot of energy for that, and I would be very surprised if you don't already see spirit. Do you see spirit?

KT: No, not yet.

PB: Not yet, but you will. They are going to start by first coming to your bedside, mostly in the morning. I am going to let Saint Germain come through right now and talk to you.

Saint Germain (SG): I am here, this is Saint Germain. I am smiling upon you my son. As Philip said, I come in spontaneously, and now is as good a time as any.

Honor the God Within

You are much loved here; first for your courage, and second for your faith. To work with us initially takes faith. Those who have this kind of faith are very blessed in the world. It is the kind of faith that helps people to believe in the unseeable and the unhearable. Like a child, you simply believe.

My son, your life in pursuit of spiritual things is going to be rewarded in these latter years. Even as you might wear a picture of me, I would like you to wear a picture of you. I do not mean this literally; what I mean is, you honor me and I honor you. God is as much in you as he is in me. The only difference is that I know it and you do not. It is only a matter of time before you shall know that God is in you to the extent that he is.

We see here that you would give up everything to know about spirit. I would say to you to please honor God within you, as much as you honor me. The secret and center of all self-mastery, which I proclaim, comes from knowing God within. You see, spiritual things sometimes take a little longer than physical things to appear in the obvious way, but you are well on your way.

You have working with you the spirit of Saint Paul who comes very close to you. We see within you the ability to write spiritual things and to speak spiritual things. Like Jesus, Saint Paul also comes as a universal master and not just as a Christian. This gentleman doing this channeling is being overshadowed by many people too, but primarily by myself and by Buddha. Some would laugh and say, "Why? Your group is not so important." From heaven's point of view, we masters are working worldwide and universally. We are not respecters of language, race, country, or any of that. What we are drawn to is sincerity and consistency towards effort and purpose. Because your group has that, we are working with you and others who have that to try to bring forward a deeper understanding of channeling.

We are not at all fascinated by our coming through human beings on earth. It has been going on since the beginning of the human race. Every culture has its channelers and prophets, and they come to every nation without exception. Of course, the level and degree of channeling varies from person to person, but through these individuals God has blessed and guided the nations. In Israel, there was the school of prophets, which I helped to oversee. They used the word "prophets," not channelers, but it is the same thing.

You and those involved with the leader of your channeling group are being overshadowed for a purpose greater than you can understand. Always, throughout human history, God prepares and brings forward such people at the right time. On this side, we join together as beads upon the necklace of God. None of this is done for pure entertainment. Among those of us who are sober and serious about this, it is done to lead others closer and closer to God.

My admonition to everyone who does or tries to do this work is to remain very humble. Forget yourself and think about being an open door for God to walk through. The more you yield yourself to that, the more deeply and quickly will your channeling come. Of course, the initial motive, which is quite all right, is to gain channeling for oneself. This medium I am speaking through often reads the transcriptions of what I have said, that he may learn from them also. At a future date, he will listen to this tape as well. In this way, he seeks to humble himself in order to learn and to grow.

Again, we want to say to you, you're in a good place, and you are on the right path, so move forward. I am going to step back from Philip now to allow him to come back, and I shall come in a little later. This is your friend and brother in spirit, Saint Germain.

PB: Saint Germain was very present, and I was out more than usual.

Now, please ask your first question.

Stopping the Aging Process and Growing Younger

KT: I want to ask a question about how to stop the aging process of the human body? From day to day, what can I do to be able to grow younger? Is it possible?

PB: You don't want very much, do you? I am joking with you. Saint Germain is going to come back to speak with you.

SG: I am back. The *length of a life* is not as important *as the quality of life*. In ignorance some humans want to remain young on earth thinking that earthly life is most desirable and needs to be extended for as long as possible.

There is nothing wrong with wanting to live a long life. Long or short, it is what you do with your life that is most important. Jesus lived for only thirty-three years and look what he accomplished while living and dying in a thirty-three-year lifespan.

By comparison, there are some people who live to be seventy, eighty, ninety years old who die as if they were still spiritual children, not having grown much spiritually at all during their time on earth. We are meant to grow old and all of us go through the aging process, it cannot be stopped.

This process varies from person to person, depending upon several factors: The first is your DNA containing or involving your genes, according to what you inherited from your parents; and a second factor is how you live. That includes your diet—physically and spiritually—and your mental attitude.

It has been observed that those who eat a balanced diet, get plenty of rest and exercise, and have a positive attitude are usually happier, healthier, longer-living individuals than others. They may even appear to not age and even look and feel younger for a time. But we humans were never intended to grow physically younger and remain on earth.

When the physical body can no longer function and remain alive—a process, called death—you as a human spirit will automatically begin having the experience of permanently separating from your physical body and on and into the spirit world. You came from the spirit world, and you will, without question, return to the spirit world.

Live a Life of Quality and Practice Meditation

My advice to you is to seek a life of quality based upon sound and proven spiritual principles: the first being, love others as yourself. Second, do unto others as you would have others do unto you. And thirdly, always remember that what you sow is what you reap.

Rather than seeking to consciously prolong life, focus your time and energies on meditation. Spend your precious earthly energies and simultaneously, your spiritual energies meditating, and you will discover who you truly are. In the process you will uplift and refine your spiritual abilities and gifts and ultimately experience Self and God-realization.

KT: May I ask my next question now?

PB: Please.

Channeling Spirit

KT: I want to know, if you are to become a trance channeler, do you need to already have a contract with somebody in spirit to come through you, or is this something that you can really practice and work very hard at, and then a master will come to you?

PB: It depends on your belief system. I never had a contract with Saint Germain. He just came through me as a medium. The only contract— I'm listening to him now—is love. If you love others as yourself, then they can work with you. That's the only criteria he ever gave me.

If you do channeling for the sake of ego, they won't work with you. A spirit may come, but it won't be a high spirit. It will be an ego-centered spirit. Some people may become very prideful and arrogant doing this work, because they think they are the one doing it, or the spirits working with them think they're doing it. As you know, God is doing it. It's all God.

I don't know if that answers your question completely, but if not, ask more questions if you want to.

KT: Therefore, it doesn't mean you have to have a contract with a spirit, as long as you have a contract for love.

PB: Be a loving person, and you'll draw a loving soul to work through you. Saint Germain is going to speak again.

SG: I am here again, and I do appreciate your questions very much.

Truth and Love

In the highest levels of the spirit world, there are those who seek to approach God through the truth of things, and that is an authentic path. But those who are the highest of the highest are those who just love purely. They may not be able to speak the truth the most eloquently or clearly but they live the truth.

The difference is this, my son. You see an old woman crossing the street, and she drops a bag of oranges. You rush to her because you know it is the right thing to do. However, another person watching the same woman with the same problem, dashes to her without thinking about whether it is the right thing to do, but because he or she could not help but do it out of love. Therefore, the second highest heaven consists of individuals who are what we call living "in the truth of truths," but the highest heavens are filled with those who unconditionally or unconsciously live the truth and have become love itself.

In this second heaven, that is the lower of the heavens, there are those masters who are very good at articulating the truth. They can quote this author and that book, and this reading and so on, but they have yet to grow completely in unconditional love. Therefore, a teacher who we would call a master of truth is not as high as a master of love.

The highest truth is love. One who loves purely and unconditionally loves without having to think about it. That is the pure and core nature of God himself. The realm from which I come is the realm of the love of love, not merely the love of truth. Consequently, I was drawn to this man who comes from that same motive. When he loves, he simply loves purely, with no motive other than seeing that person as himself, and seeing God in that person. That is the criteria to draw the highest spirits. Examine yourself and you know where you are. Are you in the realm of the love of truth, or the love of love?

KT: Of course, love.

SG: Therefore, all you need to do is be you and learn how to open yourself to the pouring in of guides and teachers who work with you, as your channel teachers teach you how to channel.

KT: Once more please?

SG: The spirit channel teacher working with you will teach you how to channel spirit. The principles of channeling are the ladder you climb, and to go to the top level you must climb it with love. From our perspective that is enough of a condition for us to work with you. If you are working with that realm of masters whose belief system is that they must have a contract, then they will tell you that, but the highest understanding from our perspective is that love is enough. Isn't it simple? Yes?

KT: Yes.

SG: Yes. Now I am going to stay here with Philip, so please ask your next question.

Turn Towards the Light; Abandon the Dark

KT: You have answered most of this next question for me already. What should I do about the deepest levels of myself that I don't like and that are difficult to deal with?

SG: That is a very easy question.

KT: And the second part of this question is, in order to love unconditionally every day, day by day, what steps do I need to take to be able to do that?

SG: The answers to your questions are short and simple. That I might have the energy, repeat the first part of the question again?

KT: I've forgotten.

SG: There are aspects of yourself that you don't like?

KT: Yes, and they're at a very deep level.

SG: Yes.

KT: What should I do about them? I have gone back over my life and looked at everything, but I don't feel it's enough. There are still many things that I feel inside myself that I just don't like, and I don't know what to do about these things.

SG: Yes. When the sun is blazingly bright, there are no shadows. And if there are shadows and you are facing the sun, the shadow falls behind you, so they are not in your view. You are so enthralled, or so centered upon the light, that you don't see the shadows.

There are two ways to take dirty water out of a bucket. Either you can pour all of the water out and pour clean water in, or you can drop diamonds into the dirty water and the water will rise up and spill over the edge and be replaced by the diamonds.

Do not pay any attention to the dark side of your nature. Like a shadow, put it behind you. Do not pick it up or look at it. And when you make a mistake, immediately forgive yourself. Always turn and face the light, then the shadows of your life will melt away.

When we focus upon our problems, they consume our energies, and our dark side has the tendency to keep us locked into that side. When one achieves self-mastery, it does not mean that the master did not at one time also have darkness in his life. What it means is that, through trial and error, he learned how to turn totally to the light, putting the darkness behind. Eventually the darkness disappeared.

Be kind to yourself and love self as you would love others. Forgive self as you would forgive others. Focus only upon that which is good in you, and it will come to replace the darkness. When you try to resist the darkness, you engage the darkness; and when you wrestle with the darkness you get caught up in it.

What I am telling you is the truth. When the doctor is operating upon a cancer patient, he takes the tumor out. He does not spend his time with the tumor, but rather turns back to the healthy body and treats it. That is how to achieve self-mastery.

God lives in you. That is the light of the lights that I speak of. Be happy about that and celebrate that presence. That presence is brought out through positive thinking, positive feeling, and positive talking. God is all light and all positive. Then if you want to bring him out of you as he already exists in you, be positive. If you do as I say, even if you have to be a good actor in the beginning, you will shorten your spiritual walk by many, many miles. Do you understand me?

KT: I am thinking over some of the things you spoke about, such as becoming an actor. At first, I couldn't understand what you meant by that. But I realized that it is like being on a stage in a play, and now I understand.

SG: Yes, you have to fool yourself. Being a good actor is a means of transforming negative energies into positive energies. Whether you are happy or not, if you act happy, then happiness will come out of you. In other words, it has to do with transforming negative energy into positive energy. Act this way and what you seek will come to you faster. This is one of the greatest secrets to the mystery of self-mastery. Let us go to your next question.

Fasting

KT: I would like to ask a question about fasting. I have studied about Jesus' life, where he went into the desert and fasted for forty days, and I believe that was so he could learn about unconditional love. I want to know if there is any reason for the forty days, or if that number of days really has no particular meaning.

SG: It's a mystical number that has meaning to those who believe in numerology. These conditions are inspired by spirit, and spirit knows the power of numbers, so people are inspired to do things for three days, seven days, eight days, or forty days. All of these numbers have symbolic meaning.

Religions around the world include the practice of numerology. Throughout the Christian Bible, if you study it, you will find the number three is predominant. Jesus suffered through the crucifixion experience for three days. He was thirty-three years old. He had three major disciples, Peter, John, and James. His life was sold for thirty pieces of silver. He was a part of the trinity—father, son, and holy spirit. These numbers, when centered upon God, have power because they are energy configurations. Because of this, the soul is inspired to use them. In this way, God's will is done.

Do you think God does not know how many days he has existed? (Laughter) Or how long eternity is? Or how far the sun is from the earth? Or the moon from the earth? God is the grand mathematician. Therefore, the earth and the universe are based upon geometric forms, and these forms are based upon numbers. Those numbers when used on earth have power. At the very least, they yield a certain kind of vibration or result. Is this helpful?

KT: Yes, it has helped me very much. I am planning on doing a seven-day fast every month, and I am fasting now.

SG: What day?

KT: It's my second day.

SG: The most difficult day.

KT: It's not very difficult for me to fast.

SG: Yes, this gentleman that I am speaking through did five seven-day fasts on water only. It was part of what made it possible for him to be used by me. But on his second day, he always had to go to bed. This body that I speak through does not have the same reserves as yours does. His kidneys are smaller than yours and his body burns energy faster than yours does.

The secret to truly effective fasting is to take an enema before doing the fast. When you don't eat, there is nothing to push the waste out, and the toxins in the body stay in and poison the body. Thus, it makes the body work much harder, and when the fast is over, the time of recuperation is much slower.

KT: I am asking, if I do that, will it clear my intestines out immediately?

SG: Yes, that is correct, and you will have no great after-effect after completing your fast.

KT: This is very wonderful information that I am hearing.

SG: I understand.

KT: It's very difficult sometimes to do a fast because so many different things come up within me during the fast, one of them being that I become extremely hungry, and I think about food all the time. Then, when it's over, I sometimes worry about becoming fat because I have been fasting for so long, and I can only eat half of what I ate before, lest I get fat.

SG: I do not mean to discourage you, but I advised my medium to not do more fasts. It is better to fast from anger, from any negative energy, and from judging others.

KT: I don't understand.

SG: In other words, when you fast from food it affects the body, and it can affect the spirit. If you are fasting for health reasons, that is one thing, but if you are fasting in order to edify your spirit, that is another thing. Rather than fasting from food, try for seven days not to be negative in any way. For seven days, in your heart and mind, do not judge anyone else, including yourself. For seven days, do not think of yourself, but only think of others, fast from selfish thought. Then you will truly bring about very high results in your spirit.

Yes, we know well that when you fast, the only thing you think of is food. It is very hard to even think of God when you are hungry. Missionaries going to other countries sometimes have to feed the people before they can teach them about God. How can someone who is very hungry think about anything other than food?

All we would say to you is just consider these points in your philosophy. In no way would I, Saint Germain, tell you absolutely not to do this or absolutely to do that. Such decisions are within your free will and within the realm of your own decision making. That is part of the path of self-mastery.

Now do you understand comprehensively what we are trying to tell you?

KT: Yes, I understand now.

SG: Yes. Do you have another question?

Who Are My Guides?

KT: I would very much like to know who my spirit guides are and who is working with me. How do I communicate with them?

SG: I am going to step back from Philip, because he can handle this portion, and if I think it is necessary to come back here again, I shall do so. This is Saint Germain.

PB: Okay, I heard the question, you want to know about your spirit guides. First of all, at the beginning of the reading, I mentioned various people that were with you. I saw Jesus and I saw Saint Germain. These two master teachers are working with you like they do with me. They are more in charge of your life than any other spirits.

Both Jesus and Saint Germain appear in my dreams and wake me up and talk to me at my bedside. It's the same for you, so don't search any further. Just come to know Jesus as much as you can and Saint Germain as well. Jesus—thank you; Saint Germain just touched me— Saint Germain and Jesus are almost like twin flames. The nature of Saint Germain in terms of love is more like that of the real Jesus than what is taught in Christianity.

Also, I just heard Buddha talking in my left ear. He works with you as well. They are a trinity, the three of them, and Saint Germain in this case is the spokesperson. He more or less teaches the high-level information of truth, and Jesus will work on the inside regarding directing your love. Buddha is in charge of the most important thing of all, which is your meditation. When you meditate, call on Buddha, and when you want to work on heart issues—issues about loving self or loving others—call on Jesus. When you want to understand comprehensively the truth of things, call on Saint Germain.

Before I came here, for your information, Buddha suddenly appeared to me in a flash of gold light, and said, "Don't worry about Japan, I will be there and help you." Buddha is here now in fulfillment of that promise. I have seen Buddha with some people here in Japan, but not with as many as I thought.

The reading for you is very different from other readings I have given. Partly it's your age, partly you have already come a long way spiritually, and finally, you are uniquely you. You are in a very good place, and I hope I see you in the future, if not on earth, at least in the spirit world. We belong to the same brotherhood. You may be Eastern, and I may be Western, but in terms of the heart, we are the same.

Another question?

Clearing Inner Pain from the Past

KT: I have read the Bible many times, and there is a certain idea written throughout the Bible, including through the words of John the Baptist, that by clearing out your inner pain you get closer to the door of heaven or words to that effect. I have already asked the question of how to get rid of my inner pain, and Saint Germain gave me the whole story—I am trying to find the right words.

PB: Say it in simple form.

KT: I am wondering if you have to go back to your own childhood, you know, when you are doing a regression on something, do you need to go back and look at all of those things?

PB: Only if that's on your path. If that's how you are inspired, then you should.

KT: As I was writing these questions, I realized I needed to look at my past. I talked a lot about looking at the past with Saint Germain.

PB: About a year ago, I was where you are now with that question, and God told me it's not necessary. He told me, "If you will just keep your eye on the light and on me, the past will take care of itself." It doesn't mean you shouldn't look at it, but you should not dwell on it or put major energy into it. Put your major energy into meditation and prayer. Then the past will die.

KT: I understood today very much how important meditation is.

PB: Do you meditate regularly?

KT: Yes.

PB: Good. That is why you are so developed spiritually. Incidentally, I see that your mother is in the spirit world?

KT: Yes.

PB: She is right here in front of me. She is crying because she is so proud of you, and she says that she follows you everywhere. She says she talks about you to everyone in the spirit world, because she is so proud. She said you have done great good with your life. Her only sadness is that she wishes she were here on earth today to help you, because you are at that place in spiritual life that you need to have free time just to develop and not have to work.

End of recording

HELPING OTHERS ON THE SPIRITUAL PATH

Hana W.—Female

Philip Burley (PB): *Our Heavenly Father and Mother, the ever-present spirit in mankind and around mankind, the essence of all intelligence and all love, we direct our thoughts and feelings toward you and the spirit world. This young lady has come today to communicate with her spirit world to receive answers to the questions in her mind and heart and on her paper. Please touch her spiritually and physically to bring forth healing and all the answers to her questions. Help me to step out of the way, that everything can come through unhindered by my presence. Thank you for this great privilege of reading for her. All this I pray in divine love.*

This is very interesting, because the first thing I see for you is a house with a white, wooden picket fence. Are you longing to get married?

HW: Yes.

PB: Yes, that is the whole feeling I get—that you want to settle down in a home, with marriage and everything. That's the feeling that came in from my guide Tiffany who handles family problems, marital situations, and so on. Energy-wise, I need you to move closer so I can be more in your energy. That's good, thank you.

Spiritual Assistance during Physical Therapy

You have many angels with you. For most people I see two, but with you I see a band of angels. It means two things: First, you literally have them with you, and second, you're a very pure soul. This is coming in from spirit. The tears in my eyes are from those in spirit, including the angelic world, who love you very, very much. When I read for you I become you, and whatever thoughts and feelings they have for you come through me, and then I have to pass them on to you.

There is a woman on your mother's side of the family who comes very, very close to you. I have seen her twice. Is your mother's mother in spirit?

HW: She is still here.

PB: Still here? Then it must be your great grandmother. This woman is very, very close to you and says she works through you spiritually. I don't know if you are in the healing field, but you have a lot of natural healing ability. Are you interested in that field?

HW: I am a physical therapist.

PB: That explains it. This woman works through you when you are working in physical therapy, but beyond the physical therapy, there is spiritual energy that comes through you that heals people. You don't know all about this, but it is one of the reasons why the angels are with you.

You have many people with you in spirit—relatives, spirit guides, and teachers, but no one is defining themselves at this point. Tiffany was telling me that these spirits are not only guides and teachers, but many, many people who are grateful to you for what you have done for their people on earth. Are you around medical doctors?

HW: In my job, I work in a hospital, and doctors are there.

PB: I get a strong feeling that the person you will marry will be a doctor. There are two or three doctors around you that I see making some kind of contact or going out with you.

Spirit says you are very, very good at what you do, and it is natural for you.

HW: I really don't think I am that good.

Meditation and Opening the Third Eye

PB: We all can improve in everything, but you are above average in your field. Because there is some tightness through here, down in the arms, and in the back, Doctor Palmer is right behind you putting a green energy into you. Do you sometimes get headaches?

HW: No, I really never get them.

PB: I don't know what this is, but do you meditate?

HW: A little bit. This week I meditated. I have been involved in metaphysics for many, many years.

PB: The central point of your life is really spiritual, and when I asked if you get headaches, it was because I have this feeling up here. It has to do with their wanting to work with you to open the third eye more.

HW: When you said the feeling here, what did you mean?

PB: A feeling in this area between my eyes. I thought it had to do with a headache, but it has to do with the opening of the third eye.

HW: I have been thinking that I would like to open my third eye, but it doesn't open at all.

PB: Yes, because you must sit more, you have to meditate more. That is how it happens.

I opened my third eye by spending enough time meditating. It is the quickest route to becoming gifted in that way. Saint Germain is behind me talking now saying that people get excited when they read a lot of books on metaphysics and imagine themselves doing things they read about, but the short cut to doing what I do is steady meditation. It doesn't have to be complicated, and there doesn't have to be a lot of ritual. The main thing is to get the kundalini energy to rise, to open the upper chakras. If you spend twenty minutes a day, five days a week (this is coming from Saint Germain) you will open up within a year. I am a professional medium and I still have to meditate to keep my energies up and open. The reason they are talking to you about this is because they want to impress you with the fact that you have ability in this area.

A Japanese master is appearing behind you—a Zen master. He has a moustache, and he is a very handsome man. He was not too heavy, but he was a stout man. He also practiced martial arts, and he tells me that he was a Zen master here in the Tokyo area. As I am watching him behind you, the energy that is in him comes to you. He just said to me, if we want to float down the river of life together, we must get into the same boat, meaning that to go where you want to go spiritually, you need to work very closely with him and with others around you. There is also a very strong Egyptian influence with you.

HW: I want to know how to feel that Zen master's presence more. Right now, I don't feel anything. I am not aware that he is there at all, so how can I have the ability to feel that energy and know that he is with me?

PB: Because you work very much in the physical world your energies are very grounded. Because of working on people's bodies every day, it is very natural that you don't feel anything right now. The energy around you is very clear, but it is not the kind of energy that is yet highly spiritualized. Meditation literally changes the energy around us and in us, making us far, far more sensitive. In order to feel him and others around you, you need to spend consistent time in meditation. There is no question about that as I look at you.

You also have a lot of gold energy in your aura, which indicates a good spiritual life, and also an attunement with God. Most of the time, I see gold on the outside of the aura, but this time it is right next to you. It means you were born a spiritual person. By spiritual (now I am listening to them) they're not meaning that you are necessarily spiritually open, but that you are a moral person of high integrity who cares about people.

I see you doing a lot of foreign travel in the future.

HW: Do you mean traveling or living?

PB: Traveling. You will attend metaphysical meetings in the Western world. Do you want to live elsewhere?

HW: No, not right now.

PB: You won't. You may go for two or three months at a time, but you will always come back here. Your home is here. You were born to serve Japan. That's your calling. You will have at least two children, and you may have more, but I see clearly two children at the very least.

Within a year, you are going to find yourself involved romantically with someone you really like, but don't just give your heart away. If this person loves you, he will respect you and work to win your love. The way they are talking to me (Tiffany is talking to me), your energies are such that you have to be very careful that you don't upset your balance, because romance can throw you way off. You must be careful in romance and really appreciate your own virtuous nature—your own purity.

HW: I am just not able to really love myself yet.

PB: I am telling you what spirit is telling me to tell you. You are one of many people I have read for in Japan, and you are the first one they have mentioned about this point. I can see your value, and I can see where you are going. Today it is very popular to sleep around before marriage, but the spirit world is saying to you, "Don't be like those people. Really prize your spirituality and protect it." That is what they are saying. The Zen master just said to me, "Dozo." He is right behind you now, and he looked at me and said, "Dozo," meaning, "please hear this."

Spiritual Guidance

Standing beside you to your left is a very lovely master teacher, a woman. She is in a kimono gown, and she was very psychic when she was on earth. What is she saying? I have to listen, because she just did something I have never seen before. Anyway, as you open up spiritually, this woman will help you in the way my guide helps me. Whatever the Japanese word is for "lily," that is the name of this woman, Lily.

HW: Yuri.

PB: Yuri? That is her name. She is a very, very pure soul. Her energy field goes out very far and it's all white, all around. She is a very pure spirit. The Zen master is there to work with you in meditation, self-mastery and discipline, and it's as if he is in charge of all the chakras. But this woman, Lily, is a master of the chakras from here up (motions to chest), so she will teach you to feel, hear, and see spiritually. That's exactly what my guide Tiffany did and does for me. You have both inside and outside clairvoyance.

HW: I do?

PB: Yes. I can see spirits and auras with my eyes open and closed, and you can have the same ability. It's all a matter of consistency toward this purpose.

HW: You mean, through meditation?

PB: That, and the reality of metaphysical responsibility.

Could you begin to ask your questions, please?

HW: The Zen master and this woman named Yuri are two of the people guiding me now; is that correct?

PB: That's correct. There are others, but those are the two that have been shown to me. Perhaps with your questions more will come out; I don't know. My guides and teachers work very systematically and logically.

Go ahead and ask your first question.

Medical Issues

HW: I just went to the doctor yesterday and found out that I have a retinal detachment, and I will have an operation on my right eye this week. I want to know if you think that the operation will go well.

PB: I want to touch in with the vibration.

HW: I asked the doctor what the reason could be for this happening, and the doctor said, for this particular problem, there is no reason that it has happened.

PB: They say it is going to be a routine procedure, so you should not be terribly worried. You will need a little while to recuperate, but it looks like it will be okay. My guide Dr. Palmer says the reason the doctor told you there is no particular reason is because he doesn't know, but it is probably dietary.

HW: I don't really have to do anything to be on a diet in order to lose weight, but are you talking about the particular foods that I am eating?

PB: Yes, and the lack of certain chemicals or vitamins or minerals. (Dr. Palmer is talking to me) You can study to learn what particular herbs help the eyes. For example, in the West we have one called *Eyebright*.

HW: It's an herb?

PB: Yes, it's an herb for people who have bad eyes. When people take it, it greatly improves the health of the eye, and some even stop having to wear glasses. But you are going to be okay, don't worry.

HW: Also in my left eye, the retinal covering is like it is in the right eye—very, very thin. The same detachment could happen in my left eye, so I am worried about that, too. What do you think about that?

PB: Again, Dr. Palmer is saying that you should study what herbs can be used for the eyes. For example, this is me speaking now, some people have cataracts caused by a deficiency of some kind. When they start taking certain herbs, the condition goes away. Most human physical disease results from problems in the diet. Is there a high level of diabetes among Japanese?

HW: Recently diabetes has been occurring more.

PB: That is due to too much rice and too many sugars. The Japanese are imitating the West by consuming chocolate and coca cola, and lots of white rice. Let's move on.

HW: I have another health question. When I was born, the muscles in my neck were extremely tight, and I couldn't move my head. Now my neck finally moves, but because of this problem, I have had trouble with my spine, and it has moved somewhat sideways. I am wondering if there is a problem in my energy field that is causing this.

PB: I had a friend who had the same problem and she was also born with it. She had it operated on and she doesn't have it anymore. For your case, let me ask spirit.

Dr. Palmer said there are two things affecting this condition. One is the kind of work you do, which really puts a lot of pressure on the whole muscle structure. The other is that this congenital problem will probably always be with you. But he said it is not going to kill you. He laughed and said, "Tell her none of the things that she's suffering from are going to kill her." It is not karmic, it's congenital, genetic. You come in with it as a baby, but it's from the genes, and it is not some kind of punishment. He said that if you consistently stretch these muscles with all kinds of movement, and do that all of your life, you can keep the muscles toned. You teach this and tell other people to do this, so the same applies to you.

HW: I tend to go like this. (moves neck)

PB: So does my wife, but she doesn't have neck problems. You will be okay. Just keep working with the muscles. There is really nothing that can be done to change it. It's not obvious, and you look very normal. Let's go to the next question.

Helping Others on the Spiritual Path

HW: I finally figured out what I want to ask. I have patients who are having problems and they are coming to me for advice. I know I can help them by talking to them, so I do. I also help them through physical therapy. I want to know what other techniques, energies, or healing methods I can use to help the people in front of me progress on their particular path.

PB: I am going to let Saint Germain come through.

Saint Germain (SG): I am here. Can you hear me all right? I am very happy to come through Philip and speak to you. He holds the crystal, that I may vibrate off of it. You see, crystals send and receive energy and they also hold energy. For this reason, they are used in things like radios. They are also used in other electronics like microphones, alarm clocks, robotics, and buzzers. Instead of always using Philip's energy, I play off of the crystal he is holding to send and receive energy, and so on. In this way, he does not drain his energy. We don't use the crystal all the time, but sometimes.

Now regarding your work with your patients: All of what Philip was guided to tell you has to do with your profession. There are physical therapists, and then there are physical therapists who are also spiritually oriented. As we have indicated by the various spiritual guides and teachers around you, including the angelic force, you were born for inner spiritual awareness, and whether you know it or not, it is the most important thing of your life.

Most people are not even aware that they are spirit. They give lip service to spirit and to spirit world and spirit guides, but truly they are not so aware. We are encouraging you to meditate and to be disciplined, because you have the skill and the potential to open up to these finer energies of life. The desire to be able to do more to help your patients is both your desire and that which has been given to you by God. So again, we would say to meditate, and you will open up to actually see and work with the chakra energy.

This gentleman before you (Philip) was a healer who worked directly with the chakras, and he could look into the chakra system and see which chakras were in need of attention. To some extent he can still do that. What made it possible are two things: one is natural inclination or being born with it, and the other was the effort he made. He opened up to see clearly. In order to be a fully developed person in your work, both as a physical therapist and a spiritual sensitive, you need to meditate. As much as possible, be with people who are spiritual; not those who just talk about spiritual things over a cup of tea, but those who are actually doing spiritual things. There are many talkers in the metaphysical field. Be a doer.

Now what additional question do you want to ask me regarding what we just talked to you about?

HW: I would like you to tell me in more detail how to meditate.

The Importance of Meditation

SG: Yes. My recommendation is to attend Philip's class on meditation. If you cannot afford it, come as our guest, because we can help you in a very simple and swift way. Philip has worked with countless numbers of people teaching them meditation, and among them are several people who became channelers like he is. To have the healing energy come through you is also a form of channeling, so if you attend the class which he is going to give, it could be very helpful to you. Rather than to take up your time today on this point, and because we need diagrams, it is better to wait. If you cannot make that class, which I urge you to do, then we will talk to Philip about having a little private session with you here, again as our guest.

Let us move onto the next question.

Self-Knowledge and the Higher Self

HW: I really feel I don't know very much about myself yet, and I would like to know what I should do to learn more about myself. Also, I would like to know where I am on my spiritual path and where I need to be going.

SG: Yes. I have been where you are. First of all, you are not this body. You are simply a soul using this body for expression. Secondly, you are not your thoughts. If you notice, thoughts just come and go, without even asking us. In this moment, we have thoughts of anger and in the next moment, we have thoughts of love. In this way, man is crazy. It is the same with our feelings. We are not our feelings. In fact, when we have thoughts or feelings we don't like, we sometimes talk to ourselves, admonishing ourselves not to think and feel a certain way.

Who is the individual observing all of this who does not want to be a part of it? That is your God self or your higher self, the one observing your thoughts, feelings, and actions. The more you practice not being attached to anything, the freer you will be from your thoughts, feelings, and actions.

The truth is that, to a great extent, we are acted upon and really have little to nothing to say about it. You do not ask to be born. You do not ask to be born in this body. You do not ask to be born to your parents, and on and on. Who decided all these things? A force, intelligence, and personality greater than us decided them. Therefore, it is better to surrender to that higher power and let it take over our lives. That's what Philip did.

Therefore, we again go back to meditation. In meditation, at least eighty-five percent of the time should be spent on observing self. In this altered state of mind, one should ask, "Who am I?" over and over. Yes, "Who am I?" "Who am I?" "Who am I?" Who is asking this question? It is your higher self observing the lower self. And what does the lower self contain? Thoughts and feelings. We came into this life to come to the realization that I am *not* my thoughts or feelings or this body. I am my own God presence observing these things. The more we observe thusly, the more detached we become from our life. This detachment puts us in perfect harmony with divine intelligence and leads us to higher and higher realization and self-management. The secret, which comes within meditation, is to find that higher self. Your higher self brought you here, and your higher self protects you from wrong decisions. It is your higher self that urges you to find out who you are.

HW: Could you say that one more time?

SG: Your higher self is urging you to find out who your higher self is. Within this higher self is God. From the outside, our higher self looks like the divine spirit, but from the inside, it is all endless, eternal, divine light and love. The God presence comes to earth as you.

Is all of this helpful?

HW: You're talking not just about me but about every single person as God?

SG: That is true, even as all the cells of your body comprise your whole body, the energy that runs through one cell runs through all cells, and there is as much energy in one cell as there is in all the other cells, equally.

So, God dwells equally in all people. It's just that some are more enlightened, and they know that, and know it clearly. Others are still learning.

My advice to you, dear one, is that you do not have to just sit in front of an altar and meditate. While you are working, while you are on the street, while you are eating your meals, you can ask yourself in your mind, "Who am I?" "Who am I? Who am I? Who am I?" Watch your soul come forth, and watch your own personal development. I cannot say more on this topic at this time. I am going to move away from Philip, and if I need to come back through again, I shall do so. This is Saint Germain.

PB: Let's go to your next question.

The Purpose of Life and Self Mastery

HW: From a universal point of view, how far have I come along in my spiritual growth? Not within the whole planet or compared to everybody, but just within my own spiritual growth, how far have I come?

PB: I am listening. You are a unique, individual manifestation of God. You have to live out your life, your dharma, through this body. Your God self, your higher self, chose this body and personality. In fact, your higher self formed this body.

The personality results partly from birth, but also partly from the societal and familial environment. Even though we are individual souls, we often imitate our siblings and parents. Sometimes we can see ourselves smiling or talking like a parent. In fact, when some people grow up and have families, they say, "I am acting just like my mother!" Our personalities form through parental and family environment, so there is some likeness of energy, but you are still walking your own unique path.

The purpose of this lifetime is to realize self-mastery. That is why this Zen master is with you. There are no accidents. You have to take yourself or your life seriously enough to cause yourself to be consistent in your spiritual pursuits. In order to do what I do spiritually I can't just do what the average person does. I have had to work harder. In my case, where other people might be having free time, I was always meditating, always praying, because I was afraid to lose my gift, and additionally, I tried to be obedient to God. It's that kind of mind that creates this kind of gift. It is often a big sacrifice, but that's the price you pay for a high spiritual life.

With respect to how far you have evolved, you are in the final stage of your spiritual evolution. Saint Germain is showing me the violet light all around you, and it is validation that your path is the metaphysical path and the inner life. While I have continued my spiritual work all my life, I have also run businesses, so this doesn't mean that you have to do spiritual work exclusively.

When you are giving physical therapy to someone, think of them as you, and love them as yourself. Become them. Then your spirituality will grow faster. The natural reality of who you are will come out. Finally, don't be afraid to step out. When I was your age, I never thought I would be doing what I am doing, and when this mission came upon me, I thought it was the last thing I wanted to be doing. But it is my destiny, so I gave myself to it consistently. By doing this, I developed above average ability, because above average effort results in above average ability. Really believe in yourself. You have it all together.

HW: It's difficult.

PB: Only if you think that way. It is also difficult to live. It is difficult to live poorly, but if we work hard, we don't have to live poorly. My favorite phrase is this: *It's not what happens to us in life that matters; it's how we respond.* Someone, a lesser soul, might be very upset about your muscle problem or about the eye problem, but a great soul just sees it as, "Oh, this is just life unfolding. It's no big deal. I am not the body."

Let's go to your next question.

Destiny and the Hand of God

HW: I have been a physical therapist now for only one year, and I am still studying. I have a wonderful physical therapy teacher right now, but in a few years, I want to go beyond physical therapy and not do only that. I don't know how to go about finding a new teacher to study something different, so can you give me some advice on this subject?

PB: First, before Saint Germain comes through, I want to say that I saw you moving away from physical therapy in the future. This is only a phase. You are going to be teaching in the future. That's one of the things you will do.

SG: I am here. I am pleased to be back with you, and the smile upon Philip's face is my smile. It's lovely to be in your presence. We see violet light around you, because there is a connection between Saint Germain and you.

If you hear everything correctly today, you will understand that your future is already set. Have faith and step into life as it unfolds. Rather than worry about the future, which can only happen when it happens, just affirm God's presence within you by saying to yourself that God is leading me to the next place. Wait upon God and he will provide you with all things.

As far as your future is concerned and what you shall do, I am not allowed to give details because you must work out your own dharma. If I tell you everything, I will rob you of the energy needed for you to go to the next level. God put doors and windows in life so as to open and close them. Sometimes he lets us in on the secrets, and sometimes he closes the door or the window. He is all-wise to know when to open and close the door, and he knows what to do with each soul.

You shall move forward in the metaphysical field, and you will study those things that have to do with spiritual awakening. Because working with those kinds of things does not make a lot of money to begin with, you are still going to have to be involved in some physical therapy work. But know this, your future is assured, and as you step into it, you will be successful. Absolutely. Yes. Do you have any more questions regarding this major question?

HW: I understand what you have said today. Do you mean that if I just stay on my path and do what I am doing, I will be successful? Is there more I have to do, in order to do what you are saying?

SG: How did you get to where you are now? Were there some magical steps? Who do you think decided that you should become a physical therapist? Who brought the information to you to capture your interest, and who brought your particular physical therapist to you? How much have you actually done on your own to be successful? Ninety-five percent of what is done in life is done by God. Only some small three to five percent is what we do. Did you decide what color your eyes would be? Did you decide that you would be living in Japan? Who decided all these things? Therefore, we are saying to you, yes, make that effort if that is what appeals to you. Do the research and ask questions. But in the end, your fate is already decided.

HW: I always feel that I really haven't tried very hard, and there is a lot more effort that I can put into everything that I am doing. Should I be putting a lot more effort into my actions than I have been?

SG: As you are impressed, so should you do.

HW: I always think, "Oh, I have to do something—I should do something," but then I always end up feeling lazy and being lazy.

SG: What percentage of human beings do you think are like you? Ninety-nine percent. That is a part of the lesson in this school called life. God created all these conditions for man to learn from. Many people resist life, but in spite of themselves, they wind up doing the thing that

God intended for them to do, even the man who becomes an alcoholic. Who decided that he should be born with genes that would incline him towards drinking alcohol? Did he pick those genes? Who decided that you should be born with an infirmity in your neck? If I keep talking, you will see more and more that you have done very little. Those who make great effort are those who are directed inwardly by God to make great effort. If it is not their destiny to put in hard work, then they will not.

Here we are. Among humanity, you have this unique opportunity. You are a young lady talking to a man from the spirit world. Who created this opportunity? Who gave you this privileged opportunity? When we say trust God, we mean *truly* trust God and truly lean upon God. If you don't know who God is, that is also part of your path. Whether you awaken to God's existence or not is also part of your path. To God, what is to be, has already been put in place, so there is nothing to be upset about or to feel guilty about. Life happens as it happens because that is how it is supposed to happen, but God makes it look as if life happens spontaneously, so we don't become bored.

End of recording

UNCONDITIONAL LOVE AND LOVE OF SELF

Kocho H.—Female

Philip Burley (PB): May I have your paper to hold please? It helps me to feel the vibration. I'd like to open with a prayer.

> *Our Heavenly Father, bless us with your divine presence, and over-shadow this room with your love. This young lady has come to receive from you and from her spirit world today, so bless her through this experience that she may receive all the information she is seeking. May all those in spirit who are guiding her and teaching her come close to us today. Thank you for this great privilege to be a bridge between the two worlds. All this I pray and ask in divine love.*

As I was praying, I saw a beautiful bright red light around you, and I very seldom see this color around people. It represents a level of pure love. Then, as it goes out from your body, it becomes pink, and on the outer edges, a light blue. This indicates that your path to God and to self-realization is not just service, which is love, but also study, which is to gain truth. You have a good balance between these two, and I don't see this very often.

An angel is standing directly behind you, and it's Archangel Michael. There is a lot of gold energy around him that flows right into your energy. The master Jesus also comes to you, and he is standing just behind you to your left. He comes with a great amount of love, but almost like an elder brother, and not just as a master. They are working on balancing your energies, and there are a number of masters here. They have not identified themselves yet, but there is one woman who particularly makes her presence known.

I don't know whether you do public speaking or anything like this, but this possibility shows in your auric field, particularly around your vocal cords. You have the ability to teach and lead people or to be some kind of speaker for truth.

If you are searching at this time, which I feel you are, this is a particular period of time when you should stop thinking too much and make your mind kind of blank. You are in a waiting period, something like a purifying period, and this is the time to throw out old things, in terms of truth, and add new things. One thing I want to really drive home to you is that God is very, very close to you. On your life path, it's almost as if God is moving your feet and not you.

They keep bringing up something about "mother," and I don't know if this is about yourself as a mother or about your own mother. Do you have a question about your mother on your paper?

KH: Yes.

PB: Okay, please ask that question since they brought it up.

KH: My sister has a sickness, like a mental illness, and she has had it for about ten years. She is feeling better, and my mother has been taking care of her. They get along pretty well now, and obviously, there has been a lot between the two of them over the years. As my mother is getting older, they actually take care of each other, and a lot of people, including all the neighbors, help my mother out with all of this. My mother has had something like unconditional love since she was a child, and my mother and I both have a very deep love.

PB: Do you mean that she received unconditional love?

KH: No, she has the nature to give unconditional love, and I received that same nature from her.

PB: Unconditional love. That's the first thing I saw reflected in your aura.

KH: How should my mother take care of my sister? My mother is seventy-nine years old, and at this point, my sister is also taking care of my mother. There is a lot of stress between the two of them, and I end up getting caught in the middle. I am hoping I can become a good cushion between the two of them, and I think I can probably do more for the two of them. I would like you to teach me what I can do for them.

PB: May I have your paper again, please? I am going to let my guide Saint Germain come through and talk to you.

Saint Germain (SG): I am here. This is Saint Germain; can you hear me all right?

KH: Yes.

Unconditional Love and Love of Self

SG: I am very pleased to be here with you today, and for you to have spent this energy to come here.

Dear one, we well understand your dilemma. It is repeated thousands and thousands of times around the world every day, and it is called life. I am not dismissing or minimizing the pressure that you feel, but as you already know, those who know how to love are often the ones who experience sacrifice in love. It happens more often that the mother, more than the father, sacrifices herself to give unconditional love to all of the family. The mother, because she has unconditional love, goes on and on, so she also may burn out. Indeed, your mother, as you describe her, has given unconditional love all of her life, and as you have indicated, it is harder for her to serve others as she is growing older. Of course, we also appreciate the fact that your sister is somewhat incapacitated, as you describe her, and your mother is becoming more that way herself, so you are caught between them.

The purpose of this life is to learn how to give unconditional love; however, the mistake most people make is to give everything they have and leave little or nothing for self. When giving out food when there is very little to spare, one also must set some aside for oneself. People must become wise enough to know that they can give out eighty percent of their unconditional love to others but must save twenty percent for themselves or ninety-five percent to others and five percent for oneself; whatever figure you choose to use. The point I am trying to make is that anyone who gives out one hundred percent to others and saves little or nothing for oneself, eventually is not able to give out anymore. Even a field in the countryside must be allowed one season free of planting to replenish itself.

My first point in answering your question is to suggest that you don't burn yourself out in life when giving unconditional love. Be sure to reserve love for yourself under all conditions as well. You ultimately can do only so much for other people, and it's not your job to make them feel comfortable by sacrificing yourself. It is not your job to take away their mental or emotional pain. Just being there sometimes to help out and to listen could be enough.

We are put on this earth plane, as you have well discerned, to learn how to love, so this experience is an opportunity for all three of you to learn how to love unconditionally. Though your mother and sister may suffer because of their problems, this is their karmic path. It is inevitable that your mother will eventually die, and how she shall go is also a part of her karmic path. Instead of pitying her, allow the karmic path to unfold. Do not try to determine what your mother or your sister does, for you cannot control that. Only determine what you do. They will act the way they will act; and they will do and say what they will do and say. At times, there may be conflict, but you cannot eliminate that between them. It provides an object lesson for all three of you to learn unconditional love. You can only do your best and learn from the situation. Give what you can give, but that is enough.

The rule of this life is balance—balance, balance, balance—and it is when life becomes unbalanced that we become disturbed. This includes giving too much love and not reserving enough love for ourselves. Take my word that everything will work out, and things will unfold as they are supposed to. You should come out of this situation an even more loving and compassionate person, but just know you can't live their lives or think or decide anything for them, even as they cannot do that for you. Listening to this recording and reflecting upon my words to you will greatly help you to remain both loving toward them and objective about their situation.

I am going to stay here with Philip. I am going to remove myself, but I shall come back later.

PB: I see a big heart that he just put in the air for you. He feels a lot of love towards you.

Kwan Yin works with you, and she is right here, all in white. The energy around her is blue, and she is holding a beautiful pink lotus blossom with the stem on it. It is for you, and it represents eternal love. She is laughing, and I can hear her so clearly. She is laughing and says she will help you with your mother and your sister. She says, just do what you can do, and we will make up the difference. Your mother also has Kwan Yin with her, and she moves throughout your family.

The other thing that appears right over your head is a crown. It's a beautiful, tall crown, and it looks like the crown of a princess. The reason this crown is appearing above your head is that you are supposed to obtain self-mastery in this lifetime. You are in the situation you have described primarily to learn that. Many people have to go away from home to learn self-mastery, but your opportunity is right here in your home.

KH: I don't live with them, and I'm trying to figure out which home you mean. I want to know if my home is where I live now or with my mother and sister.

PB: No; I am saying that the situation with your mother and sister provides an opportunity for you to gain self-mastery, so you don't have to leave this area.

Love and Healing Energy

KH: I have been working in an old folks' home, so I spend a lot of time with elderly people. I have learned all kinds of things from them and have taught them a lot, so they have learned from each other. I am extremely grateful that I have this opportunity to work with them, so I am always asking the angels to help me with my job. I live alone right now and have many friends who are always coming in and out of my house. I am in a very good situation right now and would like to be able to help my friends even more than I already do.

I want to volunteer in a hospice, but I went to one hospice to look at it, and the energy or atmosphere was really dark, so I decided not to choose that one. I know that in a hospice a patient can be in shock that they are going to die, and the family and friends who come can also be in shock; but when the shock they feel is really big, I don't feel I am ready yet to be able to help them. I want to study, grow, and develop more so I can receive as much power as possible from the guides who are with me. I also would like to be able to talk to my guides. That is what I am wishing for more than anything. How can I connect with my guides even more and bring myself as close as possible to them?

PB: I was purposely letting you talk, because you need to express yourself, but I want to back up a minute and respond to everything you are talking about. Again, this gaining of self-mastery can happen within your current environment, meaning your job and your interaction with your mother and sister. All of this is bringing you the opportunity you need to grow and develop self-mastery. You don't have to go anywhere else than where you are, and you are already in the midst of the situation where you can gain self-mastery. That is why this red energy shows around you so much.

As far as gaining insight or knowledge to be able to do hospice work, you already have more ability than you realize. You just need to continue being the person you are to be effective. You would also be trained if you joined a hospice group. My wife volunteered in a hospice for several years, and I was a guest speaker where she worked, so I know from that experience that they give adequate training. They always pair you up with another person who is more advanced. I was a speaker at hospice because hospice workers often saw spirits around people, and they wanted to ask me about that. Some of them became my students, and I taught them how to work with the dying and how to communicate with their own guides. Where you have an advantage is that you already know about the spirit world, and you also want to work with your guides.

You have very high-level guides, as I mentioned. Archangel Michael is working with you all the time, fundamentally as a protector; but the major reason he is with you is that you are a being of love, and you draw him to you. He works with the love that you bring to the world, and it is the same with Jesus. Jesus is also with you to raise you to a new level of understanding of self. He is the one that was holding the crown over your head. You have Kwan Yin also, so you have a very strong trinity working with you. My guide, Tiffany, is standing here to my right, and she says that if you just work with them and call them in to help with whatever you are doing, you will receive a great amount of help.

My guide, Dr. Palmer, who stands to my left, was just talking to me about your healing energy. He says you have a natural ability to heal, and you don't even have to try. Just be you and continue doing what you are doing with helping the elderly and perhaps working with hospice, and the healing energy will just come from you. If you want to take training in this, that is okay, but he says it's not really necessary. You are a natural healer.

KH: If I am aware of the healing energy in my mind, and I think about expanding it, does it just expand naturally?

PB: You were born with the ability to love naturally, and on the basis of that reality there is a foundation which provides for the energy of healing to just flow within you and through you. I felt it as soon as I saw you, and it comes from you naturally. The key to increasing the power of healing energy is just to continue to love. Some people have to work at it, but you don't. I am hearing this from my guide, Dr. Palmer.

Let's go to the next question.

KH: Are Kwan Yin and Mother Mary the same person or are they two different people?

PB: They are two different people. Kwan Yin is Chinese and Mother Mary is Jewish.

KH: Because all my life I have been praying to Mother Mary, so I thought instead of Kwan Yin, Mother Mary would come.

PB: She may still come, but I have no control over this. I am just telling you what I see. They both have the same kind of energy, so we will see.

Cosmic Changes and God

KH: Here is my next question. Everybody believes that in the year 2012 there are going to be major changes on the earth, and my friends say this all the time. All of us know it is very important to grow as much as possible during this time, and I would like to help my friends to grow. What can I do in my life to be able to help my friends to grow in preparation for this event?

PB: Saint Germain will come through to speak to you.

SG: I am here. This is Saint Germain.

While you desire to help your friends, each must walk his or her own path. You have the master Jesus working with you, and his best presentation to the world is the example of his life. The best thing we can do for friends and family is not trying to cause them to follow us or to believe in us, but to be an example of self-reliance, so they may become reliant upon themselves. As God is guiding you from within and without, God is also guiding each one of them. God is aware of any cosmic or local changes occurring in the earth far, far in advance, and he is preparing those who may be affected by such changes. Just trust that God is working behind the scenes with each one of your friends and be an example of following spiritual truth. Be steadfast and fixed in your own purpose.

As we have said through this medium a number of times, there are three areas of concern: God's, others', and our own. We always advise you to stay within the area of your own concern and let God take care of his concerns and others take care of their concerns. Many people are out there telling others what to do, even though they themselves fail to do the very thing they tell others to do. I am not suggesting that this is you; but I am saying to do what you need to do on your own path, and let others do what they need to do. By all means be a positive force wherever you go but use discrimination. Because of where you are headed on the spiritual path, dear one, discrimination is very serious. The use of your life energies is vitally important—how you direct them and how they bring the kind of results you desire.

As regards any cosmic change, again I say that all those who are to be aware of it and prepared for it shall be, because God is very much in charge. Even when things seem to go wrong, God is still the one behind all that is happening. God alone knows the results that are wanted and needed within humankind.

Now again I am going to leave Philip and let him come back to himself.

PB: I don't know what was said. Let's go to your next question.

A Father's Love

KH: My father died nineteen years ago, and that was a very, very painful thing for me. I feel like my father is always next to me or near me, always protecting me.

PB: He is right behind you, not beside you, but behind you.

KH: Does he have a message for me?

PB: First of all, he came around behind me because he wants to receive this energy directly, so I need to look into your eyes. He is proud of you—very, very proud—and he has devoted his whole life on the spirit side to helping you. He doesn't really leave you, and the kind of love he has for you is Christ-like; very high and very pure. I can hear him laughing, and he is saying that he is very happy. Regarding the situation with your mother and sister, he says, "Don't worry about it so much. They are going to go through what they are going to go through, with or without you. So, relax."

Wave after wave of electricity is going through my body from the top of my head to the bottom of my feet, and this energy is your father's love coming out towards you. He says that sometimes you don't get enough rest, and he is concerned about that. Make sure you save some love for yourself, because you are going to have a long life and serve many people. Therefore, you need to discipline yourself and get enough rest. He says he only wishes that he could live his life over, because he would like to be able to do with his life what you are doing with yours. There is a big, big, heart right behind you, and it has been there all the time I have been talking to you. He says it's there because you are a natural channel of love. If you want to, you can channel spirit in the future, and that's fine, but the major thing is that you are a natural channeler of love. Just accept it. He wants you to give his love to your mother and sister. He wants you to tell them about his appearing here.

Are you married?

KH: I broke up with my husband three years ago, after being with him for seventeen years.

PB: Did you used to wear a gold ring?

KH: I probably did.

PB: Do you want to marry again? Your father is talking to me about marriage.

KH: Right now, no. I am not thinking about that. I have freedom to be on my own now, and there is nobody that I have to take care of. I am free; and so, no, I'm not thinking about that at all.

PB: Okay; he is not clarifying, but he is sad to see you alone.

KH: Is he worried about me?

PB: No, not worried. It's not that you have to get married or anything like that, but he is just sad that you don't have a life partner that you can be happy with. He's not saying it's anything you must do, but he is just expressing the sentiment that he wishes you could have had a life partner to be happy with.

KH: I am dating someone.

PB: Ok; I see. I still see the gold ring, so I think you will eventually marry—not now, but as you grow older, and probably the same person you are with now.

KH: Should I try to be open-minded about it and not keep thinking that I don't want to get married? Should I get rid of that thought?

PB: He is not telling you what to do. That's all your responsibility, so he is not at all pressuring you to marry or to stay single. He was only expressing that he wishes you could have a life partner and be happy. That's all. It is just pure sentiment. Anyway, he is praying for you on the other side, and he is showing me that he is praying.

Mother Teresa

Mother Teresa is here. She is standing right here, and she said she came instead of Mother Mary. She is also working with you in a big way, and she is like a go-between for you and Mother Mary. She is laughing and says, "You know, if you want to be a nun like me, that is okay with me. If you don't ever want to marry and, instead, be like me, that is okay! Marriage or no marriage is not the question, but to love or not love is the question. This is followed by the question, what or whom do we love? I loved everyone as myself, or at least I tried, and I tried to make no exception in loving others. That is how you are trying to love also, and that is why I am attracted to you."

Even before Mother Teresa died, she was working on the spirit side with you. Being a very high master, she says she was already working on the other side before she died. So she was working with you even when she was still on earth. She came to you when you were around twelve or thirteen. Are you from a Catholic background?

KH: Yes.

PB: Were you confirmed around that time?

KH: I don't know that word.

PB: Well anyway, Mother Teresa is saying she was with you during your confirmation. She is standing there now, and it's as though showers of blessings are just coming down on you. Much of this information you can tell other people, but don't tell them all the details. Keep some of it in your heart like a treasure, so the power of this experience will grow.

Let's go to your next question.

KH: Thank you very much.

PB: You are welcome.

KH: I am very happy that I have many guides around me.

PB: There are many more, but those are the major people showing themselves.

KH: From the moment I was born, I always thought that love was really the only thing there is. I'm happy with all the information I have heard today, and I'm grateful. I want to become more one with God, and I would like to be able to feel it. I would like to feel that oneness with God in my hands and feet. I am really bad at meditation; it's not my strong point. But I would really like to be able to see the spirit world. There is a Monroe Institute in the United States where they put something over your head, and you listen to it. Is it in California?

PB: I know about it, and it's in Virginia.

KH: I have been trying to see spirits by using the techniques from the Monroe Institute, and I have been listening to their tapes. Do you think this is something that will help me?

PB: Are you hearing their tapes in English or Japanese?

KH: Somebody has translated them into Japanese, so it's all written out in Japanese. First you read the whole thing in Japanese, and then you actually listen to the tapes in English.

PB: Okay, I am going to let Saint Germain speak.

Unconditional Love and Spiritual Awakening

SG: I am back. I am so pleased again to be here with you. Dear one, there are just so many things in life that are possible, and we don't have to do them all. If there were more people on earth that loved as you love and cared as you care, this would indeed be a very spiritual place. We know that you do not take credit but give all the credit to God, and you have the most essential element necessary to become spiritually aware—the ability to love unconditionally.

All the efforts towards spiritual awakening are futile unless one loves correctly. When we become open spiritually, we want to be open at the highest level possible, and any effort made without the ability to love correctly does not take us to the highest possible level. This is why I emphasize unconditional love as the prerequisite for all spiritual awakening. You already love that way, so it's only a matter of time before your spiritual awakening comes. It is there in part already in the manifestation of love.

All of creation, including the spiritual and physical world, is built upon the matrix of love, and this is the most important reality of all. To be able to love, to give and take love at the highest level, is the greatest gift of all, and when our love becomes intense enough to reach God, then we are equipped to awaken spiritually. God lives in the temple of ourselves, and when we long for God correctly, we awaken him within ourselves. This is the means by which to become most spiritually awakened. God is the source of life and the source of the ability to perceive the spirit world. Jesus was totally one with God, so he could see and hear the spirit world. He emphasized love over and over. He was an example of love, and he allowed himself to be crucified for love. His love for God, above all, is what made him so awakened.

Fundamentally, you are already on the correct path for spiritual opening. That is the major point I am making. If you want to continue with the Monroe Institute, very well. More important than the technique you use, however, is your motive and your desire. Having a motive and desire to help others through your spiritual gifts is what will awaken you most quickly.

Please listen again to my words in this recording to truly get all the details of what I am saying. Do you want to ask any other questions regarding this?

KH: So the most important thing is for me to have the right desire within myself, is that correct?

SG: Yes.

KH: So it's not meditation or any other technique, but it's like praying inside? Is that correct?

SG: I told you from the beginning, because you were born in love, your path in life is the path of love. That path is what will lead you to spiritual awakening, and it has already been doing that for you. While the medium I am speaking through used meditation, he too was born in love, and his subordinate path to awaken has been the path of unconditional love. He has consciously sought to imitate the life of Christ. A combination of giving unconditional love and the practice of meditation have made it possible for him to be what he is today.

Have we answered your question?

KH: Yes. Thank you very much.

SG: You are very welcome. Now I am going to leave Philip and let him come back to himself. Just know that our love follows you at all times, and if you want my help just call on me, and I will be there. God has already blessed you; this is Saint Germain.

PB: Okay, we have time for one more question.

KH: I don't have one more question, because my mind is blank right now. I would just like to say, thank you very much. I am very happy.

PB: This was a wonderful reading for me. All of the people I have read for have been wonderful, but I haven't seen any that I can remember with red light surrounding them like I saw in your aura. Keep it as a secret in your heart, and it will grow and grow.

I will close with prayer:

Father, I seal this reading with love. Thank you so much for this lovely woman who is an example for others to follow. Please bless all that she seeks to do for you and hear the yearning of her heart to fully awaken. All this I pray and ask in the Christ Spirit. Amen.

End of recording

LIFE PLAN AND FAITH

Akari J.—Female

Philip Burley (PB): You have angels all around you, so you must be special to heaven. To have so many angels means you are very protected. Do you feel that way?

KH: No, I have never felt that way.

PB: Well, you are. Archangel Michael is here, standing directly behind you, and he has come to you a number of times. He just said, "Philip, this is another one I work with." My guide Saint Germain also tapped me on my shoulder and said, "Be sure to tell her I will come through."

They are showing me that you are standing in the middle of a bridge that symbolizes a transition both in life and in spirit. As you cross this bridge there is light behind you, but the light ahead of you is much brighter. It is a gold light, which means you are coming into a new and higher level of understanding of yourself and life.

There is a large tiger walking back and forth here in front of you, and he represents a very powerful Japanese master. He was a Zen Buddhist and a high master in judo, but he was primarily known for his spiritual power. He is standing right behind you with the yin/yang symbol in front of him. He says he is largely responsible for helping you make the transition I was talking about. He is known as Master Tiger, but you may just call him Tiger. Although he is not a big man, he appears as very strong and muscular. He lived towards the beginning of the era in Japan known as Edo.

You have violet and silver light all around you, and there is healing blue energy coming from your hands and solar plexus. Do you do healing?

AJ: No.

PB: Did you study healing?

AJ: A little bit.

PB: Well, you have the gift, and it is very pronounced, so if you put hands on people, you would bring about healing. In fact, this is what Master Tiger did in his life. He is working very much on the third eye with you. Do you struggle with the whole area of trying to develop and open your spiritual senses? Do you doubt yourself?

AJ: I don't doubt myself, but when I go to various seminars, some people there "see," and some don't. I put myself in the group of people that don't, so I have just decided that it is not an ability that I have.

PB: Well, I am not convinced of that because of how this master Tiger is working with you. You are going through a transitional period in which you are entering into a brighter light, with changes and greater opening of awareness ahead of you.

Are you in your forties now?

AJ: Yes.

PB: I see these changes occurring towards the latter part of your forties and into your fifties.

Do you do counseling? I see you with people sitting across from you.

AJ: No, I don't. My major in college was psychology, but I am not very interested in it now, and I have never done any counseling.

PB: Well, I probably see this because of your degree in psychology. Whatever you made up your mind to do, you could do. You are listening to your own voice, and that is good, but it's important to keep an open mind. I'm being shown very clearly that there are definite changes coming up. There will be the potential for opening the third eye and other areas of awareness.

There is a guide standing here with the name of Starlight. She is what I call a joy guide, and when this kind of spirit appears, it means the person in front of me has the potential to do what I am doing. You also have a Native American with you who is very tall and wears a feather headdress. He said his name very clearly out loud so I wouldn't miss it: Golden Eagle.

You may have been to channelers who told you about other spirit guides because different channelers see spirits from different spiritual levels, and each channeler's beliefs influence what each one sees; but it may all have some aspect of truth for you. I am seeing very high beings with you.

Do you have some questions about your health on this paper?

AJ: Yes.

PB: The Native American I was talking about is a practitioner of medicine, and he just said that you have a health question that he wants to answer. Please go ahead and ask it.

Health Question and Diagnosis

AJ: I have a tumor in my uterus, and when I went to the hospital seven or eight years ago, the doctor said the tumor had reached a size that required an operation right away to remove it. I chose not to have an operation then because I didn't feel anything, and it wasn't affecting my life. I have been living with it for seven or eight years, and since it has never affected me in any way at all, I have never had the operation.

About two or three years ago, I went to see a Japanese channeler, a healer who had studied in England. I told him about my tumor, and he said my fear of an operation was the result of my ego. He told me that I shouldn't be afraid because there are many things one can learn from an operation. I didn't believe him, and I did not like the information I received. I did not feel it was true or correct for me at all, so I'm asking, is it my ego that opposes having the operation?

PB: No, I have been listening to your guides ever since you started talking. You were correct to follow your own intuitive awareness. I have the feeling that the Japanese healer did not have a clear answer for you, and it sounds as though he was simply giving you his opinion. If he had used true clairvoyance, he could have looked into your body and seen the tumor to determine whether or not you needed an operation or if the tumor was malignant. The answer he gave you may have been from *his* ego!

In this work, we channelers have to be very careful not to get too involved. Unless I keep a healthy distance from you, I can't be a good instrument for you. To sit where I am, I have to be a compassionate lover of humanity as well as something of a lawyer. It requires a very fine balance. But as far as I can see, you didn't make a mistake, and you were right to follow your own intuition. To me, it appears that you are okay, and clairvoyantly, I don't see a tumor at all. If you develop symptoms, or if you wish to have a follow up consultation with one or more doctors, that could confirm what I'm telling you, but that is up to you. Is this helpful?

AJ: Thank you very much.

PB: The Native American who is standing here was the one who was talking to me about all of this, so please talk to him when you pray or meditate. He is very capable and can be a great help to you with your health concerns. Also, talk to Master Tiger. You have a good combination of people with you.

Right now, a lot of gold light is coming down on you, and you are receiving much healing energy. This light is originating from beyond the ceiling and pouring down on you.

I have to tell you that when I first started praying for you, I saw a four-leaf clover over your head. I asked what this meant in your case, and they said that, overall, you are a lucky person in life.

Let's go on to your first written question.

Influence of Ancestors

AJ: In many Japanese homes there are two altars. One is a Buddhist altar that stays in the family home and is passed down from the grandparents to the eldest son, and the other is a shrine to Shintoism which is placed way up high. Every day, people place offerings of water and rice on these altars and pray to their ancestors.

Last year, I received a reading from a Japanese woman, a calligraphy teacher, who told me I do not have good luck in this life because I don't pray for my ancestors. In fact, I don't feel I have good luck. What influence do our ancestors have on our present life?

PB: It is no accident that I saw a four-leaf clover over your head, that I was told it means you are lucky in this life, or that I told you about this image and what it means just before you read your first question. I am going to let Saint Germain come through and speak to you on this point. Would you repeat the part of your question about the influence of ancestors?

AJ: Yes. What influence do our ancestors have on our present life?

Saint Germain (SG): I am here. This is Saint Germain. You have asked a very good question. Since I am from the spirit world, I should be able to answer this question for you; and if I can't, nobody can! (Laughter)

It is case by case, depending on who our ancestors are and what spiritual level they reached in their lifetime. When we build an altar and pray to our ancestors, we draw them to us to some degree, but just being our ancestor does not give a spirit being a sufficient basis to interact with us. Interaction is a result of the law of attraction, and in order for there to be attraction, there must be things that you and an ancestor have in common. The other factor is the nature of your mission. If there is no one in your ancestry big enough to undertake a big mission, they will help you only as much as they can, and someone who is not your ancestor will help you further. How much they can influence you also depends upon your degree of openness. Since there are higher and lower spirits, there are varying degrees and levels of influence. If, for example, the Premier of Japan is from a line of significant leaders, it is likely that one of his ancestors who was a leader will work with him.

The factors that determine the influence of an ancestor, then, include your mission, their spiritual level, and whether they have things in common with you. In some cases, ancestors work with their family on earth just because they are family and related by blood, and that is what they have in common; but it is not always an ancestor that works with an individual. As I said, it is case by case. I really can't add any more to my answer, but I am going to stay here with Philip so you may ask any other questions you have on this point.

AJ: If I don't do any special prayers for my relatives, this doesn't mean that something bad will happen to me?

SG: Not at all. That is simply a belief system based on tradition. There are many people on earth who do not pray who have good fortune anyway, because what is most important is the kind of heart you have. That is what will determine what kind and level of individual you will draw to you from the spirit world, so do not worry about whether you pray or don't pray to your ancestors.

The reality from this side, the spirit world, is that people who focus on praying to ancestors do not grow or mature to the same level as they would if they stood individually. While it is not bad to pray for ancestors, in doing so you may draw their problems into your life. If you believe ancestors must stay together, you will be with your ancestors in the spirit world whether you like them or not, because that is what you believe. Therefore, it is better to work on your own growth with the highest beings who may attend you, whether or not they are related to you by blood.

The truth is that each person comes to earth as an individual and leaves earth as an individual. Each one must find who they are as an individual. It is very important that people understand this, and those who understand it are those who advance furthest and fastest. People often hold onto belief systems because they are afraid not to, and they are bound by either ignorance or superstition.

Spirits are always working with you, and even as I am speaking to you, there are many spirits here in the room. Whether you call us to you or not, we come. We know whom we are to serve because we are assigned in the spirit world, and we are always around and ever there to help. Do not live in fear at all regarding praying to your ancestors.

I am going to stay here with Philip, and if you have another question, I will answer it.

AJ: A yoga teacher once admonished me for eating meat and that by doing so I committed sin. I really had trouble believing him. But is it wrong to kill animals and eat them?

SG: No, it is not wrong. The animal kingdom was provided by God for the sake of humanity. As animals serve as food for other animals, so animals serve as food for humankind. The plant kingdom, which you also eat, represents all degrees of truth, and the animal kingdom represents all degrees of love. There is distant love, which is represented by animals such as the snake. The snake is cold blooded and represents a lesser love, almost like lust. Then there is the highest, most exquisite love, which is the love of God. To partake of the animal kingdom is to partake of different degrees of love. To eat plants is to symbolically partake of varying degrees of truth. Again, it is not a sin for man to eat animals, and I would not dwell on that idea any longer.

As in the first example, the information you received is based on that person's belief system. This is why we must cross the bridge of knowledge into the place of golden love where the highest truth is known. Then we can throw away many belief systems and erroneous understandings. For example, many people around the world say you should belong to this or that religion because they want to get members in order to collect more money and have more influence. But from our perspective in the golden light, when you cross the bridge of knowledge there is only one true religion, the religion of love. When you live in true love, loving others as self, you don't need religion. Such love will guide you correctly because it is the highest truth of all truths.

I am now going to leave Philip, and if I think it is necessary to come back again, I shall do so. This is Saint Germain.

PB: He had me so far out.

AJ: I was fascinated to learn about the different levels of the animal and plant kingdoms and how it all works.

PB: Good. Please ask your next question.

Life Plan and Faith

AJ: I believe I made a plan for my life before I came into this body. I would like to know how I can remember the plan I made.

PB: May I have your paper to hold? I need the energy.

SG: I am here again.

You are doing precisely what you are intended to do, and the grass is not greener off your current path. Many times, people think they should be someone else, doing something else in life. But you are exactly who you are because that is what was intended. To carry out the purpose of your life, certain things are hidden from you so you will pay the maximum karmic price to benefit your soul. I cannot say it more simply or clearly than that.

In the spirit world, we would say that living life on earth requires faith. When you buy food for a week, you buy it assuming that you are going to live that whole week, but who knows? You may die that week. When you catch a taxicab here in the city, you don't think about whether or not you are going to get to your destination; you simply have faith, hidden faith, that you will get there. So it is with everyone who gets into a taxi, but every day, a certain number of people get killed in taxis, on trains, on airplanes, and on subways. When you marry someone, you say, "I will love you forever," but is that really true? The history of the world says *no*. In today's world, fifty percent of marriages end in divorce. Therefore, when we marry, we have to have a certain amount of faith. Just to buy groceries, get into a taxi, or get married—to live life—requires faith.

When you came to the earth plane to live this life, you came in faith, so if you want to know why you came, you may or may not get the answer. It is case by case and depends on one's karma, so, you live the best you can one day at a time. Everyone in the world can only live one day at a time. Subconsciously, when you get out of bed in the morning, you simply have faith that you will get through the day. As you see by my examples, dear one, a tremendous amount of life depends on faith. My advice is to continue to be child-like and to live in faith.

You certainly do ask very good questions. I enjoy your questions because they are well thought out. Just because we cannot give you the specific answer you are seeking does not mean they are wrong questions to ask. Each of your sincere questions will lead you to higher truth.

AJ: I have read in books and heard from people that in order to realize your desires, you must have an image in your mind of what you want to do and do your best to hold onto that image while praying and meditating on it. Sometimes I do this, but only once in a while does it work for me. Is this truly the best way to realize your desires?

SG: This is how people are realizing all the time, whether they are consciously using this method or not. Consciously or unconsciously, all individuals go toward that which they have visualized inside. Does that answer your question?

AJ: Yes.

SG: Let us go to the next question.

Spiritual Guides

AJ: What messages do my guides here now have for me at this time?

SG: The major message today is that you are in a period of transition. The past is past, and you are moving into a higher level of understanding. Secondly, the answers to some of the questions you have asked today have liberated you from any more concern about them. And so we say it is a red letter day, meaning that it is an outstanding day for you. The final message from all those guides here, as they speak to me in unison is this: We love you! And that is it. Now again, I am going to leave Philip and let him come back to himself.

PB: Okay, go ahead with your questions.

AJ: Is it true that there are certain guides that are with us from the day we are born, and other guides that come and go?

PB: Well, you are assigned two personal angels that are with you your whole life. When you leave your body at night during sleep, you meet them, and they are often the ones who help you out of your body at night. Their job is not so much to educate you but to protect you and take you different places in the spirit world where you can learn. And yes, there are those that come and go, depending on the student. If the student is growing, then it is necessary that higher-level teachers come. As a spirit works with you and you grow, they also grow, so some will advance with you. Usually when ancestors are assigned to you, they stay with you for a lifetime.

Saint Germain says the word "assigned" is not really the correct word. There has to be a rapport for there to be a meaningful give and take between you and a spirit guide. I love your questions; they are really wonderful.

AJ: Thank you.

PB: I now know why I said in the beginning that you were searching for answers, and that you were on the bridge of transition going into golden light. These questions and the answers to them really lead you to a much freer, higher level of living.

Attitude of Gratitude—Everyday Jobs

AJ: I have been working in the same job for many years, and although I have wanted to quit, I have come to the conclusion that it is probably the best job for me. I am not happy in the job, but I feel it is the best for me, so I am still there. I am now studying as many spiritual things as I can. What things should I continue to study in the future for my growth, and is this the best thing to do for my life right now?

PB: Saint Germain is not going to come through right now because of my throat, but he is going to stand here, and I am just going to repeat what he says.

First of all, ninety-five percent of people are not happy in their jobs. They have a story that life should be different than it is, and most people think the grass is greener on the other side. People want to be doing anything else other than what they are doing, but wherever we are in life, we are in that situation to learn; not primarily about other people or ways of working but about *ourselves*. Evidently, that is the best place for you to be working or you would not still be there. Most people can find happiness where they are by changing their attitude. For example, there are many in Japan and in the world that can't find work and have no means to live. There are others who have physical impairments and can't work at all. Often people don't look deeply enough to see the value they are receiving from their situation, so all they see is what they don't like.

Saint Germain says the attitude of gratitude really changes everything. Taking everything into consideration, we can find reasons to be grateful. He says that, at the very least, while we are still in a work situation, we should try to get the most out of it by being grateful. He says he has advised other people in similar situations to keep a journal of what they are grateful for. It doesn't matter if it is about your family or about your job. Just start expressing in the journal what you are grateful for in every situation. At the end of the day, list three or four things. They can be the same things each day, but make a list of what you are grateful for.

When we change our attitude, the world often changes around us, and it is by divine law that this is so. What we give out is what we get back, and what we sow is what we reap. When heaven sees that we are very grateful in even the worst of circumstances, our circumstances change. Saint Germain is smiling and says, "We are not saying you have a bad attitude. We can feel you have been very patient. But if you have to stay in your job, you have to find a reason to stay, and not just say, 'Well, it must be the best place for me right now because I can't find anything else.' That is a negative attitude, and it is not fair to you. Find reasons to be grateful. If you plant gratitude there, you will come to like it there."

He says he has no suggestions about what to study but to just follow your intuition. You are at the stage in your spiritual growth where you need to work with your intuition, so ask your higher self what you need, and you will get the answer. And don't try to do it all at once; just one step at a time, one month at a time, and little by little. He said, "I will give this one piece of advice: Experience that enables us to know ourselves better and better is the best experience. I can't say any more."

AJ: I would like to clarify what you said about ancestors. Can you be influenced by ancestors whether or not you believe it is happening?

PB: I am going to listen to Saint Germain again.

Everything happens according to divine law, regardless of what we believe. The way your ancestors evolve is by helping you. Whether you worship them or not, they often have to come back to the earth plane to grow because the physical body is the secret to spiritual growth. The spirit living inside the physical body receives energy from the physical body, and that energy is what enables the spirit to grow. This is why God put us in a physical body. At the same time, through God, our own spirit gives our physical body the necessary energy to be alive. Spirits, whether they are ancestors or other spirits, can't get physical energy except by returning to the earth plane. They use the physical energy available through their interaction with us. High spirits don't draw it off and fatigue you, but lesser spirits will take energy from you.

On the other hand, false beliefs can lock you into situations that can block you. If you are Catholic and believe as Catholics do, then you will be blocked from thinking and believing as Buddhists do. If you believe as a Buddhist does, then you will block the beliefs of Catholicism and other beliefs. It is better to be able to recognize truth where you find it.

During this transitional period, it is imperative that you get away from limiting belief systems. Today, Saint Germain says, you have received certain answers that should liberate you from feeling bound, so you should go away tonight very satisfied. If you truly listen to these answers with your heart as well as your mind, you will know they are true. Above all, he says to trust your intuition.

Okay, we have time for one more question. These are excellent questions. They are clear questions, and you are receiving clear answers.

AJ: I have asked all the questions I had on this paper. Do my guides have any particular advice as to what I should do about the tumor in my uterus?

PB: What are you feeling you should do?

AJ: I will try to do whatever I think is the right thing to do. I have been thinking about using sound healing.

PB: I feel very good about your future.

End of recording

Spiritual Reading Thirteen

THE PATH OF SPIRITUAL WORK

Asahi N.—Male

Philip Burley (PB): Saint Germain works very spontaneously like I do, so I don't know when he will come in. He overshadows me and speaks when the time is right. I don't know how many people have read for you before, but I am very relaxed, and I want you to be relaxed. As you may have read in my literature, I open with a short prayer that connects me to spirit, and they begin to bring light around us so everything here will move harmoniously together. I am very happy to serve you. May I hold the paper with your questions?

Let's begin with a prayer:

Our Heavenly Father and Mother, we feel your presence and the presence of many guides and teachers as we begin today. We direct our energies toward heaven that we may make solid contact and be totally overshadowed by you and spirit. Please bless this young man with your presence, that he may go from here feeling and knowing that he has been visited by you in spirit. May his guides and teachers surround him and bring information through clearly and directly. I thank you for the privilege of being a bridge between the two worlds, and I pray and ask all this in divine love.

The Search for Spiritual Truth

First of all, I feel peace in your energies, and it seems that you practice staying peaceful. When I first saw you, I saw expansive blue light around you. There is a small band of gold light on the outer part of it, which is the kind of light mediums see around me. It indicates that you are an individual who deeply appreciates and searches for the truth of things. The outer gold light indicates that you were born ultimately for spiritual things. You may work in the outer world, but the core part of you is very much involved in spiritual things. My spirit guide, who stands here to my right, just said, "Yes; he was born to do above-average work."

Several things are happening. Saint Germain just greeted you, saying he is connected to you and wants to come through and talk to you, and now I understand what I felt when I met you a few moments ago. The feeling is that you are like my brother, a real brother. You and I, meaning you and Philip Burley, belong to a kind of spiritual circle on the other side where we have met before. The second thing I saw while Saint Germain was talking was an image of you looking to the East. You have a lot of questions about your spiritual progress. They are also telling me that you have a very important decision coming up in about three months. It's a major decision that will require choosing between two things having to do with finances, and they are showing me a vision of you signing an important contract. Whether you believe in God or not, know that God believes in you, and he has his hand directly on your life. I also see that you are the kind of person that really enjoys having a good time. This is a time of your life to allow yourself the freedom to really enjoy life. We are not talking about being irresponsible but about being joyful inside. You are very capable of making other people laugh if you just let yourself go.

Do you have a question on your paper about a woman? My guide just said this is one of your top questions. That is how they are seeing it. Please read your question out loud.

Finances and Marital Issues

AN: I am having financial difficulty right now, and my wife and I are in the process of getting a divorce. I have a very strong feeling inside of me that my wife and I just do not fit anymore. I would really like a hint to help me see if I should stay with my wife because we have three young children. I would like to know how things will go in the future if I get divorced, because the children need to be taken care of.

PB: This relates to the decision I saw ahead of you. Whatever you decide will definitely affect you financially in terms of alimony, child support, and maintaining two homes or not doing that. I know you have thought about all of this, so let's ask upstairs (pause).

Someone just touched me. Is your grandmother, your mother's mother, in spirit?

AN: Yes, she is in spirit.

PB: That's who is touching me. I knew immediately that she was from your mother's side of the family. She is not used to communicating, so she couldn't impress me strongly. Some spirits are able to impress me very easily, approaching forcefully, while others are very shy. She is shy, but she is touching your face with a great deal of love toward you. She just said you were born for God, and your life circumstances presently don't give you the peace you want. Whatever decision you make, they will back you up.

You will be guided to the right decision, and she says they want you to detach from the outcome. In other words, follow through on what you are impressed to do, and trust that whatever decision you make will work out. The major thing, and she says this very emphatically, is to do whatever you do out of love. If you feel the highest love is to separate, then do that. If the highest love is to stay together, then so be it. The energy field around you shows a second marriage may be in your destiny. It doesn't say absolutely or even probably; it just says possibly.

You will be guided, and you will make the right decision, and you will be much happier.

As I am touching in with your energies, I don't know exactly what it is, but I am feeling heartache. Are you very deeply pained about this situation? The pain is very hard, very heavy here. But when you leave here today, you will feel a greater resolution about this problem. Saint Germain just said to me in my right ear that he wants to talk to you about this point.

Saint Germain (SG): I am here. Can you hear me all right?

AN: Yes.

SG: Because I come through the physical body of Philip, I have to ask that question. Until I get further into him it is like reaching down into darkened water to find something. When I feel the vibrations from your voice, I know I have made contact. The longer I stay here with Philip, the more clearly I can experience you.

My son, here in spirit, we do not look upon divorce as something negative but as something that is sometimes a part of an individual's course. Two souls walk side by side for a period of time, get what they are supposed to get, and then separate. Therefore, if you should decide to take that step, do not pay attention to society or the culture around you but only to your own heart. In your culture and in some other cultures around the world, people feel obliged to satisfy society and family; and to make others happy, they remain miserable. But it is not what we do in life that matters, but how we do it.

On the other hand, we do not encourage divorce if it is possible for the two to work things out. Two lives have been blending into one—yours and hers—and each of you has your role to play. You cannot play her role and she cannot play yours. One must consider asking oneself, "Have I done everything I can do to play my role correctly?" This question is important because whoever or whatever appears on our path, it is for our own karmic walk and for our own dharma. If we have not worked everything out in a relationship, we may meet a similar kind of person and go through a similar situation until we learn what we are to learn.

For example, some people continuously marry someone who is alcoholic, or who wastes money, or who has sexual problems. Why does this happen? Why do they continue to marry the same kind of person? They are drawn back again and again to the same kind of person to finish some kind of karma. Therefore, it becomes vital for one to look at oneself in any relationship and ask the question, "Is there something here I need to learn that I have not yet learned?" If one determines that one has done or learned everything they can, then that karma is finished, and one can move forward without looking back. Am I making sense to you?

AN: Yes, I understand.

SG: Not that you haven't thought about these things, but you are sitting here before many spiritual beings, and in this context you can be more deeply impressed, and we can help you more. I was guided by your teachers and other master guides to come through and express all of this to you. In reality, our entire walk is a spiritual walk, and it is all about self-mastery; mastering self to pay off all karma and discerning the right dharma. In that way, the soul can fly free when it leaves the earth plane, having fulfilled both correctly.

Sometimes an individual we meet on our path is there as a master teacher for us, but we don't know it. They reflect back to us our own personality and character, and we see in them what we are. Therefore, it becomes very important to discern the actual reality of the circumstances in order to make the right decision.

Now I am going to step away from Philip, but I will come back again. This is Saint Germain.

Samurai Spirit; the Path of Spiritual Work

PB: Let's go to your next question.

I want to tell you that you have samurai energy around you. Do you know if you have samurai ancestry?

AN: I don't know.

PB: Well it is there, from your father's side. There is a group of about five or six samurai, and it means two things: First, ancestors are involved, and second, you have the spirit of a samurai, which means you can make decisions clearly and move on. You have the ability of a samurai to detach. That is in you. You have this ability more than your wife does, and that is a part of the problem. She can be very subjective, and you can be very objective.

AN: I actually don't know what those words mean.

PB: She can be very emotional, while you have the ability to observe with more detachment. It is not that you don't appreciate her emotion, but you just don't see it as being constructive. If she were less emotional, your life situation would be much easier. (Pause) Love her but maintain your detachment. That is what they are saying to me, and I am listening with this ear as they are talking.

AN: Right now I am not making the money I expected to be making, and in the future I would really like to do spiritual work and be able to get paid for doing it. Do you have any advice about that?

PB: If you remember, I told you in the beginning of the reading that you were born for spiritual work. I had never met you before and knew nothing about you except your name. Your grandmother also came, put her hands on your face, and said you were born for spiritual work. Let me touch in with spirit and see what else they say. I want to tell you that you are in the right place at the right time, and I am referring to your heart.

You're going to realize your future through working with a group. Do you belong to a group now?

AN: It is not a strong group; it is just a group of friends who get together.

PB: Yes. You may stay with them, but you are eventually going to be in a strong group. For a period of time you will have a guru or teacher. You may have already met that person, or he or she may be still ahead of you. Ultimately you will be your own teacher.

They are showing me your spiritual mind, and it is very well organized. As I look at you, I see you are a person that is able to master himself by taking self-responsibility. The teacher that will help you will be the one who will teach you even more about how to be self-responsible.

They tell me, whether you are aware of it or not, that you have many visitations from God himself. I have had those kinds of experiences since childhood, and it's a rare gift. The ability to have contact with God or be able to awaken the God presence within you is what puts you above average, and it is important that you continually humble yourself to that higher power within yourself. Whether you feel or know you communicate directly with God or not, express your heart's desire continuously to that energy within.

The hardest thing for most people, and I see it for you also, is to be consistent and steady toward your purpose. Saint Germain is going to come back through.

SG: I am here again. We have been emphasizing to you your own spirituality because we're trying to confirm and affirm the reality of who you are. People do not buy spirituality the way they buy rice, and most people are spiritually dead—that is, dead to the fact that they *are* a spirit. They run around busily making money, buying things, or doing other things. I am so joyful to be with you because you are an exception. As your lovely grandmother who is standing here beside me indicated, you were born for spiritual things. That gold band that Philip saw around you is a great indication of this.

This is not said to flatter you. I am telling you this so you can live fully. I came through to tell you that I do not want you to give up on your dream. Love your dream above all, and pursue it as life itself. With all of your heart, hunger to wake up spiritually. Within reason, and in balance with the physical life, pursue God as much as possible. If you do this, then in this lifetime, you will realize your dream. Even though most people do not buy spirituality like they buy rice, when they see someone who is outstanding spiritually, they are drawn to them. Those who are successful in this work are those who pray and meditate regularly and those who know their power does not come from themselves.

Philip is one of those individuals who works all the time to get his ego out of the way, but it has not been easy for him. He prayed and prayed and prayed and shed many, many tears, often staying up through the night to pray until morning. The biggest barrier for him was his own self, but like you, he wanted to find God or the spiritual life more than anything. What you think about and long for all day long, is what will manifest in your life. What Philip wanted above everything was to find God. So again, don't forget your vision. And know that it is not only your vision; it is God's vision for you. You have to train, discipline, and direct yourself, and then step into the role that you see for yourself.

AN: Can you say that one more time?

SG: You have to discipline and direct yourself, and then you can step into the role you want to play. Make yourself so trusted by God that he opens the doors for you, and you don't have to do it yourself. That is what Philip did. He did not ask for this work in Japan; it was offered to him. He had absolutely no plan to come to Japan, but God had a plan for him to come, maybe just for people like you. After all, God is neither of the East nor the West but universal. God opened the door for him to come here to work for the sake of people like you. Our point is that he was just consistent toward his purpose, and God opened doors for him.

Do likewise. Become an outstanding instrument in the hands of God through obedience. Want God more than you want anything else. Love all people as if they were God, because they are; and love them as yourself. Whether you like what they do or don't do, love them. God is searching and searching the earth to find such people to do his work. And unequivocally, you can be one of them. Don't worry about the details; let us take care of those. I, Saint Germain, have come here to tell you that I am also going to be working with you. I came here to work with people like you, and I will not be the only one.

That is enough on this topic. Let us move on, and I shall come back if necessary. This is Saint Germain.

Psychic Ability and Spiritual Growth

AN: I'd like to have information about psychic ability. I understand that you don't have to have psychic abilities in order for your soul to grow, but I would like to have these abilities. I struggle with the desire to have these abilities, and I would like to know if you have any advice about this internal struggle.

PB: I would like to invite you to the group meditation seminars as my guest without payment. I would like to make an exception for you. This is what spirit wants, and I see it. I would like you to come to any and all seminars as a guest. You are the first person for whom I have made such an exception.

AN: I knew you were going to at some point.

PB: Because God wants it. I saw who you were from the beginning. You have an important role to play in this country, and you need as much help as possible. Whatever I can do to help, I will do. You remind me so much of myself in the beginning. How old are you?

AN: Forty-four.

PB: That is exactly how old I was when I started. I was gifted from childhood, but I started my spiritual walk as a medium at the age of forty-four. I know how to help you get where you want to go, so please come to as many of my seminars as you can, and take this as a gift from God.

Now, I just need a moment to go back over in my mind and with spirit the question you asked about psychic abilities versus spirituality.

AN: I would really like to know more about the psychic ability itself.

PB: They said, "Philip you can answer this, so you don't need us." They are talking, and I will tell you, because this is what I do. There are two kinds of mediumship or channeling. I was told that the Japanese don't like the word "medium."

AN: We don't know the word "medium."

PB: In the West, in the tradition I come from, we use the word "medium" more than "channeler."

AN: There is no word "medium" in Japanese yet, and I think "channeler" is better than "medium," if you are going to choose between the two.

PB: In the Western world, "medium" just means a bridge between the spiritual world and the physical world. There are essentially two types of contact: One type is more like mental psychic energy, and it is more of the mind. The other type works from the emotion or the heart. Some channelers have both, and some have only one or the other, but it is ideal to have both. From the standpoint of deeper channeling, those who come from the point of love usually have deeper messages. Those who are primarily psychic are more left brained, unemotional, and objective.

In truth, both attributes are needed, because the channeler who just feels everything may be mistaken if he doesn't guide the process through reason. On the other hand, one who just sees the spiritual reality but can't make emotional contact with it may leave out something very important for the listening soul. Both are absolutely necessary, and because Saint Germain will be working with you, and he is that kind of being, you will get both.

Your eyes show you to be very open to spirit; you have a significant ability to see the spirit world that may be even better than mine. You also have the ability to work on the intellectual level with this information. So you have a good combination in your soul, and you will be able to do both, just like I do. I work on both levels. Sometimes I can be very objective with the information that comes through; I just say this is the truth, and I don't think about how they or I feel. At other times, I can be very compassionate. Both qualities are necessary, but I try to work in a balanced way, which is especially important when doing higher spiritual work.

Saint Germain comes to do the highest level of this work, and he sets up a kind of ideal model for people who want to do this work. He seems to know how to touch the hearts of people but also bring direction that guides the heart and leads to objective understanding. Unlike some guides I have met, he is very well-rounded. He doesn't emphasize one thing at the expense of another but tries to include everything. He doesn't talk about some of the things that other spirits talk about, such as UFOs and ETs, but at the same time he does not deny these things or try to convince people one way or the other. He can work with anyone, regardless of their beliefs.

To answer your question more specifically, you can raise your spirit without being psychic in terms of seeing or manifesting spirit in some outwardly dramatic way. The goal of all spiritual growth is to reach God, and some people are actually very distracted to be the point of being misled by spiritual or psychic phenomena if they are not careful. God is here within each of us, and they are trying to find God. But they can become fascinated with some psychic phenomenon about healing or esoteric information from their spirit guide or an angel or whatever, and they get all involved in that and become distracted. To be successful in accessing the highest truth and the deepest love, you always have to keep your mind on God. If you do this, with a generous amount of common sense, you will find the greatest satisfaction, the greatest stability, and the most profound reality. You will achieve the correct balance between love and truth so that you can be most accurate and helpful in your service to others.

More than any other time in history, spirit is wanting to raise up the kind of medium or channeler who can talk about any spiritual phenomena, but at the same time always remains centered on God. This will enable bringing through the highest information and the highest spirits, which makes for the greatest and most meaningful success.

Some mediums go off on a tangent and talk about only one aspect of spirituality, and that is where they dwell. They lead people to concentrate only on that area as if that one subject is the be-all and end-all. But there are many spheres and realms in the spirit world, and by staying centered on God, we can look upon all of them as one. We then have the deepest, highest, wisest, and most complete perspective.

As a future teacher, if you stay spiritually centered, you can talk about all of this while leading your people to God. There are many people, particularly women, who raise their spirits to a very high level just by giving love to their families. The idea that you must have psychic experiences is false, but at the same time, very high-level spiritual experiences are often achieved through having loved other people. It is an automatic result of loving self and others properly.

The key and the core to truly high-level channeling and spirit communication always come from the place of God's love. Love people as yourself and make no exception. See God in every person. You have to *live* this and not just give it lip service. When I embrace and hug a person, I always feel like I am hugging God. At the same time, I feel like I am hugging myself. With that kind of heart, you can be very successful. You have all of this recorded now, so you can write a book!

Do you have another question?

The Future of Planet Earth

AN: I have been told and have read that this is a very important time on the planet, and there is supposedly a big shift coming in the future. I don't know if this is true or not, but I would like to know if Saint Germain has any information about this, even if it is fun information.

PB: I will let him come through.

SG: I am here (laughing), and I am laughing at your wanting to have fun. If I told you that in the near future, Tokyo would be leveled by an earthquake, would that be fun? Or that you will be in the spirit world by that time? Neither of those things will happen. I am just joking with you. As I have said to many people, earthquakes and floods and all those things are going on all the time.

This earth is a living being, so just as a young lady moves around to change her position and readjust her clothing, so does the earth move. When Tokyo shakes, just think that Mother Earth is adjusting to be more comfortable. There is truth to the fact that human thought forms collected in a particular place cause some negative results, but there are those who would like to make more of all this than there really is. They, like you and others, are fascinated by these stories. But even as we sit here, parts of the earth are quaking on the other side of the globe, and the earth is struck each hour by thousands of bolts of lightning. I know, because they are telling me, that it is raining in 360 different places on earth right now. There are floods here and there; and there are places where the entire earth is being moved and reformed by floods.

There will be events affecting the earth that will happen, not only in the near future, but beyond. If you have a cut or sore on your body, and you look and look and look only at this spot, you may think it represents the whole body; but in truth, it is only one cut, and it takes up only a small area in relation to the entire body. Those who focus on latter day phenomena of catastrophes are concentrating only upon the catastrophes, so they are getting an exaggerated view of these phenomena. But as all kinds of things are happening right at this moment on the face of Mother Earth, you and I are sitting here peacefully. As a matter of fact, most of humanity is at peace at this moment. Only a small proportion of humanity, at this very moment, is being affected in a negative way by such phenomena.

I say these things because I am reasonable, and I want to put all of this into perspective. As for you, I want to say that none of this will affect you personally. You are meant to live a protected and long life. Make it your duty to teach people to look at the sun and not at the rain. Help them focus on the positive and not the negative, and on what they have, not what they don't have. Then they will not draw adverse circumstances to them. Lastly, if it is anyone's destiny to die in any form of catastrophe, that is their destiny. If it is their time to go and to go that way, that's it. A thousand angels can't stop it. Did I answer your question adequately?

AN: Yes, I understand.

SG: Do you have a final question?

Cultivation of Spiritual Gifts

AN: Is there is any particular spiritual work or study that I should be doing at this time for my own growth?

SG: Much like the instrument I am speaking through, you are innately guided to those things you need. When he goes to a bookstore, he can touch a book without looking at its title and tell if it is for him or not. Regardless of the price, he will buy it if he knows spirit has guided him to a book for a good purpose.

It was I who impressed Philip to invite you to come as a guest to the seminars, but there is no intention here to make you a follower of this work. It is simply a gift to you, and you are under no obligation. Through the experience, you will get insights that you have not had thus far, and there will be information given that you can utilize for your spiritual life if you so desire and are so inclined. As I said in the beginning, you are in the right time at the right place, and this is a significant turning point in your life. Why would we bother to bring this gentleman (Philip) 7,000 miles to Japan if the answers were already available here? Surely, among the millions of Japanese, there may be someone equal to or better than him.

The truth is that he came here to meet people like you who could not find the answers elsewhere, and in time you will know the full meaning of these words. Our desire is to take you as swiftly as possible, in the most direct way, to the fulfillment of your mission on earth, both because it is your destiny and because we love you. From our perspective, that is all that matters. You are not in our hands, but in the hands of God who lives in you. As we masters have awakened to the God presence within us, we want to pass that on to as many people as possible, and you are one of them. It is for this that you were born.

In conclusion, I will say that you will not be easily understood. Unfortunately, the last people to appreciate and understand a person who does this work are those who are closest to that person. This is a way of telling you not to worry about what others around you think. Don't expect them to understand you or believe in you; that is not important. What is important is that you understand and believe in yourself. Yes, yes, yes, and yes.

Now I am going to go, but I leave you with the fragrance of my love. I want you to know me better and better, and I will help you to do that. This is Saint Germain, and my love follows you always.

PB: Let's close with a prayer:

Father, I am very humbled by this experience today. It makes me so happy to find someone like this young man. There is both the purity of heart and the sincerity of interest, and your light shines on him and from him so clearly. Let him know his deep inner self that he may know you who dwells there. Bless him in all that he does and in all of his decisions, and thank you for the great privilege of serving him. I pray all this in divine love. Amen.

End of recording

Spiritual Reading Fourteen

SPIRITUAL HUNGER AND LIFE'S PURPOSE

Chikao B.—Male

Philip Burley (PB): I will ask to hold your paper with your questions so I can have your vibration, and from that point we work spontaneously. When I read for people, I go between trance and semi-trance. Do you know of Saint Germain at all?

Introduction to Saint Germain

CB: No, I have never heard the name before.

PB: He knows you. He is standing right here and just said, "Tell him I know him." From the spirit side, he said there is a place in the spirit world where the East and the West meet. It is a crossing over point between the cultures, a literal bridge in the spirit world. He is just telling me this and says you and he met on that bridge, but you crossed over to the West side as he crossed to the East side. Anyway, you have met in a group, a universal group in the high realms. He says where you met is all golden light, and there is no shadow there. You met several times, not just once, though you don't know this yourself yet.

The Dynamics of Prayer

PB: May I hold the paper with your questions now? I'd like to open with a short prayer. What is the word for "prayer" in Japanese?

CB: Inori.

PB: Vocal prayer or otherwise?

CB: Either one, inside or outside. You make your heart very quiet, and then you ask for something.

PB: Okay. It's the same thing from the Christian point of view. From life experience, I see God literally, or I see an energy form, and when I start praying there is white light that comes down over both of us. It is a literal light. Whenever I begin to pray, all of my guides and teachers draw very close. This has been true ever since I was four years old, so when I pray it is not just a routine or some kind of ritual. I am truly aware of addressing the Creator; not a vague energy, but an intelligent and loving being. I sometimes dream of him, and he will come and literally talk to me, not as spirit but specifically as the Creator. I haven't said this to anyone else in Japan, but because they asked me to explain this, I am telling you, not to impress you but just to inform. I will pray now.

> *Heavenly Father, thank you for the privilege of reading for this distinguished gentleman. I ask for healing for him in any area of his life or for any of his family or friends. Inasmuch as we all come to earth with certain goals, may this reading help him in reaching those goals. May his guides and teachers work very closely with my guides and teachers to bring answers to the questions written on his paper or in his heart and mind and to give new answers or confirm what he already knows to be true. Help me to step out of the way*

so that everything can come through unhindered by my presence. I pray and ask for all of this in divine love.

First of all, there appears behind you a huge tree. It is a gold-colored oak tree, and it represents two things: one is your ancestry and family, and the other is your spiritual power. My guides show me that this is a time in your life for the smoothing out of things. I don't know what that means exactly, but that is what they are showing me. You have a genuine, sincere interest in spiritual matters, but it doesn't look as though you get enough time for that.

Do you have a question here about your wife? Yes, that is what they just said, so please ask that question.

Spiritual Openness and Physical Health

CB: My wife sometimes gets terrible headaches, like migraine headaches, and I want to know if there is some reason for this.

PB: There is an entity that comes around her, and it's a woman. I know this answer is going to seem simplistic, but I saw this immediately. I used to remove such entities from people. I would go into trance, and they would appear so that I could see them and talk to them. The headaches come not just because of tension, though that is part of it, but because of a certain somber mood that affects her. Sometimes the headaches just come, regardless of how she has been feeling.

This woman who is around your wife died of a blow to her head, but she is not an ancestor. Your wife seems to have a very empathic heart toward people, so her energy field is open, and she picked up this entity through that openness. You, she, or a priest of some kind—it doesn't matter whether the person is Shinto or Buddhist—should pray for this entity to move on. Just use common sense and sit down and talk to her. Call to this entity, especially when your wife has one of the headaches, and just tell her, "This is my wife's body, not yours. Please leave."

In my healing work, people obsessed with spirits would come to me, and after my guides and I removed the spirit or spirits, the person became a different person. I feel very confident in what I am telling you, so just use common sense, without fear, and talk to the entity.

CB: Should I do it?

PB: Whatever you feel. You could do it, yes. You can tell your wife, so she can also talk to this entity, but be sure you tell her this is not because of anything wrong that she did. It is nothing negative about her. Everyone gets something like this once in a while, and it is not anything to be ashamed of. This is not an evil spirit, just an ignorant spirit without malice. It is your wife's compassion for people and her open energy that allowed this entity to come in. My guide just said not to do this just once, but at least three times. Did you have any other questions about your wife?

CB: About her? No, that's the only question. I have questions about my children, though.

PB: Sure. I am just sitting here tuning in.

CB: Can I ask the question about my children now?

PB: Just give me one second. I am looking to see if there is more surrounding your wife's situation, and this paper helps me tune into the vibration.

I have a guide who works with me named Dr. Palmer, the one who created chiropractic. He just said to me that when you work with your wife to remove the entity, if you will call on him, Dr. Palmer—in your mind or verbally, it doesn't matter—he will come in and work with you. When he comes, he usually works with a green light, green energy, like the color of leaves in the spring. I was listening, because sometimes when I work with people, my guides go directly to that person and do the healing while we are here.

Spiritual Development in Latter Years

Before going on to your questions, because they are showing me this, I want to talk about the energy around you. First, the energy around you is very wide, wider than I usually see. This shows that you are a more developed soul than the average person. You were born with natural wisdom, and your fundamental nature is very philosophical. Even though you have been successful in life, there is still some part of you lacking self-confidence, but the energy around you shows that you have no reason not to be confident.

A master teacher is working with you. This individual lived in the last century, and he is also a doctor. Did you have a favorite professor that you were close to when you were in college or dental school who would be on the other side? Or did you attend a dental school founded by a well-known man?

CB: I would not call the man famous at all.

PB: Well, he doesn't have to be famous, just the founder.

CB: Yes, of course, there is a founder of my school.

PB: Is he on the other side?

CB: Yes.

PB: I can't say definitively, but this energy comes to you and works through you. While you do your work as a dentist, there is a large part of you that is still not satisfied with life. You are still spiritually searching. He said he was most attracted to you because, among the many people who graduated from that school, you were among the top people spiritually.

He says he is working with you not on the dental work but on the spiritual part of your life. There is a plan in your life, as you move more into your sixties, for what I will call a golden door that will open for you to realize the fullness of your spirituality.

CB: From age sixty on?

The Path of Service; Influence of Buddha

PB: According to the preparation from the spirit side this is planned to start after age sixty. Your path to enlightenment is not so much meditation but more the path of volunteer service such as helping people through charitable work, perhaps by volunteering to provide dental work, giving free service in your retirement years.

You may sit and meditate, but from the spirit side, you don't look like the kind of person that would enjoy just sitting. You are the kind of person that needs to be active, and that's your path to your spiritual enlightenment. This does not mean that you will not meditate, but the predominant means to enlightenment for you is human service.

The light in this area is a very faint violet color. This means that the metaphysical, the spiritual—this light ray came with you to the earth plane. Your soul cannot be satisfied with mundane nine-to-five living. The soul searches for spiritual fulfillment. Unlike some men who may think they are just too masculine to pay attention to nature, you pay attention to nature—trees, flowers, birds, and so on—and you should spend a lot of time in nature. You don't have to meditate or pray, but sit by a stream or walk in the woods. Spirit wants to contact you in that setting and awaken you spiritually that way. Are you from a Buddhist background?

CB: Yes.

PB: Yes, because Buddha just appeared right behind you. I was just listening and all of a sudden saw the explosion of gold. Before I left America, I was in a neutral meditation, meaning I wasn't thinking about anything, but was just passive. Suddenly there was an explosion of gold light that startled me. When I opened my eyes, there was Buddha, standing all in gold. He pointed at me and said, "Don't worry about your work in Japan. I will be there, and I will help you."

You are one of the people that he is coming to in the fulfillment of that prophecy. I have various master teachers like this who come to me. Jesus comes to me in dreams, and I have seen Buddha many times, as well as Confucius. The point of this is to say that I am seeing him with you now.

Buddha is saying to me that his path of enlightenment was like yours. He didn't meditate as much as he spoke the truth. This is what he is saying to me now. He has been with you since you were around twelve years old. He is there all the time. He is your master teacher. Did you ever know that?

CB: No.

PB: Well, you know it now. Call on him, even in the situation with your wife. Call on him, believe me. I am not trying to impress you, but if I tell you something like this, it is literally true.

When I was on radio shows in America, this kind of information came in when people called. I got many letters and phone calls from people confirming that certain things I said were true. Some of them had a dream, or spirit came to confirm a message I gave. When you are on radio or television, you must speak the truth, or you don't have much of a future! I am just telling you so you can feel confident in what I am saying. Buddha is the one preparing you for these latter years, and he will work with you. It is the same for your wife. You work side by side. Buddha is also with her. You and your wife are like twin flames.

Let's go to your next question.

CB: In my dentistry practice, the number of patients is lessening recently, and I am wondering if I am going to be able to make enough money to keep up my salary. I am very worried about this, and I want to know if you know the answer.

PB: It is a phase, that's all. Your practice will pick up again, and you will not have to work outside of your field.

Right now, as I am looking, I am seeing a boy. You have questions about your children, but is there a question specifically about a son?

Father and Son

CB: I have a son who is in the second year of junior high school, and I want to know what my son can do for a living.

PB: Well first of all, he is not going to stay in this locality.

CB: No, my son wants to go to America and study English, and I am wondering when I should let my son go to America to study? Also, my son has stated that he wants to be a doctor. Is this really the right move for him?

PB: That is true, absolutely. As soon as you mentioned him, I saw the word "doctor."

CB: There are many different kinds of doctors; a doctor of dentistry and other kinds of doctors. Do you know which kind? Will he go into dentistry or something else?

PB: I don't think he will go into dentistry; it doesn't appear that way. But he will go into medicine.

CB: I would really prefer him not to be a dentist.

PB: Yes, I know that.

CB: I want my son to work with the entire physical body.

PB: Yes, he will. He loves and respects you very much, very deeply inside. He's a very loyal son. Your words have much influence. I don't see him going to America until perhaps the latter part of the high school years, maybe for a summer program to study English. It will be on the east coast, and he will be educated in America.

CB: Would he go to a university in America?

PB: Yes. Is that what he wants to do?

CB: We don't know yet. Right now, all he is saying is that he wants to study English.

PB: That is how it appears.

CB: That is what you are seeing now?

PB: Yes, but what they want to add is that while spirit can see in advance, the way they work is not only spontaneously, but also by using common sense, so don't just take whatever spirit says here literally. Take it as you feel moved to take it. In your son's case, this is a quest of his soul, and therefore it is his karma and yours to work out the timing. As you and he, especially you, are impressed to think about this, know that is God working through your situation. Trust that.

Spirit doesn't do everything, because you have to master yourself, and that is quite literally true. Sometimes, like the question of your business going down, they may not give you a clear answer because they see that you must live through your situation and master yourself through it. You have to create the energy and the circumstances to make it all happen to bring your business back up, not through advertising as much as by having the right attitude. You should put out the energy for more people to come, and then watch them come. Just hold onto that image.

That's what I'm doing here in Japan. I don't care about numbers. In my mind, all I think about is that I see more people come, more people come, and more people come. When you get to a certain level of self-mastery, inevitably that vision is fulfilled. You have the merit, you see. I want to tell you, you are there. This is confirmed especially as you have Buddha working with you! (Laughter) I don't see Buddha with many people. I've read for a number of people here so far, and I've only seen Buddha with a few people. You are one of them.

Your son is going to be a doctor, a very good doctor. He's also going to be the head of a staff of doctors, and you will be very proud of him. They are showing that he will go back and forth between America and Japan many times.

CB: My son went to Massachusetts last summer, and he always says how much he loves America.

PB: In addition to his going back and forth, you will also go back and forth, so don't worry about seeing him. He is going to be very good.

Now, what is your next question?

Father and Daughters

CB: My oldest daughter is in her third year of school to become a doctor, and she wants to know when she is going to get married.

PB: She is in her third year of medical school?

CB: It is her sixth year of school, and she is in her third year to become a doctor. She is half way through.

PB: What kind of doctor?

CB: We don't know yet; she has lots of energy, but that is all.

PB: And she is how old?

CB: Twenty-one.

PB: In two years, she will meet the man.

CB: When you say "the man," what do you mean?

PB: She will meet the man of her life.

CB: There is one guy that she's with already, right now.

PB: I feel there is going to be someone else. There may be competition. That's how it appears from the spirit side.

CB: That would be good.

PB: I just don't feel that the man she is with now will be the one, but don't say anything to her. Her soul has to work things out, so let her work through it. There are things happening that she is not telling you. Not bad, just things going on inside. She is more awakened than you realize. You look at her as your little girl, but actually, she is very much a woman. Does she want to do research work, or do you know?

CB: I don't know.

PB: I see her working in a hospital and doing some kind of research work. Is she very studious?

CB: Yes, she really is.

PB: Yes, that fits. You don't have to worry about her.

CB: Ok, I would like to ask about my second daughter. She is living in Iowa right now.

PB: Iowa?

CB: Yes, she lives in Iowa.

PB: Before you say any more, I want to say something about this younger one. She is—what do I want to say—a firecracker.

CB: Maybe, yes. I am wondering what kind of work she will be doing in the future. This is the famous Japanese question.

PB: Well, they ask the same thing in America all the time and in the same way. The image spirit brings up of her is that of a teddy bear. That is the feeling or the energy they bring. Is she very much into music? I am hearing a lot of music with her.

CB: Yes, I think she likes music.

PB: Does she play the piano?

CB: No, she doesn't.

PB: She doesn't have any musical ability?

CB: I think she just listens to it.

PB: I don't know, but it seems that her path is not going to be as easy as the other two. You don't have to worry about her, but it is not going to be as easy. She is not like the other two. She is "Miss Independent."

CB: Yes, she is quite different from the other two, and she is already talking about how she wants to marry an American in the future.

PB: She will do her own thing. I was hesitant to say it before, but when I was reading about your son, I wanted to tell you that you are probably going to wind up with at least one American son-in-law or daughter-in-law. This will be good, so don't worry.

CB: It is probably my second daughter then. As soon as she sees a foreigner, she is just so happy.

PB: But the fortunate thing is that you are a broad-minded father.

CB: I keep telling myself that is just my daughter's soul, and that is the way she is.

PB: That is the way my wife and I raised our three children. We have a son and two daughters, and the only thing we ever asked of them was to be their highest and best selves. That's all. We learned that they didn't belong to us, and they have to learn to live without their parents. They each went down their own independent paths, and they are all three very happily married and they have given us a total of 7 wonderful grandchildren!

We never judged them or criticized them because they have to make their mistakes to learn. Therefore, we are very close, and they still come and share some of their inner lives. They are twenty-nine, thirty, and thirty-one years of age. Your children are lucky to have you as a father, because you have a very broad mind. They will always come back to you.

Let's go to your next question.

Health and Rhythm of Work

CB: I have been told by somebody else that I will live until age eighty-four, and I have a question about my health. I want to know, between now and the age of eighty-four, am I going to have any major illness?

PB: You don't want to know much do you? (Laughter) I have the same question, so if I tell you, would you please tell me, using your psychic ability? How old are you now?

CB: I turned fifty yesterday. My birthday was yesterday.

PB: Let me tune in. (Pause) If anything happens, it will be around the upper part of the body, but it will not be major. It's just the natural process of growing older. You will probably live beyond the age of eighty-four, and when you pass on, you will pass on with a very clear mind. Your temperament is such that you've learned how not to get filled with stress. As I see you working, you seem to take your work in stride, in a kind of rhythm. That is your nature, and that is how you work. Because of that, your health will stay very good. Your wife worries much more than you do. You are okay, and you will live to see your grandchildren.

Spiritual Hunger and Life's Purpose

CB: The other thing I really want to know is what is my mission or my destiny in this life? What am I supposed to be doing? What is the life purpose I was born with?

PB: The answer was given to one of your previous questions; that as you grow older, you will be doing charitable work. But Saint Germain is going to speak now.

Saint Germain (SG): I am here. This is Saint Germain. On earth there are many, many roles. There is the outer life, which is the occupation or work, and people are born with those talents. The seeds of what you are to become are planted in the soil of your spiritual self before your birth. For example, in your son, the seeds of interest in the medical field were planted before his birth. This is for the outer work of life. It is the placement of the soul in the field where that individual has talents. As to when those seeds begin to grow and germinate, it varies from person to person. Some people spend much time in life trying to find their purpose, but even that characteristic is sewn into the fabric of the life of the spirit.

CB: The characteristic of searching for the outer purpose?

SG: Yes. In Hindu teachings this outer life has been called dharma. Your dharma has been your dentistry, but the seeds of spiritual hunger for your inner life were also sewn into your spirit.

As we can see, the number of people seeking the spiritual path is small compared to what most people choose to do. Out of all humanity, a rare few actually seek the spiritual path. In many, there is only the awareness of their inclination towards an occupation, and they do not even think about the inner spiritual path. The average person on the street does not consider these things. Therefore, humanity at large is not very awakened.

Most people are satisfied to work from nine to five or whatever hours and earn a weekly paycheck. Even if they are part of some religious activity that has a spiritual purpose, they have mostly external involvement. They often attend religious activities out of obligation or tradition in the family, but they are not spiritually very alive. Those who are awakened on the inner plane of themselves think about spiritual things.

Even for those not yet awakened, there is a hunger for the spiritual. They do not know what this hunger is about, so some of them fill their life with alcohol, sex, books, music, movies, or just wasting time. Many people are in this category. It's sad but true. But it's only sad if one thinks they should be elsewhere. It is their path, so they do not suffer for the lack of spiritual truth.

In your case, there is a spiritual hunger that you are aware of. You know your life is not complete if you are just looking into peoples' mouths. It is a very important work and service to humanity, but it does not feed your soul. If you have nothing else in life but this awareness, we could say that you are very blessed. How very, very fortunate is he or she who has this hunger and knows it.

Meditation, Education and Service

This life, as you well know, is a kind of school. In human society there are many, many interests, and each person goes toward an interest according to their nature and inclination. But from God's perspective or point of view, the real thing to be interested in is one's own soul, and to realize that this physical world and this physical body are only temporary. The degree to which we are awakened on the earthly side of life is the degree to which we will be awakened in the spirit world. Therefore, the goal is to pass into that life as awakened as much as possible.

The path, classically and practically, to that awakening is meditation, education, and service to humanity. Some peoples' path is through knowledge or education, some through meditation, and some through human service. In most awakened human beings, all three of these practices are important: education, meditation, and service. However, one of these paths will usually be the most appealing to an individual, more so than the other two. The one who meditates also needs to be educated and to give service, although his or her pastime or basic investment in self will be through meditation. One who spends time getting an education can become very incomplete without serving others and going inside to meditate. And the one who is always working, as many wives do—by just serving, serving, and serving, but taking no time out to learn anything new or to go inside and meditate—becomes empty and tired. People need all three practices to some extent.

My son, you came into this life to awaken to your own spirituality, and the center of that spirituality is the God presence. The kernel of life, the center of human life, is God living in man as the temple. You came into this life to awaken to that reality to know God within you—not merely theoretically, but practically, through life experience.

As was indicated earlier in this reading, your path is a path of service as you have already been doing. By serving others, you come to serve self. By loving others, you come to love self. By doing both, you will awaken to God within. When you serve your patients by fixing their teeth and taking away their pain, and you see them happy, you find joy. The essence of that joy is God. God is pouring himself through you, through this service. When entered into fully, this service cannot help but lead you to enlightenment.

Again, you were born to awaken to God within through service, but you also need to educate your spirit, and you need to meditate. A table cannot stand on one leg. The table of spiritual life cannot stand only on service. It also needs the legs of meditation and of education. Then it can stand on three legs. But your predominant path is service, human service. You are still a young man. Even today, before retirement, you can turn your office into a temple of God. Educate yourself in human nature and the love of human beings and meditate upon this reality. And when you serve your patients, treat them as yourself, or as God within.

Yours is among many occupations on earth that is privileged to repair the human temple or the body. You enter the very personal part of the human being where the mouth eats, and the tongue speaks. In this area, the body is nurtured, the temple is maintained, and the individual speaks his or her truth. With the right attitude, your work is not merely a mundane thing. With the right attitude or by lifting your mind to heaven, your work suddenly becomes a sacred work, and your office a holy place. You are in service now.

Therefore, for the third time, I say your purpose in this life is to awaken to God within, on the path of human service, sustained and balanced by education and meditation. This is a long answer to a short question. I, Saint Germain, give comprehensive answers to leave little or nothing to doubt, but also the merit is here with you so that I can do this.

It has been my great, great joy and pleasure to serve you in this way. Thank you for being here and allowing us to serve you. It is in the love of the Father who created us all that I bid you farewell. Call on me, with Buddha or Jesus or any of the masters, and we will help you. These are not mere words; this is fact, and you can count on it. Our love follows you always. This is Saint Germain.

End of recording

FINDING THE GOD PRESENCE THROUGH MEDITATION

Sakiko K.—Female

Philip Burley (PB): When I'm working with you, I go in and out of trance and semi-trance, and I will hold your paper for the vibration and give it back to you periodically to ask your questions. Spirit often answers a question before you ask it and before I know what it is. Saint Germain comes in spontaneously, and there is no specific time when he comes in. He usually talks quite a bit with each person. If I may have your paper, I will begin with prayer.

> *Our Heavenly Father, we step away from the world outside to come to you. You are as real as our breath, our heartbeat, our thoughts, and you are the essence of them all. As we turn to you, we ask especially for any healing needed for this young woman or any of her family members. Please open the door between the two worlds very wide for her and pour in all that she needs and desires. May her guides and teachers coordinate very, very closely with my guides*

*and teachers to bring through the answers she seeks. Because you
are the invisible yet real force behind all this work, may your will
be done. Thank you for the privilege of being a bridge between the
spiritual and physical worlds. I ask all this in divine love. Amen.*

I don't know what this is, but ever since I started praying for you, I've
had tears in my eyes. The feeling is very holy. You have an East Indian
master teacher and guide working with you. I see him very clearly, and
it is Krishna. Do you know Krishna?

SK: I have heard his name before.

PB: Right, you may not know much about him, but he works with you,
very clearly. As a soul, you are quite capable of significant diversity. If
you have found yourself searching among different spiritual concepts,
that's a reflection of your inner nature and you need that. Do you find
yourself interested in many different ideas?

SK: Yes.

PB: Yes, that's your nature. In this lifetime, your purpose is to accumulate
knowledge for your own personal growth. I don't know what kind of
work you do, they don't show me that, but in the future you will come
out of that work and go more directly into spiritual work.

You may ask your first question.

Life's Mission

SK: I want to know what my mission is in this lifetime, why I was born,
and if there is anything I need to do to fulfill that mission.

PB: Some of that has already been answered. You were born to accumulate
knowledge for your own personal growth, and ultimately for spiritual
work. You may work in an ordinary occupation, but in terms of the
state of your soul, you will not be satisfied until you get into spiritual
work. Is that how you feel?

SK: Yes.

PB: Yes. There is a deep hunger in you. As I examine it, I feel the reason for my tears is that deep hunger. I have a guide that stands here whose name is Tiffany, and she is talking to me about your extra sensitivity and the importance of taking care of yourself. It is very important that you love yourself properly. Coming here today is for your benefit more than for other people. That's why you were guided here, she says. You have not yet built your spiritual foundation. You are trying, but you haven't yet completed it. Are there people around you who are opposed to some of your interests in spiritual things?

SK: I think there is probably somebody that is opposed.

PB: I am feeling there is some kind of mental force in someone around you that works against you. Just keep pursuing your heart's desire in spiritual matters.

Spirit says that you have the innate ability to *hear* spirit. As you develop spiritually, this will be a major feature—your ability to hear spirit, or clairaudience. You may not think that now, but as time goes on, that will change. They are showing me a circle of people around you.

Spiritual Circle

SK: Are you talking about a spiritual circle?

PB: Yes. I don't know if you are in such a circle or not, but they show you should be, or if you already are, that it is a good thing. It's for spiritual fellowship and development. Are you in a group now?

SK: No.

PB: Over the next three months, they are showing you will be. Just pray, ask questions, and search around yourself. They show you need to meet on a weekly basis with a spiritual group of people who are very interested in this specific kind of work: mediumship, healing, channeling, and all of that. Have you been thinking about this kind of work?

SK: I was just thinking that it would be nice to meet some people, but I have no idea of what I should study. I don't know what to study at all.

PB: They are saying that you should study in these fields, but they also say that you are going to retain, more than most, your individuality.

Your energy field, your aura, is silver, and that's very unusual. I usually see colors, but not silver, which is usually a band on the outside. It's a good sign. It indicates that in some way you will be speaking publicly. But right now, search for a group and attend regularly to learn so you can expand your spiritual understanding and lay your foundation. Then all these other things will develop. You have a very good spirit for all that I am talking about.

My guide Tiffany says that the primary purpose for you in joining any group is to learn meditation, because that's the building block or cornerstone of your spiritual foundation. By closing my eyes or looking down or away from you, I can see happenings all around you, because I am looking with my spiritual eyes and not my physical eyes. Have you been to America?

SK: Yes.

PB: Because I saw the American flag over your head. You are going to go back there. In the future you will spend quite a bit of time in America, not living there or moving there, but spending time, particularly in the western part of the United States in places such as California, Seattle, Los Angeles, or even Arizona. I don't know the purpose, but it is going to happen. You will travel several times to visit, but it will also be for spiritual purposes. I also see you in Hawaii. Have you been there? You will go in the future. Let's go to your next question.

Finding the God Presence through Meditation

SK: I want to know exactly what my work is going to be.

PB: You are going to do a lot of meditating and you will open up to clairaudience and probably clairvoyance too. You will be used a lot for natural healing. As you develop your openness and sensitivity, your thoughts and prayers focusing on an individual will be very effective in helping to heal that person. Spirit shows that the chakra energy, particularly in the palms of your hands, is potentially very strong. Do you understand chakras? When I started this work, I didn't know exactly what I would be doing. By trial and error, you will try, and you will see.

The more you are around this kind of work, the more you will know who you are in terms of your particular work, and you will be naturally drawn to what you are to do. Most people attracted to this work want to do everything in the beginning—heal, channel, and all kinds of things. But in the end, what usually happens is that people find one or two things that they are good at and focus on that.

Saint Germain is standing right behind me, and he says the next thing that we are going to say is probably the most important of this whole reading for your future. He says those who are most conscientious and who most aggressively seek to know themselves are the ones who find their own gifts the quickest. That doesn't mean knowing yourself externally but knowing yourself internally by asking, "Who am I spiritually? What is my inner power? Of what did God make me?" He says the only way to find the answers is to go inside. He is going to come through now and speak to you.

Saint Germain (SG): I am here. Good morning to you, young lady. I am very pleased to be here with you. I simply stepped from the spiritual vibration into the earthly vibration through this medium to be with you. He is like a door, and he allows me to use him, to open him up to come through. For your own understanding, I will say that I am primarily using him by my thought. I *think* myself into his vocal cords, his mind, and his emotions, aligning myself in this way with his energies. This is the way I harmonize myself with him, and his allowing me to do this is his way of harmonizing his energies with me.

He came to this work by the very means of which I just spoke—of knowing self. Because such phenomena are new to most people, they question it, as you shall do also. Questioning is healthy, but it is important not to dismiss it. Rather seek through it to know the truth of things.

The primary question to ask in order to know self is, "Who am I?" Seeking the answer to this question will take you deeper and deeper into yourself and closer and closer to God within. The source and power of life is within each human being. It is not in the food and air completely. The source of life for every human being is God himself in each person.

When you go deeper and deeper into self, more and more of the God presence in you is uncovered. It is much like when you are wearing many layers of clothing in the winter, and you take one layer off at a time to gradually expose the physical body. In this case, it is the removing of layers of ignorance, misunderstanding, fear, and insecurity to uncover God within yourself. How is it that your heart beats and your lungs breathe without your conscious participation? The God presence in each person makes it possible for us to breathe and for your heart to beat automatically.

There is breathing and there is our heartbeat, but deeper than that is the element of love. Why is it that human beings want to love and be loved? It is God within them, who *is* love itself, who wants to give and receive love. People ask, "Who am I?" because the outer aspects of self will disappear when you die. Ultimately, you will reveal to yourself your own God presence.

Some of what I say may not make sense to you now, but as you hear it on the tape and contemplate it, it will make more and more sense.

You are very, very fortunate to be here and for this truth to be given to you at such an early age. You did not come here to meet Philip or me; you came here to meet your true self. We do not care whether you remember us at all. What we care about is that you find your authentic self and remember it constantly.

This authentic inner self is the source and power for all of life. You are a spirit living inside of a physical body, like the butterfly living inside of a cocoon preparing to emerge as the beautiful, fully grown butterfly that you are. You have all the makings of significant self-mastery and spiritual attainment. If it were not so, we would not be allowed to tell you. I am going to remove myself from Philip and let him come back to continue with your questions. Do you find all of this helpful?

SK: Yes.

SG: We know. It is what your soul came here to learn. As I said, this is the essential, most important answer for this whole session today, because based on this understanding you can truly build an authentic spiritual life. That is all we are interested in. This is Saint Germain.

Channeling and Spiritual Guides

PB: Okay. Have you witnessed channeling before?

SK: Yes, I have seen it in the past but was never sure if it was really true.

PB: It is good that you question it. The most important thing about channeling is not the phenomenon itself, but whether there is truth in what's said. If there is truth, you can know it is authentic channeling. The more developed the channeler, the more universal the truth spoken. It will apply to everyone around the world, past, present and future. That's the major test. Let's go to your next question.

SK: I want to know who my guides are and about channeling. I have heard from someone that a person channels only one spirit, and I want to know who that one spirit is that I am supposed to channel in this lifetime.

PB: I have also heard the teaching that a spirit works through only one person, but I take exception to that. In the West I have worked with highly developed teachers who have three or four entities working with them, so my experience says it's not entirely true that a spirit channels only through one person. Two highly qualified teachers I knew channeled three or four high-level entities, and that's typical in the Western world of spiritual channelers. What we believe to be true usually happens to us, so if you lived only in Japan and never went anywhere else or knew anything else, you would think everyone ate rice and ate with chopsticks.

What I'm saying to you is to be broadminded about the possibility of channeling more than one spirit. It is true that I only channel one, Saint Germain. But, standing around me are other guides whom I can see and hear. They come in dreams and wake me up and talk to me, so they work as a team.

If there were no light coming into this room, no matter how perfect your eyes, you couldn't see anything. It's only as the light reflects off of things and objects that we can see them with our eyes. Understanding is the light of the spirit world. To be able to see truth or phenomena accurately, you must grow in understanding. If your understanding is that there's only one entity that can work through you, then that's what you'll experience. But if your understanding is that there can be more than one, then that is what you will experience.

I am listening to them as I speak to you. They are telling you this information because they want you to be broadminded. If you remember, in the beginning of this reading I told you that you are a person who would be diverse in your abilities. You are not the kind of person whose mind can be stuck in a small space. You need the freedom to explore.

The longing you have to channel will probably bring that phenomenon to you. Potentially, we are all channelers. Anytime you become inspired and try to inspire someone else, you are channeling higher truth, because you are channeling energy outside of yourself. Truth comes from God or from high-level master teachers and spiritual guides, so when you are speaking the truth, you are channeling God. Any time you are speaking the truth, you are channeling. The difference between that and what I am doing here is that the spiritual beings identify themselves to let me know as they bring the truth through.

SK: I didn't understand that.

PB: Let me back up. The difference is that we know the source of the truth because the spirits who bring it through identify themselves. Remember, we are all overshadowed by spirit, and people who do very good things have good spirits around them. As we on earth move, they move. We work as a team with our guides and teachers, whether we know it or not.

Someone who does evil is overshadowed by a low spirit or spirits, and they become a channel for wrongdoing. There are all degrees between the highest and lowest spirit influences, but we are all channelers. It is very good that you hear about this in this context.

You are already a channeler, because you speak the truth of things. Whether it is a little truth or a big truth, it is the same idea. Now you will step across the line in your life. You may need to know a specific entity who will use you, not to enlarge your ego, but so you can cooperate in bringing truth through. Saint Germain is so real to me. He comes in dreams, and he touches me. He woke me up yesterday morning, talked to me, and just sent love into me. That is the kind of relationship one needs.

It's not a question of *if* you can be a channeler. You *can* be a channeler, and you will be a good one. You have the background and the sincerity for it. It is not a question of *if;* it is a question of *when*. Again, it goes back to the point made earlier, that those who are most diligent get results fastest.

You asked who is working with you. Earlier I told you that you have an East Indian master teacher and that Krishna overshadows you. You should come to know as much about Krishna as possible because he is a universal master like Saint Germain.

As I am looking around you, there is a woman that keeps coming up on your side. From the moment you sat down, there she was. She is on your mother's side of the family, and she is dressed in a classical Japanese kimono, which is what they wore when at the time she lived. She is from the last century, so it is either a grandmother or great-grandmother. I feel it's your great-grandmother. She is nodding her head to affirm this is true.

Sometimes when we do this work, we have to ask questions because there may be a spirit who is not educated about communicating with us. Those who are most experienced will come in and tell me directly, "I am her grandmother," or "I am her great-grandmother," but those who are not accustomed to this are not as capable. For example, Krishna came in and identified himself immediately. Because he has communicated countless times with me, he doesn't hesitate to say, "I am Krishna."

Your great-grandmother was highly intuitive. She didn't talk about it, she says, but she had the intuitive ability. She is a very prayerful person who prayed a lot in life. Because she served others, forgetting herself, she is a kind of master teacher. You need to find out her name if you don't know it, because she is working with you.

I just heard a voice and looked up to see that you have a doctor teacher. He was a medical doctor in Tokyo, and he worked on a hospital staff. He lived during World War II, and he died in his eighties. He just said to me, "Because of the war, I became awake to spiritual things. During the war so many people were dying, and we couldn't handle them all, and that environment brought my heart out. At night I had very bad dreams, and I worked really hard to get rid of them. After one and a half years of struggling with these dreams, things finally changed. A spirit guide came to me and told me about my spirit. It was not in a dream; the spirit woke me up in the morning. He told me about the spirit world and about how to develop spiritually. I still remained a doctor, but I worked from a very different perspective." This man's last name begins with a "W," or at least that's what he showed me. I don't know the actual last name. He is working with you and very much wants to work through your energies as you develop a healing ability.

Let's go to your next question. I keep seeing a little boy with you. Did someone in your family pass over as a child?

SK: I don't think so.

PB: It's a little East Indian boy who died very young. When I was tuning into him, my body began to move. He was a holy man in India.

SK: In Japan when we talk about Indian people, we think of American Indians. Before when you were talking about Indians, were you also talking about a man from India?

PB: Yes, East Indian, not American Indian. Do you understand?

SK: Yes.

PB: From now on, I will say a man from India or a boy from India. Anyway, this boy was so highly developed that even as a child his kundalini energy was very elevated. He went into trance very easily and spirit used him. He is probably more important than the other guides, because he is very capable of working with your core energies.

From my point of view, I would ask that you please apply yourself according to the directions being given to you today. If you do, you will be very, very blessed, and you will be happy. I don't say that to many people, but you are very blessed. Next question.

Exploring Spiritual Groups

SK: I have been to many different groups and, as we say in Japanese, put my face in the door. But I think that many of the groups are very strange, and they do weird things. There was one particular group that was really a mistake for me to join and I got out of that as fast as I could. If you could give me more direction or if you see something particular in my energies, maybe I could try studying that. I'd like more hints as to what I should study so I know which group to work with.

PB: Meditation is most important. If there is a group that teaches general meditation, go to that group. You don't have to participate in all their activities, but just go to the meditation part. I went to many crazy groups, and sometimes I just walked in the door, looked, and walked back out. But one of the craziest groups was a group I wound up with, and I found out that I had to change my perception. I had a kind of superior attitude, though I'm not saying this is true of you; I am just telling you my experience. The people at first appeared strange, but I found among them some normal people.

I don't know about here, but in the West, I have found that good channelers often come from strange groups. Such groups draw all kinds of people, and among the strange people, I found normal ones. In one group of about fifteen or twenty people, I found about five normal ones. I humbled myself and just went to get what I could. Later I learned from the spirit world that they purposely put me in that group so that I would learn to love all kinds of people.

If you sit in the role where I am sitting right now, you meet all kinds of people. I have read for people who have stolen things and people who have murdered people. I have read for people dying of AIDS or other illnesses, teachers, college professors, policemen—the whole gamut of types of people. What I learned in the end is that I have to do this work with detachment, so I had to learn how to love everyone equally and not judge them because of any external reality.

I have found that to do high-level work, you must have a very big heart and be universal. It is very hard to find a group that is not strange in some way, so I agree with you. But go into several groups and stay awhile to find the normal ones. I am going to let Saint Germain come though because he wants to speak to you in these closing minutes.

Meditation is the Foundation of Channeling

SG: I am back. This is Saint Germain again. The things that Philip is saying are quite true, and that is his experience. We advise you to take from it what you know to be true for yourself, as it applies to you. The most important thing for you is to study and practice meditation. It is the foundation of all good channeling, all good healing, and all good spiritual work. True and consistent meditation attaches us to our higher self and God within. God within is the power behind all effective channeling. Find a place where you can, at the very least, go and consistently meditate.

With all that has been said to you today, we hope you don't feel overwhelmed. There is no effort here to try to flatter you. My medium is used only to try to bring to you a comprehensive understanding of yourself and spiritual life. Because he has been effectively used by us in the past, we are using him in the same way for you today.

Now for the remaining minutes I am going to step aside and let Philip come back and let you ask any further questions. This is Saint Germain.

PB: Do you have another question?

Public Relations Work

SK: I have been working at the same company for nine years, and I am thinking I want to change my job. What would be a good job for me to move into?

PB: May I have your paper? I don't know what you do now, but spirit shows me you should try to work towards being in public relations at a public relations firm. Do you understand?

SK: No, but I will look up "public relations firm" to find out what it means in Japanese.

PB: In this case it has to do with your working publicly, meaning as a representative for a company; not selling, but as a spokesperson or information coordinator. In fact, what I see is that when you go to another company, they are going to train you. There is some kind of training for this work, and you will be happier. When I am in your energies, I feel like you are bored with your present job or tired of it? True?

SK: Yes.

PB: Yes, that is the feeling I get, and it is time to move on. All you have to do is put out, either on paper or in your mind, the affirmation that God is guiding you to the next job. You don't have to ask to be guided, but just say, "I am being guided." Then start searching and asking questions, particularly in the field of public relations. You have a very good appearance and a very good presence energy-wise, and you can meet people easily and not be afraid to speak. Many of us are shy sometimes, but fundamentally, you have the ability to speak out. My guide just said you will teach in the future also. You will teach spiritual things. How old are you now?

SK: Thirty-two.

PB: Yes, I thought you were around thirty. To the Western eye you look like nineteen, so every time I meet someone in Japan, when I think of their age, I have to add about ten years to be accurate. I met a man yesterday who looked to be about twenty, but he was forty-one years old.

Just be steady in life, for you are going to be successful. You *are* successful, and you are going to continue to be successful. I don't know if you are asking for a child or wanting to have a child, but I see a child with you. Do you have children now?

SK: No, I don't want to have children.

PB: You may change your mind as you get older, because as soon as you sat down I saw a child. That doesn't mean that you have to have a child. If you choose to have a child, it will be a boy. It's one area that I am very accurate in. Okay, was that your last question? We have time for one more.

SK: I have three things that I am very good at: languages, music, and art.

PB: Do you play the piano?

SK: A long time ago, just a little bit.

PB: Yes, because I saw a piano in front of you. Music, languages, and art . . .

SK: Pursuing any of these areas requires a lot of time, money, and determination. I am asking if you feel through my energies, which one of these might be a good idea to pursue?

PB: It's in the language area, and it goes with work in public relations. You remember that I told you I saw you going to America a number of times? Somehow the study of languages, work in public relations, and your talents generally are all tied together.

When I give readings in America, people believe most of what I give, but they are skeptical of some parts. I tell people that it's okay to be skeptical, but don't throw everything out. Just put it on a shelf in your mind and watch to see if things unfold as I said. Many people call or write me and say, you know the thing I doubted? It just happened. None of us really knows what is going to happen tomorrow. Like anything, you need to build a foundation first, and then all the other things that are prophesied will come to pass. Rather than to feel overwhelmed or fearful, do the one thing today that you can do to move yourself forward toward these goals. You can only meditate one day at a time.

SK: It sounds as if you are saying you can only meditate once a day. Is that true?

PB: No, I mean you can only meditate one day at a time because you can only live one day at a time.

SK: I understand.

PB: You can't live tomorrow, you can only live today. Have a clear vision of your ultimate goal, but more importantly, have a clear vision of today. A person becomes a master at meditation, not suddenly, all at once, but one day at a time. You know from studying music that you have to practice, practice, practice. It's the same with meditation. You are headed in the right direction; just ground yourself in focusing on today, each day. You have that in your nature anyway, I see it. The energy with you is very together. You have a lot of integrity, and you are very disciplined and structured. When I first met you, and as you sit here, I can see that you have a lot of integrity.

SK: I have to look up that word "integrity" to see what it means in Japanese.

PB: You are born for success and long life, so go for it. Go for it. You have a need to be an individual, and in Japan that is difficult. But you're not a typical Japanese person, I can see that. Okay, we are finished, and I am going to close with prayer.

Thank you for this opportunity, Heavenly Father, for this reading. May the content help her in decision-making. May she equally believe in its content as well as in herself, and may your presence become increasingly obvious to her.

End of recording

ENLIGHTENMENT AND THE ETERNAL PATH

Mei W.—Female

Philip Burley (PB): I'll start with a prayer. Can I have your paper? I will give it to you and take it back from time to time.

> *Father, as we begin, I feel your presence very much and the presence*
> *of several high masters. I ask your blessings upon this young woman,*
> *that all the questions she has written here may be answered by you*
> *and spirit. All of us are looking for specific answers in life to walk our*
> *spiritual path correctly, but the truth is there are never any mistakes*
> *on that path. Every up and down and every turn right or left is on*
> *purpose. All is to teach us about ourselves so that we may learn of*
> *our earthly self and of our higher self, and in that higher self, know*
> *your presence. Therefore, may this reading contribute significantly*
> *to the answers she seeks in the quest of her life. I thank you for all*
> *those gathered here in spirit for her and for their coordination and*
> *help. All this I pray in divine love.*

First of all, you have a very beautiful blue aura, a very deep blue. It shows psychic ability. They show a gold ladder here in front of me and this is the spiritual ladder of your life. As far as where you are on that ladder, that is a little past halfway. When we say a little past halfway, we are talking about how much knowledge you have acquired for your journey. You have a very good and solid foundation, but what you are going to gain in the second half of climbing this gold ladder is more important than the first half, and it is going to take longer to acquire. This portion of your path has a lot to do with proper self-love.

Lao Tzu, Jesus and the Path

You have the significant influence of a Chinese master. I want to say Lao Tzu. Do you know Lao Tzu?

MW: Yes. In Japan we say *Loshi*.

PB: *Loshi*. He is just standing right here, and the energy he has, that he *is*, just pours into you and becomes you. Also, at the throat chakra there is a very large amount of light, and the yin/yang symbol shows over that area. One part of the yin/yang is the ability to channel spirit, and the other part is clairaudience, the ability to hear spirit. In whatever you are doing, they are working a lot on the third eye right now. You are already seeing, but the final step that you need, they show me, is to believe. It's not a question of whether you have the talent.

MW: Other people have said this to me already.

PB: You are already seeing clairvoyantly, but you have yet to recognize its subtlety. Right now, you are going in circles spiritually. They show you walking in a rut, and it is getting deeper and deeper; you are not going anywhere. But God has a plan for you, and you are going to climb up and out of that rut.

MW: Will I do it by myself?

PB: There are three steps to take. What I see is a path and it's deep. How shall I say it? I watched, and heaven placed three steps down inside that space. The steps are turquoise, a combination of green and blue. In this case, the blue of the turquoise represents that you will climb these three steps through higher truth by just continuing to live. Life will teach you.

I believe there will be more teachers for you. When I first started praying for you, the master Jesus came in. He is talking to me right now, so I know the reason for these three steps. The major thing in working with self has to do with the development or opening of the heart chakra. Right now, they show that you are doing things having more to do with form than content. It's like building a beautiful, beautiful box that you can use in many ways, but you have to put something in that box. It represents the body without a spirit. Therefore, the next phase in your spiritual growth, simply speaking, has to do with growth in personal love and expanded love.

Lao Tzu has been with you for a long time, but he is working on the truth of this, the blue part of the steps, and Jesus is with you to work on the love part.

MW: What was the role of Lao Tzu? I remember Jesus is the love master.

PB: Lao Tzu is working with the truth of things, the information, the explanation, the theory, and so on.

You also have Kwan Yin with you, do you know that? She is standing right there as big as life. As with Lao Tzu, her energy comes into you and becomes you. I am listening to my guide Tiffany saying to me, "Tell her that by all means she is the kind of person that must pursue spiritual things above everything else." It doesn't mean to become a nun, but working on the inside, the heart.

Do you have a question on your paper about marriage?

Marriage and Spiritual Growth

MW: I am not really interested in getting married or having a mate or anything like that. I never have been. But other people around me have been saying it is time for me to find a mate. They say it is time for me to find my spiritual mate. A lot of people keep saying this to me. Why do people keep saying this to me when I'm not interested? People here say that if you don't have your spiritual mate, you will never be able to grow any further.

PB: This is my opinion. It's up to you. I had a woman come to me who is in her sixties and is Korean. She was worried about what would happen in the spirit world if she was not married. She asked Saint Germain through me if you have to be married to get into the highest levels, and he said no. It's up to you. No teacher, not even spirit, can tell you what you must do. And as many of the great masters have said, the highest truth is to know yourself. Shakespeare wrote, "To thine own self be true, and thou canst not then be false to any man," or something like that. Be true to yourself, and then you will always be true to other people.

One time Jesus channeled very directly to me, about a year or two ago, through a woman channeler in America. Because I am clairvoyant, I know it really was Jesus. He said, "I thought the highest service to God was a single life—being married in spirit to God, but if I had to do it over, I would get married in the earthly sense." The truth of his life is that he didn't get married, and there are no accidents or failures. He didn't get married because of his karma, and he wasn't meant to get married. He could see the benefits of earthly marriage, but his destiny was to not get married. Otherwise, he would have gotten married. Respond to your own heart, and you will not make a mistake. It is up to you.

My guide Tiffany just said that people often project onto us not something from spirit, but their own thinking. She said, when people say to you that you should get married, just be silent. Like a wise woman, just smile and don't say anything. Don't give them any basis to get into your private business. That question belongs in the trinity of God, your earthly self, and your higher self. That's where it will be decided.

Mother Teresa is now in the process of being canonized as a saint. She was a single woman who did great, great work. I have seen her in spirit, and she is a magnificent spiritual being. She doesn't look like she is suffering from not marrying.

Let's move on to your next questions.

Deepening through Internal Work

MW: I have no idea why I came to earth; I am not interested in this planet at all.

PB: (Chuckles) That makes two of us.

MW: And I don't know what to do about it. Everybody says I should be having a life of serving. Everybody says I should be focusing on peace or something, but I have no idea how to take action or what to do.

PB: Then you have to listen inside. I told you earlier that Jesus is working with you. As you know, among all of the masters, he is considered to be the master of love. The biggest obstacle to your knowing what to do with your life is that you need to realize you have to go deeper into yourself and to love yourself properly.

Both teachers and students have their stories, and they want us to live their stories. But where God is truly speaking to us as individuals, is inside of us. Jesus clearly indicated that he and the Father were one and Saint Paul taught that we are the temples of God.

The Bible tells us that at the age of twelve, Jesus went missing. Mary and Joseph, his parents, didn't know what to think and filled with considerable concern they searched all over for him. Finally, after a few days searching, they found him in the temple—their house of worship—speaking with various spiritual teachers.

Upon finding him they said something like, "What are you doing here? We have been looking all over for you!" In a seemingly calm and mature manner Jesus indicated that he was at the temple because he had to be about his Father's business, meaning God's business. **Luke 2:49**

Well, how did Jesus, at age twelve, know about God's business? Because he could communicate with God directly, even at that age he knew many things that no one else could know because of his calling and mission in life.

Jesus learned to listen to God speaking to him inside and habitually so and doing so made him most secure and confident in himself; "I have to be about my Father's business!" He *knew in no uncertain terms* who he was and what he needed to do in the role of messiah. He listened more to the voice of God inside than to human beings outside.

I am taking quite a long time to get around to answering your question. They are telling me to do that because it is necessary to impress upon you to listen more to your inside voice. Right now, for example, if you feel anything about anyone or anything, and that feeling won't go away, then you need to listen to that. That's your higher self talking. Things that don't go away and just keep coming back are things we all must really listen to. If you have certain thoughts or feelings about those people or situations and thoughts about them keep coming back, you need to listen to those thoughts.

For example, if you are dating a man, and you keep getting a feeling like this is not going to work out, even though everything seems to be externally okay, and the message that something is not right keeps coming back over a month or two, then you must look at it seriously. That is God speaking to you, through you. In many cases like this, people have such feelings, and then later they find out that the person they were dating was actually being unfaithful to them. This was spirit's way—or God's way—of helping them get out of that relationship.

Jesus is very prominently supporting you in this part of your life. The next phase of your life is stepping up and out of that rut, learning to go inside more, and coming to know and love yourself more. Your spirituality will develop higher and broader. You will be able to stand alone with confidence and climb up those spiritual steps.

MW: Maybe you are talking about the guy that I am dating now. I have been with him for seven years. I am scared of what I need to do. I need to do something to take action, but I am scared of doing that.

PB: Again, it is because you don't know yourself. The highest truth is to know yourself, but to do that you have to go inside and look around and listen. That's really what meditation, good meditation, is about.

In authentic meditation, one should spend about eighty-five to ninety percent of the time looking at oneself, not in some negative or judgmental way, but just observing. Then when you know yourself, there is no basis for any fear. I understand you very well, because I am walking the same path. I have had a number of people in my life whom I loved, and I have had different teachers. I don't know your business, so I don't know anything about the details of your life, but in the end, I had to walk away from all of them, because I was not finding myself. I was living *their* stories, and not my dream, not my story.

Are you a little bit anxious that this man has not asked you to marry him, or does it matter?

MW: No, it does not matter to me.

PB: When I gave that example about a man being unfaithful, I was not referring to any man you are dating.

MW: I think it's good that you said that the example does not refer to me. In my experience in Japan, I find that when psychics speak in examples, ninety percent of the time people think they are speaking to them personally.

PB: I am not saying that he is unfaithful to you at all. It was just an example of learning to listen to the inside voice. What I said didn't specifically apply to your life with him.

MW: Could I give you a name and you could read the energy of that person? Even if he had somebody else in his life, I wouldn't care. I don't have any feelings about that, even if he liked someone else more. Still, I am afraid to move away from him to be on my own.

PB: Are you telling me that after seven years that you like him, but don't love him?

MW: I don't know whether it's that I like him, or if it's some kind of love attachment.

PB: I believe it's attachment, because that's what I am hearing from spirit.

MW: Can I ask spirit to cut the attachment and help me to be alone, or be on my own?

PB: You will. It's a part of stepping out of that rut. You don't know it, but you were born for great things. So, you have to be careful that you listen for and answer the inside call, the inside voice, and not the voice of the world.

My point again is that in life you have to listen to the inside voice. It will never, ever mislead you. You have to deepen your spirituality inside to be able to hear that voice clearly. What I am saying to you during this segment of the reading, I would like to say to the whole world. Jesus never apologized for what he did, all the way to the point of death, because he knew one hundred percent what he came to earth to do. So, he did it completely.

The problem with human beings is that we are cut off from God inside. Most of us are ignorant about God being inside of us, so our life just goes up and down and in all directions, and we are confused. Those who have an authentic relationship with God inside and communicate regularly don't go through such changes. They are the ones who go all the way to the top, and that's your path. That is your path, to go all the way to the top, to be victorious in life, and to grow in the inner relationship and follow the inner voice all the way to where it's leading you. How old are you?

MW: Thirty-one.

PB: Thirty-one. Yes, so you have a long time. You are going to live at least into the early part of your nineties. It's not totally decided, but that is how they show it. You have plenty of time, so don't get panicky.

Let's go onto your next question.

Clairvoyance and the Third Eye

MW: For a long time now, I have been trying to see with my third eye, and you said that I can already see with my third eye. But when I close my eyes and look, it's absolutely, totally, one hundred percent dark. I see absolutely nothing. I went to a channeling school a couple of years ago, and even before that, I have been trying to see. I went to a number of other teachers, trying to see, and I still can't see. I've had a number of readings, and they all say basically the same thing: I *should* be able to see. This is where I am confused. If everyone tells me I'm supposed to be able to see already, and my brain can't see, then what on earth am I supposed to do about this problem?

PB: Okay, it's all about understanding. I've taught hundreds and hundreds of people to see clairvoyantly, and the biggest problem is that their idea of how you see spiritually is not consistent with how it really works. The imagination is the path, the key, and the door to the spirit world. I am going to be teaching this tonight at my class.

Imagination has to do with the right brain, the creative side of the mind. With the use of imagination, you access the right brain, and through the right brain you make the connection to spirit. Both the front and the back are points of seeing. The medulla oblongata in the back is actually where God makes contact. That is where the energy comes in. The impression or the energy that spirit uses can be read from this part, and for most people it is there. In any case, it is all one.

In my classes, initially I don't teach people to see clairvoyantly. It's not how I learned. I teach people how to use their imagination. So, for example, would you please close your eyes? I would like you to imagine your home, where you live now, your apartment.

MW: I have never been able to do that, even since I was a small child.

PB: That is okay, I know. Just close your eyes. Now I want you to feel the presence of your mother, can you feel her? It doesn't matter whether she is alive or dead, but can you get a feeling? Did she have any kind of distinctive marks on her face like a mole, or did her eyebrows look different? Turn your eyes up into your forehead. Now, do you have a picture of anyone in your home that you keep out?

MW: No. In Japan we usually just put up pictures in our house of dead people, dead grandparents, not living people.

PB: You work in an office? Where do you work?

MW: I don't work.

PB: Okay, do you have a bed where you sleep? You don't even have to close your eyes; in your mind, can you see that bed?

MW: Yes.

PB: Yes. That's clairvoyance, that's the beginning of clairvoyance. Can you see the blanket on the bed?

MW: I am not seeing it. I am just thinking that I am seeing it.

PB: That's right, but you are—that's clairvoyance. Because of language it is hard to say, but when you turn your eyes up like this, you are accessing the right brain. Often when you go to a restaurant and you ask the waitress about desserts, she will say, well we have hot fudge sundaes, we have this . . . , and she is looking upwards. She is triggering her memory, but she is also tapping into her imagination. She is "seeing" the desserts.

Clairvoyance is really seeing and feeling at the same time. When I saw Jesus and Lao Tzu behind you, and I also saw Kwan Yin, I *saw* them and simultaneously I *felt* them. That's ultimate clairvoyance. When spirit comes, unless you are very advanced, the image is so quick that if you don't know what you are doing, you don't catch it. But I can tell you, because I have worked with many people like you, if I worked with you, I could teach you how to be clairvoyant.

My wife sat in all my classes for twelve years, and not until the last part of the twelve years did she begin to see clairvoyantly. In the end, she learned she was looking in the wrong way and in the wrong place. My impression with you is that you are one who is more attuned to sense from intuition. The energy from intuition is above the head, and through that you *feel-see*.

MW: Feel-see?

PB: It's like intuition, but more than that.

MW: I have just never heard anyone say that before.

PB: No, because I coined the phrase. But again, look at your bed. Don't close your eyes, just look in your mind. While looking at your bed, look over to the left side. Just look up like this and see if you can see the bed up there, in your mind. Do you see the bed? Let your eyes go naturally wherever they need to go. Where do you see the bed the best? You are looking up. What do you see on the bed?

MW: There is a pillow and a dryer.

PB: Hair dryer? What color is the bedspread?

MW: White.

PB: See, you looked up, triggering the right brain. In your learning so far, did your teachers teach you to turn your eyes up into your forehead?

MW: Well, I was taught that, yes, but what I was taught most was to picture something like a square, and then close my eyes and picture the square being right there. That is the way I was taught to be able to see something.

PB: That's one method, but it is less direct than through the proper use of the imagination.

MW: Somebody else tried to teach me to picture myself writing the number one and taking ahold of the number one and putting it down, and then picture myself writing the number two.

PB: I know all these methods, but they may not work for you, because you are not that kind of person. Part of self-mastery is learning to discover what your type is—what learning style will suit you the best. But all I have to do is watch your eyes to know how you access the spirit world. Once you understand that about yourself, you will stop blocking your own vision. It will come more naturally to you.

Artists, writers, and actors are all highly right-brain oriented, and they're also highly inspired. They have very vivid imaginations. For the actor Mifune to know how to be a samurai, he had to imagine what a samurai looked like, and what a samurai did. It is the same with someone writing a book; they have to see the characters in their mind, and all the details in the scenery—everything. Their primary gift is having a very, very vivid imagination.

That is how spirit world passes on the inspiration for inventions. You have that facility, and the more you think of it in these terms, the easier it will get for you. Finally, you have to start giving yourself the message, "I can do this. I can do this."

Do you have another question?

Mystery School Studies

MW: I have been studying with the Rocky Mountain Mystery School for a while, but recently I am not sure if this is the path I am supposed to be on. I am kind of going around in circles about this. Part of it is really a lot of fun, but there is a part of me that is not sure I am supposed to be at that school. Instead of making the decision, I have just decided not to think about it all, just to make myself totally blank.

I am the type of person who decided as a small child that if I tried to, I could see what's going to come next, and that was always so much fun for me. It is the only way I have lived my life—just doing something and then being able to see what will happen next. It is not that I want to study a certain thing so I will take a certain road. I take the road and then end up studying whatever I find. I never plan ahead of time, I just act and then decide, "I will just do this and then I will see what happens next." That's the way I have always lived my life, but now I have stopped that part of myself.

PB: You stopped doing that?

MW: I just decided to stop and don't feel like doing that anymore. I am trying to decide if studying at this Rocky Mountain Mystery School is a match for me or not.

PB: What do you think your inside voice is saying?

MW: Both answers come up inside of me, so I am not sure what to do. A while ago I made the decision to study until the end of this year. I decided I have already studied whatever I am supposed to study, and then I am done and finished. That's what I was thinking, but now I am going to this seminar where I get to see everybody who is there, and all my friends are there. Everybody seems to be having so much fun, so I started thinking, "Oh, I will attend more seminars now, because it is just so much fun." But now I am going back and forth. Actually, what I would like to do is just forget everything and go climb inside of a mountain and just stay there for good. All I am thinking about is going inside of some cave in a mountain and just doing nothing for the rest of my life.

PB: I am going to let Saint Germain come in.

MW: This question is not written down on the paper.

PB: It doesn't matter. It's the vibration. I am going to let Saint Germain come through and talk to you.

Enlightenment and the Internal Path

Saint Germain (SG): I am here, God bless you. This is Saint Germain. I am so pleased to be with you today. Even though I have met many people through this medium, this channeler, no two are alike. They are like individual snowflakes. Each one is different.

All of us go through seasons of the spirit. Everyone I know personally and any master teachers whom I have spoken to would at times like to go off into a cave somewhere and just sit and do nothing. In fact, some of us do that for a time.

Again, beloved one, you have to learn what your own soul is telling you. Many people go to all kinds of organizations for social reasons. In fact, there are people who for years and years attend certain meetings in which they get nothing from it except friendship, and there is nothing wrong with that. Then there are those who go both for friendship *and* to gain higher knowledge and that is good too. The larger question is the eternal question: Am I growing spiritually higher from this experience? If you come up with the answer that you are not, then it is time to look around for something new.

If a parent was feeding a child and the child didn't grow, they would question the food they were providing to the child. They would change the diet, add more, or take something away, and they might have to experiment. Then when the child took certain things and started growing again, they would know they had the correct diet. The fundamental way to know you are growing is to ask yourself whether or not you are happy and gaining greater peace. Only you can answer those questions. If the answer to those questions is no, I am not getting happier, and no, I am not getting more peaceful, then you must question whether what you are doing is of value for eternal purposes.

A true master always does that which edifies the soul, and he or she leaves behind those things that do not do that. Because our reason for being on earth is to find higher and higher truth, then many times we masters live a very lonely life. True self-enlightenment does not come in a group setting. We may get certain knowledge in groups and certain edifying loving experiences, but for the actual growth of the soul, we need to be isolated. All the great masters went off by themselves. This was not because they didn't love people, and not because they were negative, but because their experience taught them that they needed to be alone to go inside where they could commune uninterrupted with their higher self and God.

By these criteria, we cannot tell you what to do, but we can imply the best path. You have to discern the truth of what we say and act from your own consciousness. If you were a lesser soul, I would tell you do this and this and this. But you are not called to live just the average life. You are to be a master of self, and to do that, you must learn how to discern truth from falsehood.

I can say this however: whether you leave that group now or in the future, you will leave it. When a child grows into adulthood, it no longer wants or eats baby food. It wants solid food. If you are truly living what any group has taught you, you will grow out of it eventually. When anyone seriously lives any truth from any group, they eventually grow out of it. Life is progressive, moving ever upward and onward. It is not stagnant and repetitive. This is why we go from the first grade up through the various grades and into college, learning higher knowledge and expanding our life experience.

Now I am here with you, and I have tried to cover the answer to your question. But if there are any other salient points or tributary questions, please ask them now.

MW: I'd like to ask a question about humans, about people.

SG: Yes. (Laughter)

Stay in Your Business

MW: I am not able to understand what other people are thinking.

SG: Not important.

MW: I don't need to know what other people are thinking?

SG:No, you only need to know what *you* are thinking. Many spend too much time in other people's lives or business. The true master tries to figure out only what he or she is thinking and needing to do *on their path*. What *concerns you and your life* is what needs your attention the most and in a concentrated way.

What is God's concern depends upon God and God's response is according to his will. As for other people's concerns or business, for the most part, leave all of that up to them. Yes, if someone asks you to help with some part of their life and you are available and can, then perhaps you may lend a hand or give some needed advice. You will find yourself, however, doing better and making more positive strides forward in your life if you focus mostly on your own business and not God's or other's. Is this helpful or not?

MW: Yes.

SG: Just, yes, or more than yes? Is it very helpful or a little bit helpful? (Laughter)

MW: Just a little, because I don't really understand it yet.

SG: Yes, you have to figure it out. The Japanese culture or society is one in which many people are in other people's business. You live so close to each other, and a favorite thing is to go about talking about each other—but not those who are aiming towards self-mastery. You will not find them among the populous, the common crowd; they are not the people who will achieve self-mastery in this lifetime. Those who gain self-mastery will be the persons working quietly, often in isolated ways. They are more concerned about the afterlife than this life, and they want to do everything they can to arrive at the best place possible in the spirit world. Therefore, they spend their time directing their own life towards that end.

Now I am going to go, and I know that you will make all the right decisions for yourself. You are being guided, and you have very powerful, high forces working with you. Learn how to call upon and use them and let them help you. Do not die with regret that you did not use us. Be both loving and wise in life and you cannot go wrong. This is Saint Germain. We bless you.

MW: Thank you. It's very difficult for me.

PB: Well, you can listen to the recording. Why are you scratching your head? What is confusing you?

The Reality of God

MW: I am saying God, just—God. I have never had any interest in God whatsoever for a long, long time, and don't even want to get to know God. That is probably what is holding me back.

PB: You are right. That is the very thing. But God has an interest in knowing you. You didn't come from nowhere.

MW: Everybody always says to become one with God, but I have zero interest in that. No matter what I study, I am not really interested in anything that I am studying. I have no idea why.

PB: Well, that is your path.

MW: Does it mean that I should probably learn about God and study about God?

PB: Well, the thing you don't realize is that you are already one with God. You couldn't live if the energy of God was not in you. The heartbeat behind your heartbeat is God's heart. The reason why your heart beats when you are asleep, and you keep breathing when you sleep is that God's heart is beating through you, and he is breathing through you. God is the intelligence, the force, and the energy behind all of your existence. You are exactly where you are supposed to be. Don't change anything, except learn to go inside. God will reveal himself to you. It is not that simple, but yet it *is* that simple. Let's close with a prayer.

> *Thank you for this time, Father. I would ask that you guide this young lady in however her life unfolds. The more she knows her own heart inside, the more she will find you. You never push yourself on anyone, but like the rose that is opened by the warmth and heat of the sun, so the more we experience love and light, the more we open to you. May the content of this reading progressively help her to find her way. All this I pray in divine love. Amen.*

End of recording

Spiritual Reading Seventeen

UNDERSTANDING YOUR CHILDREN

Yuna G.—Female

Philip Burley (PB): The Star of David appears above your head. Just now, my guides are showing me the light around you as a very beautiful silver blue, and it means that you have a high intellect.

YG: Did you say blue or silver-blue?

PB: It's a silver blue, indicating high intelligence. You are searching for some very important answers for your spiritual life. They show you with a magnifying glass looking at the globe, and the earth is floating right in front of you. You are searching over the globe—not literally—but looking everywhere. It is very, very important for you to finally come to the realization that all the answers are inside of you.

Do you have a question on your paper about one of your children?

YG: Yes.

PB: Yes, I thought so. You may ask that question.

YG: I have three children, all boys.

PB: Yes, I saw a boy.

YG: My oldest son is twenty-seven years old. He does whatever he feels like doing and he listens to no one. Just recently, we were finally able to have conversations. He is still living with us. He has the feeling to go off on his own and be independent, but I am wondering how he's going to be able to leave the house. I think about this all the time. My second son knows how much I worry about my first son, and he is always taking care of me because he knows how much trouble I'm having.

I read in a book that before they come to the planet, souls choose their parents and make a contract with them, and I'm sure that my second boy came to the planet to help me. My third son has a more advanced soul, and I'm sure he is more advanced than I am.

PB: How old is your third son?

YG: Twenty years old.

PB: And the second son?

YG: Twenty-five.

PB: Twenty, twenty-five and twenty-seven.

YG: The younger two sons are doing very well, and I have nothing to worry about with either one of them. I am worried most about my first son.

PB: That is what I thought. I saw a void. I am going to let Saint Germain, my guide, speak to you. He does not usually ask, but for some reason he has asked if that is okay.

Saint Germain (SG): I am here. This is Saint Germain. God bless You. You can hear me all right?

YG: Yes.

Understanding Your Children

SG: Thank you. I need your energy in order to connect. Your faith and belief, combined with your response to me, helps me be here and stay here. Every state of existence is a state of energy, and faith and belief are also energy forms. This is why certain teachings have power over us. It is also why prayer works. We are sending forth energy we believe will help someone.

First of all, your oldest son, your twenty-seven-year-old son, is the victim of being the number one son. We are always harder on the first child, because we as parents are experimenting in a way with raising the first child. The first child in the family often has a difficult time being able to feel truly free. Since that child is the eldest, we expect more of him. We expect older children to set an example for the younger children. At times, consciously and unconsciously, they resent this.

You can help your son most by believing in him. As I said, belief is energy. If you think of him with disparaging ideas or concerns, that energy will reach him, and it *is* reaching him. You can help him best by being rather silent, and in your mind and heart, whenever you think of him, think of him being successful.

When we know what we want to do in life, and we have a very clear vision, we simply step out and go for it. It is obvious from our side that your son does not have a complete vision of his future and is therefore insecure about stepping out. You can help him best by being very loving and silent, and by encouraging him whenever you see something good that he does. In his heart of hearts, he would like to leave, but because he is not clear about himself and about having self-confidence, he cannot do this so easily. In this insecure position of not having a vision, he becomes defensive.

Be aware that your beliefs, your prayers, and your thoughts have great influence upon him if you hold them steadily. Each day in silence, and in isolation, sit thinking of him. If you need to, use a picture, and in your mind see him first as being more secure. See him catching a vision, a clear vision, and in that same effort on your part see him leaving your home, going out, and being happy and successful. Keep repeating this exercise for at least one month. This energy will reach him and influence him. I have seen many miracles take place by using this method.

The other thing, dear lady, is that your son is a part of the transition that is taking place in Japan. More and more youth are going to depart from tradition. Many are not listening to their parents. This can be very disturbing because it breaks the harmony that normally exists, but you cannot change what is already in motion. More and more, it is becoming one world, and old ways everywhere around the world are breaking down. Before a new thing is born, there are always birth pains. Your son and many young people of his age are in this category of transition, and they are all somewhat confused. It is part of the birth pains of your nation as it emerges into a new nation. As the new Japan is being born gradually over a number of decades, part of the old Japan is fading away. Like most cultures, your culture has gone through various phases to come to modern times.

We know it is difficult for you as a parent to sit by and watch your son, because you have a certain idea of how he should be and you see that he is not living up to your expectations. This causes you to struggle. Instead, try your best to see him in the larger context of the transition of your nation. If you can, ask him what he is thinking about himself. Rather than criticizing him, just listen—listen, listen, listen. As you listen, he will be somewhat surprised, but he will open up to you more. Hear what he has to say, but listen in order to let *him* hear what he has to say. Then he can get a better view of himself.

Instead of criticizing him, say something like this: "Son, I know you are doing your best, and I will stand beside you under all circumstances."

With that kind of love, he will feel much better about himself. We see in his soul that he is not a bad person. Not at all. By using such dynamics, you can help him to further his progress along his own path.

Finally, remember that he is a unique soul. Not all people awaken at the same time in the same way. We daresay that across the land of Japan, particularly in the large cities, many of the youth, twenty-five years old and above, are still living at home. With the economic struggle in your country, it has become more and more a necessity because, as you well know, living alone can be very expensive. Even the smallest and cheapest apartments are not cheap. Money goes so very, very fast in your culture.

Taking all of this into consideration, give him three months more. Keep doing your part to be very positive, and influence your husband to be positive. Then just see what happens.

In a former time in Japan, all you had to do was to demand something of children and they would obey, but now that is not so. Young people are living in a very different world than the world you grew up in. Those in this generation are more independent *internally*, if not so much externally. Yes, we understand your dilemma, and if you ask us, we on this side will help as much as we can.

I may come back again to you to speak to you on other topics. I am deeply pleased to have been able to serve you. This is Saint Germain.

PB: Let's go to the next question, please. (Pause)

Excuse me. Do you have a teaching background?

A Teacher's Intuition

YG: I will talk, in a moment, about my work when I was a teacher.

PB: Yes, because I saw teacher written over your head. Go ahead.

YG: I want to know if I was correct about my two younger sons when I said I thought the second one was born to help me.

PB: All that was correct.

YG: And was I correct that the third one is here as a more advanced soul?

PB: You're exactly right, so you have very good intuition. In teachers, intuition develops naturally. When Saint Germain was just now taking leave of me, he showed me a vision of your other two boys and said, "Let her know what she is thinking about them is correct." But as I was coming out, I forgot what he said because of the state of mind I was in. When you asked the question, I remembered. Your two younger sons will be fine.

YG: I started teaching thirteen or fourteen years ago when my children were still young. Now that they are older, I feel I have more free time to be able to teach. I wanted to work as a substitute teacher, but here they will not allow people to be substitute teachers who are over fifty years old, and I am older than fifty. I went to another prefecture and to another school to try to teach, but that did not work out. Now I have a part-time job working for a particular city in a different prefecture, but even that is not going that great.

I am wondering why there are continuous blocks or walls being put up on my path—why all of this is happening. I am ready to teach, but it is difficult to get a job when they don't want to hire people my age. I want to know what will happen with my job in the future.

PB: When you say these teaching positions didn't work out, what does that mean?

YG: For example, I went to the education office and made a contract for work for this year, but the person in charge did not make a good contract. I am a science teacher, and they came to me saying, "We have space for one science teacher." Then they came back and said, "We are very sorry we made a mistake. We did not need another science teacher." They actually needed another social studies teacher, so they let me go and hired a social studies teacher. It was that kind of problem: I thought I was all set up with a job, and then they came back and said, "We made a mistake, and we are really sorry." Suddenly I did not have a job.

PB: Spirit has given me an answer. I will ask you some questions, because they are telling me to ask some questions first. How does this make you feel about yourself?

YG: In the beginning, I felt a big let-down, but I was sure that God was making these choices for me. God was saying that I should not go into that school, and that I should have a part-time job which is better for me than *that* job. God made that decision for me. That is the way I think about it, and that is what I personally accept.

PB: That is exactly what they said. My guide, Tiffany, is standing here, and she adds that your life on earth appears to include many mistakes, but there are no mistakes. Your deduction that things did not work out because they were not supposed to work out is exactly correct. You have been given these situations as an opportunity to work on your own character. You often work with students to help them solve problems. My guide says that as a teacher, you know that attitude makes up about ninety percent of whether you will be successful. It's not what happens to us in life that matters, but how we respond to what happens. God is still in charge of your life, and God still has a plan.

One of the major reasons you came here today is to understand that you are on the right path in terms of your faith and to learn to trust your own intuition more. You will change jobs in about six months, and it will be good—a teaching job. But to get to that particular job, you had to go through these other steps. In the meantime, it is like when you are swimming, and you cannot swim anymore; you just have to float and tread water.

Your oldest son and you are kind of in the same position right now. Neither one of you knows exactly where you are going, so you can have some appreciation for how he feels. When you don't know where you are going, it can create insecurity. Rest assured that you are being held in God's arms as his child, and he is taking care of you. Coming through my body I just feel a great amount of God's love for you, and this is true for your son also.

I am looking behind you right now, because guides and teachers are starting to come in. You have with you the spirit of Einstein standing to the side. He has influenced your work. Have you done some writing in your field, meaning how to teach certain things within the teaching field?

YG: I write when I am planning for the lectures and for teachers who teach the classes that I do.

PB: Yes, that is how you are influenced by him.

I also continue to see the master Jesus behind you. Are you from a Christian background, or have you studied Christianity at all?

YG: No, almost nothing.

PB: Because Jesus is very strongly with you, and he is nodding "yes" in front of me. This is a time in which you have to show faith in your life, and his example of faith in the face of great suffering is a good example for you. He is not coming to you as a Christian but as a universal master. He works with me a lot. Since childhood, I have met him in dreams, and he often wakes me up in the mornings and gives me messages. I used to have a radio program heard all over the world, and sometimes he would wake me up and give me messages to give to listeners when I did my radio show that morning. One of the reasons he is here is because of his work with me, and he just very much wants to encourage you not to be discouraged.

You have a lot of Buddhist energy with you, and a number of Japanese teachers are around you, fighting over you (chuckles) as to which one gets to work most closely with you. Evidently, you're a very good teacher and very devoted. You have an ideal character and personality to be a teacher.

There is a man here, I don't know who he is, but he said that he's working very, very hard to open doors for you for a teaching job. He was probably a principal from your grade school years. Would you know who this is? Do you have any idea?

YG: I have no idea.

PB: Well anyway, you might go back and try to find out who he is, for he is very much helping you.

Let's go to your next question.

Marriage and Husband

YG: I want to ask a question about my husband. We married out of love, but my older son is causing problems between us. All my husband ever does is work, so we really can't discuss this problem together. None of our conversations about it have gone well. Because of these problems, my husband and I really can't communicate well together at all.

I've heard that there is a difference in relationships where one has the energy of love that will last forever, and others don't have this kind of love. I know there are relationships where love isn't there, just relationship energy. When I chose to be with my husband, when we got married, I thought that he was the perfect one for me and that we had the kind of love that would last forever. I am always thinking about what is going to happen about us in the future.

PB: Yes. It is very interesting, because during the whole time I was talking to you about your first son, I kept looking for your husband, and I could not see him in the picture.

YG: I think so too.

PB: He still loves you, but his pride has been hurt. His oldest son is not turning out the way he wanted him to. Partly because you are the mother, he thinks you are at fault, because the mother has more control over the children than the father on a day-to-day basis. Since his male pride has been hurt, he is sulking to a degree.

Saint Germain just said to me, instead of thinking of it negatively, when you sit down to meditate and pray for your eldest son, do the same way with your husband. Right now, the situation with your eldest son, your husband, and your job is like a hurricane. But in the center of every hurricane is the eye, where all is quiet. During this time, you need to go into the eye of the hurricane.

While everything is storming around you, you need to become very calm yourself. Take on the whole energy of being the eye of the storm—unaffected, unmoved, unchanged, because you are not in charge anyway. God is doing all this, and because he is doing it, you can have faith that he will also work it out.

Everything will work out exactly as it is supposed to; not the way you or your husband think, but the way God thinks. It is very easy in this situation to lose yourself and to have your own peace disturbed, but you can't let that happen.

They show that you are really the power center in the family, and as you take on these peaceful energies, this will bring about the dying down of the storm. Rather than trying to figure out your husband's thinking and feeling, work only with your own thinking and feeling.

Sometimes we can go crazy trying to figure out what other people are thinking. You can't control your eldest son's life, and you can't control your husband's life. Whatever they are going to do, they are going to do. But again, don't lose yourself.

(Pause) I am listening. I am kind of like a translator from the United Nations. I am listening and just repeating what they say to me or show me. Saint Germain further says that as you deal with your son by going into daily positive visualizing for him, do the same thing with your husband. Just visualize your husband being at peace and being positive, and keep doing this every day. Then watch what happens. Your energy will affect him. If you worry and become negative, you will be a part of the storm.

The way Saint Germain shows it to me is for you just to walk calmly through life completely confident that everything is in divine order. No matter what happens, keep smiling—not a pretend smile, but a smile that comes from deep inside from the peace that you have. Soon, they are going to start asking questions because they notice your energies. You can have great influence over time.

This is me (Philip) talking now: When I worked in business, I had to negotiate contracts with many people, working within a very tight budget with millions of dollars. I had to be very wise about how I directed that money. I was very anxious in the beginning, because it wasn't my money, and I had to answer to people above me. I would get into strong discussions with the higherups and feel a lot of anxiety, but I learned that I had greater influence and was more powerful by being silent at times.

It really is true that the quiet one usually wins. Growing up as a child, I had a Chinese guide who taught me always to win in life with my mind and also by remaining silent.

God is very much over you. I see the hand of God over you. When you leave here today, walk in peace. Leave behind all the anxiety about your job, about your husband, about your son—just leave it behind. Stand in the light of your own peace and confidence, for God is in charge. The more you have faith in that, the more God will be in charge and work things out for the best.

You can ask the next question.

YG: I read in a book about soulmates and twin flames. I want to know if I have met any of my soulmates or twin flames and if any of them are around now.

PB: Your second son is both a twin flame and a soulmate, and he will always, always be close. I wouldn't be surprised if many wise things come out of him.

YG: I have a question about my health. I am talking about my kidneys. For the most part, my health is pretty good, and I don't really have any problems.

PB: I would say exactly that.

YG: But I feel sometimes that my kidneys are not working correctly. Also, I have really stiff shoulders and am wondering why.

Worries Affecting Health

PB: In your case, right now your disappointment in your husband is affecting your health. You want his love, and he is not giving; you are used to being close and affectionate, but that is not happening. The worry about your son is going into the back of the neck. The energy of God enters in through the back of the head. When we have tension related to worry, we cut down on the influx of that energy. It is as though we filter the light, cutting down on its power inside of us. In people to whom that happens, people who have a tragedy or people in grief, their energy just goes way down. They can't sleep, and they don't want to eat. That is why it is important to learn how to go inside and meditate to restore our energy by connecting to God.

The whole explanation that Saint Germain gave regarding visualizing your son and your husband in a certain way each day is a form of meditation for you. The intention is so that you will move into that space within yourself where peace already exists. God is already in us, but when we move out of the center of ourselves, we lose the peace of our whole life. Meditating on your son and your husband, as Saint Germain described it, will move you back into a peaceful center. It's a process of turning them over to a higher power. Then you can stop worrying about them and let the higher power, God, take care of them. The tension will go, and you will be simply amazed at how beautiful it feels to be so peaceful. If you practice that method the rest of your life, you will maintain that peace.

As for the kidneys, the symptoms are linked to these same problems. As I look inside, I don't see anything wrong with your kidneys. I see only tension, as the lines of energy—the meridians running through this area—are affecting your kidneys as well. Do you have a problem with your feet or the soles of your feet when you walk for a length of time?

YG: No.

PB: One thing you might do is work on this area of the bottom of your foot. This corresponds to the kidneys in reflexology. Just work across this area and you will probably get relaxation of the tension in your kidneys. Do it with your thumb, and don't do it too much. May I demonstrate? Just along here. Usually if there is a problem, there will be some soreness.

YG: It doesn't hurt.

The Importance of Meditation

PB: Yes, I know; but if you feel around this area, you will find the tension. In any case, the tension should go away if you do the meditation exercise you've been given.

You think your life is in a kind of crisis right now, but that is only in your thinking. There is no real crisis. You think life should be different than it is. Your son should be the good son and do everything you want him to do, and your husband should love you like he always loved you, but that is not what is happening.

They are not living your story, and because their reality doesn't comply with your story, you're disappointed and worried. Accept them exactly as they are, and in doing that, turn them over to a higher power.

This is my experience also, and the experience of many of us. When we change, the whole world changes, because we are all integrated, and we all affect each other. I am telling you for the third time, you have more power in your family than you realize. The mother is always the center of power. The husband likes to think he is, but love is the center of power, and the woman often has more ability to love, so she has the power. If a woman is wise, she will know how to use that power in very quiet and subtle ways. You have that ability. Does this help?

YG: I already feel that the part of me that was really tired is beginning to leave.

PB: Of course. Often when people are with me, they receive healing. It's not because of anything I do, but because under these circumstances, the spirit world and the power of God work with us. Ever since I walked in and met you, my whole body has been humming, kind of like a hummmmmmmm. I don't know exactly why, but it has something to do with healing. Let's go to your next question.

YG: I came to the meditation class the other day and I had never known how to meditate before. I have been practicing what you taught, but I am not able to see images of anything. Every time I try to picture the top of my head, I can't see anything. If I just think about the top of my head and keep working on it, will I get better and better at it?

PB: Yes. Clairvoyance is not seeing the way we see with our physical eyes. Clairvoyance is what I call "feel see."

YG: If I keep working on it, will I have the *aha* experience?

PB: I'm not sure what you are asking.

YG: It's like when you are working and working on something, and finally, *aha!* Wow! Now it has come to me. I get it; I see it. I have not had that kind of experience yet at all, and I want to know if that day will come and when.

PB: My comment would be not to have any expectations. It's a combination of your effort and the effort of the spirit world. Our responsibility is more to just get in place and do the exercise, and our spirit guides and teachers do the adjusting in us. A spiritual master teacher who would like to open our spiritual sight can do it immediately. Some spiritual masters just touch the forehead here and the disciple is suddenly open.

Do you drive a car?

YG: Yes.

PB: You know that when you first start driving, there are many little things you have to be concerned about: making sure you are in the right gear, making sure the street looks safe, watching how you drive so you don't hit anyone, looking in the rear view mirror to make sure there's no policeman, (laughter) a thousand and one things.

When children learn to ride a two-wheel bicycle, the parents run beside them. Until they practice and practice, they are nervous and shaky, but still parents are there to say, "You can do it," and to help them stay up or pick them up if they fall down. The meditation experience is not different. You will learn to meditate. Just be patient. Trust your guides and teachers.

Kwan Yin works with you. She is right behind you, and that's the first time I have seen a master teacher with you. She has her hands on your shoulders and on your head, so I know she is guiding you directly. As far as having the *aha* experience, it happens case by case. My wife sat through my classes for a number of years and couldn't see anything. After some time, she gradually got it. Now, in some ways, she is much better than I am. Her intuition grew.

When you are trying to work while trying to relax your body, if you can't imagine the top of your head, just feel it. Just feel that part of your body with your mind, and continue that way with your mind feeling each part. Gradually your spiritual sight will open.

Okay. We have about five minutes left.

The World and Me

YG: I am a Capricorn? I'm not sure . . . but anyway, a goat?

PB: Capricorn, the goat.

YG: Goat, yes. I have been looking at this world for all these long, long years, watching the wars and seeing all the different things that have happened. I always want the world to become one, so when I sit down and think strongly about the world becoming one and everything becoming peaceful, does this have real value?

PB: It has value because you are the world. This world is contained inside of you. This is a very hard statement to understand, but if it weren't for you, this world would not exist. This world exists in your consciousness, so the center of the universe *is* you.

I am only a projection of your consciousness. We all exist in each other's projections. You understand very well, don't you? It is very beautiful, isn't it? If we see it all as one, then we have to realize there is only one consciousness and we are all characters in that consciousness. Does this help?

YG: What you said right now I have read before in a book, so I know it and understand it in my mind, but I can't understand it inside myself yet.

PB: That is because you don't know yourself completely yet. There are volumes of self-explanation you have not read about. For consciousness to know itself, it has to know everything, and consciousness has created eternity to make it possible to know everything. It happens when we reach this super-conscious level where we can see all is one, and we can know everything instantly. This is most likely to happen through regular meditation and other methods that are rather secret. They are available, but they can't be known by the student before the student is ready. Right now, in terms of meditation, you are where you should be. Otherwise, you would be somewhere else. From here, you can develop to that super-conscious level.

Okay, I think we have finished. I am happy to have served you. You are a very worthy soul. You have lovely energy, and I very much appreciate working with you.

End of recording

Spiritual Reading Eighteen

LOVE RULES THE SPIRIT WORLD

Rina W.—Female

Philip Burley (PB): I'm very honored to read for you.

RW: Should I sit here? I want you to know that I'm going through a very difficult time right now.

PB: Yes. That's a good time to come for a reading. Most people come when they are in trouble or struggling with something. If you didn't have questions or problems, you wouldn't be here.

Okay. I'm going to open with a prayer.

Our Heavenly Father and Mother, we now enter into the world of prayer and solemnity. We move our minds to the higher levels of living—the inner world of spirit. We ask for your presence and all of this woman's guides and teachers. Thank you so much for her spirit. I feel greatly honored to sit before her and to have this opportunity to read for her. Please bless her with all the answers she's seeking. Bring healing to her, and to her family and friends in any way they need it. Please open the door wide between the two worlds for her sake. All of this I pray and ask in divine love. Amen.

When I was praying for you before you came, the spirit world showed me the heavens, with many stars representing highly evolved souls. They weren't famous or wealthy, but the essence of their lives was love and spirituality, and consequently, in their case, silver and gold light radiates from their aura. I saw you as one of those stars, and this is why I feel honored to read for you.

Spirit told me that you have lived what many people only talk and preach about. You are probably unaware of your value and your spiritual beauty, but heaven and God love you very, very much. That is what I see and feel. When you make your transition to spirit, you'll have many greeting you, and there will be a significant celebration. You're very much loved by those in the spirit world.

Himiko and the Founding of Japan; Sisterhood

PB: There's a classically dressed Japanese woman here with long hair and a white kimono with a deep blue obi around the waist. The energy around her is gold, and she stands behind you. The gold color shows that she is a very high soul. In the Japanese spirit world, she is like an angel, and she lived in ancient Japanese history, almost at the time of the founding of Japan.

RW: I think her name is Himiko.

PB: Himiko?

RW: Himiko, yes. I have actually known her for a long time.

PB: Oh, really?

RW: It's the first time I have been able to really see her. She is the woman who founded Japan.

PB: Oh, really?

RW: Yes. A woman named Himiko. Everybody knows who she is. She's very famous in Japan.

PB: I have to get spirit's train of thought. I'm waiting for Himiko to talk. (Pause.) First of all, she acknowledges what you have said. She *is* that person. She is telling me yes; she is that person. She says she is the one who hears and carries your prayers heavenward, and not just your spoken prayers before an altar, but even the prayers of your heart. She says that her reason for coming today is multiple, but she wants to tell you that the difficulty you are going through right now is that you are paying karma to get a great blessing. Just trust God that everything is going to work out.

When Himiko came here, she bowed all the way to the floor, and she honors you like a sister. On the spirit side, you belong to a kind of sisterhood. When you have been out of the body, you have talked with her and many sisters in this very special group.

God uses this group to guide and protect Japan. They are like a mother group. She says that Japan is spiritually anchored by women, and if it were not for this force, Japan would have suffered much more through many millennia.

This group is connected to other groups of women in the Far East. She says you don't have to understand all this, but when you come here, you will. It was very important to have this appointment today, she says, so you could see your life in a larger context. This is important information for you.

Jesus and the God within

I also have the master Jesus that comes to you as well as the master Buddha, Confucius, and many others.

RW: But I am Christian.

PB: Yes. Jesus comes first. When he comes to a Japanese person, I'm always surprised because I think of Japanese people as being typically

Buddhist or Shinto. But Jesus comes first, and he is a direct master and master teacher for you. He's standing all in gold light with his hands on your shoulders. The reason why Confucius and Buddha and others come is because all masters are beyond religion.

RW: I believe that, too, yes.

PB: Yes. Buddha, Confucius, Jesus, all these master teachers are honoring your spirituality.

RW: But I'm very low.

PB: You see, that's because you don't know your value. Before you pass over, they want you to know. Jesus just whispered in my ear, saying, "Tell her that God is as much in her as he is in me, and it's only a matter of her understanding that. Christianity has confused many people because it taught that human beings are not worthy of God. But God lives in man. As you know, I taught that the Father lived in me, and St. Paul who followed me taught that human beings are the temple of God. Man and woman either contain God, or they don't. There is no in-between. The true nature of human beings is also God's nature."

RW: Could you say that one more time?

PB: "The true nature of human beings is God's nature. There are some false ideas about human beings from the earthly perspective."

RW: About God?

PB: "About human beings and also about God. False teachings separated human beings from God. But rather than focusing on your sins, focus on God within you. I came to teach emphatically that God lives in each of us. When we deny that, we hurt God. God wants us to know clearly that he lives in us. If we center on that idea and on that presence, sin will disappear from the earth."

Jesus says that here in Japan, people often deny their own value, putting themselves way down. It's okay to be humble, but if God lives in us, we must celebrate and honor that. Yes, we make mistakes, but God doesn't stop loving us because of that. God does not separate us from him because of that. It is only our confused thinking, based on false teachings, that makes us feel separate from God.

The Religion of Love

Jesus is laughing and says, "You know, I'm not Christian; my religion is love. The highest religion is love. And it is in love that God can be active in our lives." He says, "Beloved one, because of your merit, before you come to this side, we are able to come and tell you this to liberate you from falsehood. If you want to know if what Philip is saying is true, pray and ask me, and I will tell you. I will confirm to you that, yes, all that he has said is true. This is not to criticize Christianity, nor to accuse it, but to separate for you the truth and the falsehood within Christianity. Please listen to this tape many times, and I will lead you closer to God than you have ever been. Because God lives in you, you are worthy of God. Rather than saying 'I am very low,' say, 'Because God lives in me, I am high.' That's what I came to teach. But that part of my message is not present in mainstream Christian teaching."

"I have come to this medium in dreams many times. Sometimes I appear at his bedside and wake him up. He and I have met many times in spirit, and I have taught him many of these things."

You're not sitting before an average Christian but one on whose shoulder I literally cried in a dream. I told him in that dream that many Christians do not understand me. I want you to take comfort today. And please, please, think about these things, and you will come to a whole new level of self-awareness and God-awareness." Then he gestures like this and says, "And now I must go. But my love is always with you."

RW: Thank you so much.

PB: You're very welcome. It's they who are doing the work. While all this is happening, I'm in a trance. Even now, I'm about seventy-five percent in trance, yet I see them literally, as though I'm watching a movie. That's how it happens. This is the first information spirit wanted to bring to you today. It's a lot, but evidently, they know it's important. I'd like to take your questions now, so you can begin asking them. Just take your time.

The Loving Grandfather

RW: I have a whole list of names here of people from spirit I would like you to bring through. My grandfather is the first person I would like to have come through today.

PB: (Chuckles.) He's right here and he's laughing. He shows a tremendous amount of love for you. He's so happy to be here. He says, "Thank you for remembering me. I could never forget you. I have been working just off the stage of your life, in the wings of your life. Indeed, I am one of those background guides and teachers. I thank you so much for your prayers. Your prayers have reached me, and through that energy, I was able to go higher."

Talking in my left ear, he says, "Your humility towards God has taught me much. I was standing here watching Jesus talk to you with tears in my eyes." Now he (your grandfather) and your other guides and teachers are touching me, and there's electricity going through my body. This is healing energy for you. Give me your hand, please.

I have your mother here who is a very humble woman, and your grandmother. Do you also have a brother in spirit?

RW: Yes.

PB: He's right here, too. A lot of people from both sides of the family are here. Do you have an altar in your home where you pray?

RW: I don't have an altar, but I have a place with pictures.

PB: That's what they're talking about. They're talking about that place. That's a very, very holy place. Spirit is showing me a great amount of light energy in that area. When you're in that state, there is a lot of healing energy that goes out from you to other people.

RW: My father left my mother when I was nine years old, so I relied on my grandfather.

PB: Yes. It feels that way.

RW: He was my grandfather and also my father. Even now, I am always thinking of my grandfather.

PB: Very much so. And he's also such a high soul. He didn't love out of duty; he loved because he loved.

RW: He loved anybody?

PB: You. He loved you out of love, not duty or obligation. He's crying too. He's just crying and crying.

Family Relationships

PB: Your mother just said to me that she wants you to know she's always there for you, and she's doing very well in the spirit world. She, too, is a high soul. She is showing me where she lives, and it's a beautiful, beautiful place. There are many birds. She apparently loved the sound of birds very much.

RW: My mother?

PB: Yes. I see where she is. It looks like some of the places in Kyoto—that kind of energy and those kinds of buildings. It's not Kyoto in the spirit world, but the energy is like that.

Did your mother come from a religious background originally?

RW: From a samurai background.

PB: Okay.

RW: I think my father may not be in the same heaven.

PB: Let's see if we can find him.: He seems to be very much in the business world in spirit. Was he a businessman?

RW: He was a journalist. And he was educated in the West, in America.

PB: In America—yes. Well, he has the feeling around him of business—not necessarily money, but I want to say worldly. He is not in a low place in the spirit world. He is in a higher-than-average place because his heart was pure. He says that when he left your mother, he was a very confused man. But from heaven's point of view, you, your mother, and he were intended to live together for a period of time and then separate. That was God's plan. It was your karma. Each got what they were supposed to get, and part of your karma was to lose your father. It was vitally important—this is how they're showing it—that your grandfather be the one to take care of you.

RW: I want to ask about my brother.

PB: Was he a "black sheep"?

RW: He was a bachelor who had no children. My brother was two years older than me.

PB: Yes.

RW: And he became the heir of his grandfather when he was fifteen.

PB: Yes.

RW: He was a bachelor who had no children, and he was sixty-seven years old when he died in 1985.

PB: Yes, he's the one I saw.

RW: He was a serious person, and he loved the piano, especially jazz piano. But he was not very scholarly. My grandfather was very scholarly, but my older brother, who was my grandfather's heir, was not the scholarly type. However, he was a university professor when he passed over.

PB: He's standing here listening. He has been saying, "Everything she's saying so far is true."

RW: I am sorry I was not kind enough to my brother. I wanted him to be like my grandfather.

PB: Yes. Now he's laughing.

RW: I want to say to him, "I'm very sorry."

PB: He says for years he's known how sorry you are. But it was your "script" and his script that you should treat him that way, and that was the way he was. He said, "In those days, your views were narrow, but you've changed. So it was a growing experience." He has no bad feelings towards you. He says, "My regret is that I didn't marry. Sometimes I thought too much of myself. And you are right; I wasn't serious enough about studying. But that's the nature that God gave me—and I don't apologize for it. I didn't create it. Who you are is based on the nature God gave you, so there's no need to apologize. Some people come here with unresolved human relationships."

RW: When you say "here," do you mean . . .

PB: Spirit world. But you have the merit to resolve things before coming to spirit. After today, you will feel lighter. After today, you will feel freer. You'll walk lighter. But it was you who, through faith, came here to this meeting, and that's your merit. There are places where you will now smile that you have not smiled for many years.

RW: Places inside myself?

PB: Yes. There have been no mistakes, just the living out of God's script.

My guide, Saint Germain, wants to speak to you. Please stand by.

Saint Germain (SG): I am here; this is Saint Germain. Can you hear me all right?

RW: Yes.

Love Rules the Spirit World

SG: God bless you. I often stand with Jesus. As Philip said earlier when he spoke about Jesus, Buddha, and Confucius, we are all universal masters. That does not mean we feel superior but that we learned experientially that all people are the children of God. We all came from one creator, but in man's ignorance and blindness, and through time, everything became confused.

Beloved one, where you are headed after you leave your body is to the universal spirit world. There, the ruling principle is love; not religion, nationality, or language, but love. There, you will look Japanese, but your heart will be as if you are a citizen of the world. That is partly what Jesus was trying to tell you today. I come as a part of that group. Because I have a significant rapport with this medium, I can use him to come through and speak to you this way. I just want you to know, though, that I do represent the Christ light.

I wanted to step through the veil for a few moments to make this contact, and if it's necessary for me to speak again, I shall do so. Please let us have your next question.

Tribute to Family History

RW: I have two questions. The first one is a bit of a story. I come from a very well-known family in Japan. I am the last granddaughter of this family that goes back 400 years. I have had a lot of pressure from people around me to continue this line because I'm the last granddaughter; but I have one fifty-seven-year-old daughter who does not want to get married, so there are no children. I am very sad about this because now it is the end of the line.

My grandparents were very exalted and very noble, so what I have been doing is taking their diary and collecting pictures and trying to put them together to leave the legacy and history of my family here in

Japan. It's very, very difficult work for me to be doing at this age. I'm eighty-three right now, and I am feeling very weak. My body is getting weaker. But since I received energy today from you and the masters who are around, I feel stronger.

My question is that I would like to have ten more years on this planet to be able to finish this work. Do you feel that I may become weaker and pass away next year? I would really like to know how much longer I have on the planet, so I can get this work completed.

PB: First of all, I'm listening to you and just listening to them on the other side, and on the other side, they're laughing. Your ancestors are laughing. Not at you, no. But they're amused, and they love you so much. And if you have been impressed to not marry . . .

RW: That's my daughter.

PB: Whoever it is that's impressed that way, it's correct. Yes. Saint Germain just said to me, all good things must eventually come to an end. He came from a noble family and was himself a prince, he says, but while our families may be honorable, the higher purpose of the individual soul transcends family concerns. In other words, your daughter's individual situation, from God's perspective, is more important than the carrying on of the family name or line.

RW: What does God want for my daughter? I am confused about that.

PB: Yes. You said your daughter doesn't want to marry, correct?

RW: Correct.

PB: They say that this is God's providence for her. That's God's plan for her life. She is being impressed in her soul. She is receiving the correct knowledge about her own soul not to marry. That's correct for her. Yes, the family can be honored, and this 400-year history can be written up and pictures lined up and everything. But more important than all of that is this one individual soul, your daughter.

RW: What should I do then?

PB: Well, you indicated that you were willing to put all the pictures and history together, and that would be the end of it.

RW: Right.

PB: Then the question that comes from them is, "What would you like to do beyond that?" That seems to be the closing for this long line of family history, you doing something formally to give it recognition; and since there will not be anyone to inherit the name, the line will end with your daughter, as you have said.

RW: Family things are all over the place right now. More than anything, I want to bring them together, and I do not want to die before I can put everything into a kind of neat package.

PB: I understand, and they understand, too. I see you finishing that project, and you should not hesitate to call on other people to help you. It's important for your family and for your soul to complete it. Just don't worry about it too much. Ask Heavenly Father for extra energy, and he's going to give it. Believe me, if Jesus comes in my ministry to someone, it means that person has a tremendous amount of backing from Jesus and from his spirit world. Just ask Heavenly Father for that extra time and energy. And do it in a light-hearted way; don't take it too seriously.

Jesus is back, he's standing right here. He said, "My daughter, when you come here, this earthly world will be like a dream. Even if you didn't finish the work, it wouldn't matter."

RW: I feel so much better now. I feel comfortable.

PB: He says you do not have to finish it. But if you want to live long enough to finish it, and you ask Heavenly Father, he will give you that time. When I look at your energy, I do not see you going to the spirit world soon. You may be eighty-three, but your soul is more like fifty-three.

And you will not, as you grow old, become senile or demented. You have the merit to ask, just go to spirit in your sleep and just ask. "When the time is right," Saint Germain is saying, "you will probably have a dream that will tell you approximately when you will go."

RW: I have seen spirits.

PB: Oh, of course.

RW: Not many, but some. When I was nine, a male spirit came. I was very scared. I went into my mother's room and then he would disappear. And when I was playing alone again, all of a sudden, he would show up again. After I got married, he came one time, and then he never came again.

PB: Yes, because you closed him out. When we leave childhood and go into adulthood, this happens to almost everyone; but it didn't happen to me. I had many, many experiences from childhood, and even today, Jesus often wakes me up to talk to me.

RW: You have a very pure spirit.

PB: I try. But I give all credit to God and spirit, because I know I am not perfect.

RW: One night the room was so hot that I thought my daughter had brought a stove into it. So I called out to my daughter, "It's nice and hot in here. Thank you so much for turning on the stove. Don't worry, I'll get up soon." When I opened my eyes and looked, there was a man standing there. He was wearing a kimono, and he looked like my grandfather when he was younger. He was wearing a grayish-blue kimono.

PB: That's who it was, your grandfather.

RW: I tried to touch him but couldn't. I tried to ask, "Who are you and what is the reason you came today? Is there something that you want or need?" I tried to say this, but though I was opening my mouth, my voice wouldn't come out. And he faded away. I have been wondering, why, why, why?

PB: How long ago did this happen?

RW: Maybe twenty-eight or thirty years ago.

PB: It happened because your grandfather is like an inner master guide to you, and he loves you very, very much. If you had had training like I did, your spiritual senses would have developed, and you would be able to see, hear, and communicate with spirit in the same way I do. But this was not your destiny. Your destiny was your destiny, and our meeting today was also your destiny.

RW: I am very thankful.

PB: Well, you know, Heavenly Father told me that I would meet very special people in Japan, and I know you're one of them. None of us, and I was raised Christian also, ever thinks we're special. But today, as soon as I saw you, they showed me you as a star in heaven. I knew you were one of those people that Heavenly Father told me I would meet. I'm just so very happy that I could be used to bring in your ancestors. This whole experience is overwhelming to me.

RW: I still have some questions to ask.

PB: Yes.

RW: About my eyes: As I get older, my eyes are getting weaker, and I'm getting cataracts. I want to know if you can ask to see if I am going to go blind, because I have this project, and I don't want to go blind.

PB: No, you will not go blind. Your eyes are affected by age, but also by diet. There are certain herbs you can take to either stop the cataracts or eliminate them. Do you like the taste of salt a lot? Sometimes there is too much salt in the diet. My eldest sister's husband had cataracts, and he had them operated on. He is in his seventies. They operated on his eyes, and there was no pain. If you have a problem as you go along, you can have an operation. I do not see you going blind. Again, just ask Heavenly Father to strengthen your eyes. That's his job.

RW: I am afraid of any operation.

PB: I understand.

RW: I think I am too old to go under anesthesia.

PB: Ask God to heal you. You're a Christian; in these last years, this is the most important time to practice your faith. This is the most important time to have faith in God. I'm telling you, he loves you, and he's taking care of you. He would not send Jesus like he did, and this great female spirit I saw behind you, if he didn't. It really blew my mind to see them here. Without knowing your history, I saw . . . and now I understand. Your family goes back 400 years and is a founding family of Japan. That brings great merit to you. Your family was important to God for the establishment of Japan.

RW: Not that big of a family.

PB: It doesn't matter. It's in the portion of responsibility they had.

RW: The pressure has been tremendous, and I have been—what's a good word in English? I have been . . . not criticized, but it's like I have been bullied like children in school.

PB: Yes.

RW: Also, because my grandmother was American, I was bullied for that, too. Then I became quiet about it.

PB: With the privilege and the status of your family, there's a price. But it's a very small price to pay for the fortune you've had in life.

RW: I've really received wonderful things from my grandparents, and I'm very happy.

PB: Yes.

RW: I really shouldn't be saying this now that I understand, but even though I was unworthy, my grandmother still loved me anyway. (Laughing.) I talk because I have a need to tell this. My family lives in Nagano. We would go through it some days to get to my parents' home. It's called Karuizawa, and it's where all the well-known people in Japan have their second homes. It's like somewhere in Florida.

Years ago, my family had a house there, from the Meiji period, which is many, many years ago. But over the years, they were running out of money, and they had to sell the place. Just recently, my eighty-year-old friend and I went to Karuizawa and actually found the place where my family had lived! It's still there, and no one's living in it. It's still exactly the way it was many, many years ago. My friend and I walked by the house . . . No—not the house, but the land.

PB: You walked past the land?

RW: The house itself was destroyed by somebody; just the land remains there. My family would like to buy the land and build a museum there for my family—this 400-year-old family. They want to build a museum, because I guess there are a lot of artifacts they want to put in it. But now, I am eighty-three, and my friend is eighty years old, and neither of us has any money. We are kind of thinking we'll buy a lottery ticket and maybe win the lottery.

Here we are, eighty and eighty-three. We're old, and we're acting like two little silly schoolgirls with this dream of buying the land and building a museum. Do you think that from God's point of view, this is at all possible, or is it just a silly young schoolgirl's dream that we are just having fun with?"

PB: It's not a foolish dream. Spirit is saying "Not a foolish dream." I don't know how, but there's some kind of foundation. What they were showing me is some kind of institution or foundation that would be interested in your family and would take this on as a project and be able to get the money for it. This is a possibility; yes, from the spirit side. It's not just for your ancestors, but for the sake of Japan that they would like to see it done. You need to talk it up, and you need to find someone to help.

In America, when I had a radio program, people would call me about such projects and ask what I would see. Sometimes the answer was no, but when the answer was yes, usually what I told them happened. I'm saying this to give you faith in yourself and faith in this project.

Are you feeling better than when you came here?

RW: Yes. Yes!

My daughter should be coming to you soon. My daughter is weak, and I am not able to help her. Almost everybody thinks my daughter should help me as my secretary for this project, but she will not. I understand it's a big project and that you said I should have people help me, but we're not wealthy, and we can't pay people to help. I'm wondering if you have any ideas about this?

PB: Again, get people involved as volunteers. This is what they're talking to me about. Your family history is famous. There are people in your society who would consider it an honor to help you, if you just acknowledge their contribution in some way. The secret is to find someone to manage the project. Let them know from the beginning there will be no money, but you're looking for volunteers. If God could create a mountain, he can create a manager for you.

A moment ago, my guide came up and said, "But if you don't get the project done, don't worry. Don't worry yourself to death. If the project can't be done, it's okay. Make your last years on earth happy and peaceful." Your grandfather is right behind you, right now. He has his hands on your shoulders. The major thing he's saying to me is to know that he's strongly, strongly supporting you.

End of recording

Spiritual Reading Nineteen

PSYCHIC ENERGY AND SERVICE TO OTHERS

Sakura T.—Female

Philip Burley (PB): When I read for you, I will go between a trance and semi-trance state, and I never know when Saint Germain will come. He will be here, and you will have plenty of time with him. I like to open with a prayer, as the energy will start coming in, and I can focus on spirit. Already I am able to see your aura, which has a lot of gold light.

> *Father, thank you for this opportunity to spend time with you. We are all on a spiritual path, whether we know it or not. You are guiding us on this path, and the map is in your hand. Through this experience, please bring the information being sought and lead the content for full enlightenment. May this young lady leave here deeply enriched and filled with peace, and may her guides and teachers come close to me to impart the information she is seeking. Thank you for hearing our prayer. I pray and ask all this in divine love.*

Well, the only thing I know about you is what you told me—that you drink beer, and you like it! (Laughing) I don't know anything else, so we'll see what spirit has to say.

Master Jesus comes to you first. Do you have a picture, statue, or something about him in your home?

ST: No, but I have wonderful pictures of Jesus on my phone.

PB: Yes. Well, I'm seeing something about him with you. He works with you, and you have a number of masters with you. Right now, what you need in your life is focus, because you already have enough information and material to walk your path effectively. They are showing me that you have collected a lot of information. The master Jesus is talking to me about the necessity of now putting it all into order, so the concern here is *focus*.

Influence of Indian Masters; the Path of Teaching

You have masters from India around you also, and I am seeing the sign of OM in your heart area. Do you use the mantra *OM*? You must use it a lot because I have never seen this before. I am hearing an almost constant OM-M-M-M-M.

ST: I go to India all the time, and I just got back from the airport. I have vibhuti (Indian holy ash) and other things right here.

PB: That is amazing. The OM sign or symbol is outlined in gold in the area of your heart. I meant to say the symbol is gold and it's outlined in orange. Whether you know it or not, you are very attuned to the OM, and you are a more advanced soul than you realize. I also see the word "teacher" written over your head. Do you desire to teach, or have you taught?

ST: I would like to teach.

PB: Yes. I see "teacher" in gold written over your head. My guide is telling me that now is the time to take all you have learned and put it into some kind of form. For example, you might tell your stories about going to India, or you could even teach about meditation and the spiritual path. You are a born teacher, with or without beer! (Laughing)

ST: I talk about my experiences all the time.

PB: You see, I didn't know that; I am just telling you what I'm seeing.

ST: People have spent hundreds of hours listening to my stories.

PB: I also feel that you didn't have an easy childhood.

ST: I thought it was pretty easy actually, but I have never really thought about it.

PB: Did children sometimes make fun of you? Even a little bit?

ST: They may have, but I didn't notice, because I didn't pay any attention to any of that.

PB: You came into this life already very advanced, and it was your destiny to go to India many times. I just heard someone say "Shirdi Sai Baba" in my left ear, and he is one of the people with you. Have you ever visited his site?

ST: No, but the guru I study with runs an ashram of Shirdi Sai Baba.

PB: Oh, is that right? In my left ear they are softly saying "Shirdi Sai Baba, Shirdi Sai Baba," just like that.

ST: Shirdi is the master of one of the gurus I have been studying with.

PB: The energy of Shirdi Baba works with you. You also have many spirits other than Japanese who work with you. They are from the Middle East, the East, and the Far East.

When you really get organized and begin to teach, people will listen. You are already teaching people just by talking informally, but as I said, you are a born teacher. Out of all the people I have read for, I have never seen the word "teacher" written over someone's head before. Here in Japan, some of the people I have read for are teachers or potential teachers, but when I see the word in gold over someone's head, it means that person is a born teacher. Is all this making sense to you?

ST: Yes.

PB: It feels right, doesn't it? You are on the right path.

Are you planning on moving?

ST: No.

PB: How long have you lived where you are?

ST: Twenty years.

PB: I don't know the details of it, but there is something coming up about moving. It may be an additional place or something, I don't know, but I see you teaching there.

ST: That is what I have been thinking about. I am not planning to leave my house because I have a nice big home, but I have been thinking about getting another small place and teaching there.

PB: Yes; that is what I am seeing. I am going to let Saint Germain come through and talk to you, so please stand by.

Saint Germain (SG): I am here. Can you hear me all right?

ST: Yes.

SG: I am so happy to come directly to you. Unbeknownst to you, you are a great soul. You have been like a chess piece in God's hand, because whenever and wherever he moves you, you move. Therefore, you are the kind of person God can use.

Dear one, do not wait to have everything perfect to begin to teach. Just plan a theme and purpose, make an outline, and begin to tell some of your friends that you are going to have a meeting to talk about a certain subject. If you have pictures or objects that relate to this talk, bring them too. Before the meeting, whether there are two, three or four people, just pray and ask God to bless your efforts. It is not important that you gather a large number of people in the beginning. Most great teachers start out with one or two, and that is a good place to start. Just share your heart and the information you have on that particular theme. About one half to one third of the time can be dedicated to questions and answers, and you will be used by spirit. Then plan to do something again in a week or two and invite the same people, asking each of them to bring one more person.

Keep your fee very low in the beginning. More important than making money is the truth people will receive from you. Be yourself and share your knowledge and your heart. Share your enthusiasm about your experiences. If you are enthusiastic in a natural way, it will be contagious. Do not hesitate to step out and teach.

I have the master Jesus standing to my right, and you may wonder, he says, why he came. It is not because you are Christian, for neither is he; it is because you have a great heart of love and that is his hallmark, too. This is the hallmark of the Buddha, the universal Christ, and the heart of God. That is why he has come. You, too, are to be a universal teacher. You won't teach just about Hinduism or Buddhism, but about various religions. Ultimately, you will teach about the religion of love. How does this feel to you?

ST: Yes; I think it will be just as you say.

SG: So, begin now. Give yourself maybe forty days to prepare and talk this up with your friends and contacts. I, Saint Germain, will be working with you as well, and you will have much help. There will be several Indian saints also working with you. You will also be helped by a Tibetan Buddhist monk and other various lesser spirits. You have inherited part of your spirituality from your father's side of the family. There is a woman from about four generations back who looks much like you. She is working with you and helping you, and she is also a universal spirit.

When things do not go the way you expect, do not be disillusioned or discouraged. As the teacher, you must go through suffering to teach others how to overcome suffering. Therefore, take whatever happens positively. Many times, my medium, Philip, was discouraged. Fundamentally, he had a pessimistic personality, so I taught him how to be positive under all circumstances. We see here that you already have a positive personality; therefore, you are ahead of the game and more advanced than he was when he began. You are at the right time and the right age to begin this.

I am going to leave Philip now. We will go into your questions, and I shall come back and speak again. This is Saint Germain.

PB: Okay, what is your first question?

ST: Basically, they have all been answered already. Do you want me to ask the questions again anyway?

PB: Yes, so we will have them recorded. You see, they knew your questions before you came here, and the fact that they already answered them is proof of the authenticity of this experience, so you can believe and trust what happens here.

ST: My first question is this: What is my reason for coming to the earth, and how can I serve people?

PB: You were born to be both a teacher and a world traveler. You are to be a master teacher, but your ultimate purpose is to teach and master yourself. Has your guru in India asked you to give up beer? He teaches you how to enjoy things without getting too attached to them. That is the self-mastery part of your path.

What is your next question?

Moving on and Traveling

ST: My guru is twenty-eight years old. My question is whether or not I should continue studying with him.

PB: Let me have your paper. You have a sense that maybe you should move on, right? You should follow your sense. This doesn't mean that you should leave immediately, but watch how things progress. When the time is right, your soul will know. As I told you, you are an advanced soul, and you need to learn how to trust your inner voice so you can get to the point where you don't need a guru or a psychic.

You are a person who can learn to get your own answers and trust them, and these next five years will be a turning point in your life. Where you have been crawling and walking, you will now take off and fly. I see another trip to India, but I feel it will be your last or next to last trip.

Let's have your next question, please.

Psychic Energy and Service to Others

ST: I would like to know if I should focus on opening up and using my psychic energy. Will that help God? And will it help me serve people?

PB: Saint Germain just said that yes, it would help. Your initial path is to be a teacher, but your psychic ability will open up when you focus on that. Are you not already taking some channeling classes?

ST: Yes.

PB: I see you doing that in the future.

ST: I organized channeling classes in my home, but I didn't really participate fully as a student.

PB: You are in a very different place now. It was your destiny to do what you did in order to come to this point in your life. We are all like a dog on God's leash. He lets us run around and play and play, and then after a while he says ok, enough. That is where you are now. The other night when I spoke at my event, you had some kind of a spiritual breakthrough or new awareness about yourself. You were touched.

ST: I had a number of insights, but I really haven't put them together yet. I saw a number of good things for myself.

PB: Yes, that's what they just said to me—that you are waking up more. I am going to let Saint Germain come through and talk to you again.

SG: I am back. Everyone wants to be used by God and spirit. Everyone wants to feel valued in this way. This is human nature, and it comes from the Creator who also wants to be used. God wants to feel valued, and he finds great joy when people call upon him. Because he *is* everything and *owns* everything, nothing burdens him. When you ask him for something, he would like to give you more than you ask for. But like a good parent, he gives you what you need, not what you want.

You are one of those individuals who has been close to God, so you, especially, want to be used. You have learned that just living does not bring happiness. You may own a car, have a nice house, and have this and that, but you have realized that such things don't really make you happy. You have an inner hunger to be used to find the kind of happiness that is permanent. So, by all means, formalize your work and get on with it: Teach, share, and pray to open psychically, and the way will open for you.

There is a saying in certain religious circles in the West that through praying, the way will appear. Have faith in what is being told to you here and now. Have faith that you will be used, and the way will appear. Whatever we deeply desire in this life is a form of energy, and the kind of energy we put out is the kind of energy we get back. We bless ourselves, you see. Even though this instrument is here giving to you, he is also being given to. Therefore, if you give out of your storehouse of knowledge and love, more knowledge will come, and love from God and your students will be abundant. This path is the secret to personal self-mastery, so don't let anything stand in the way of *action*. It is easy to talk and to theorize, but *action* is what brings us to you. Through action, the way will appear.

Do not think that what you are trying to attain is unnatural or peculiar. You are asking to open up to the existing and natural reality that is simply hidden from most of mankind. These gifts are natural to all human beings to varying degrees. Again, I say, step out, have faith, and the way will appear.

We did not bring Philip here for nothing, but so that people could benefit from his mediumship. He came to share with groups like yours, and out of such groups will come individuals like you. Individuals like you are the target of God's sending him here, and it is people like you that God is seeking for the world.

Again, you are in the right place, at the right time. There is no obligation for you to do anything that we talk about. Indeed, unless you do it out of your own volition, your own free will, it will not work. But if all of this speaks to your heart, your reason, and your psyche, then act on it, and in time it will prove itself.

I am going to step aside from Philip and come back again before we finish. This is Saint Germain.

PB: Do you have another question?

Universal Personhood

ST: I am focused on enlightenment, so I would like to know what the specialties of my soul are, like a specialty in a restaurant that a chef prepares on a certain day. Can you tell me about my specialties?

PB: Well, the first one is that you are a universal person. You don't look Japanese, and you could pass for Thai, Chinese, or Tibetan. Many people don't know who I am when they first meet me. They don't know if I am Japanese, Korean, Jewish or Arab, and they always think I am one of them. There is a reason for that, and it is the same for you. God created me and you to look like we do so we could be used universally. You could move throughout all the Middle East, the East and Far East and teach people of all backgrounds. The most prominent characteristic, then, is your universality.

You could capitalize on your universality by teaching the one simple principle that is applicable throughout the entire world, and it is a most outstanding characteristic of your nature: Love. Teach love. In the Far East, particularly in Japan, love equates to service; but heavenly love is a passion for other people—to want for others what you want for yourself and to treat others as you want to be treated. You have that desire, and I saw that in you the other night when I sat with you. You're not prejudiced, and you seem to like everyone. In addition to being universal when you teach people, pour love out upon them to let them feel their value, and let them feel that they are very special to you. Even if you teach 120 students, interact with them as if each was ultra-precious. This is your second and most important characteristic. Let this love shine through your work.

The third important thing is that you know how to have fun, and you know how to laugh. Don't get so serious that you lose your sense of humor! Laugh and joke a lot and make other people laugh, too. Some of the deepest and highest truths can be slipped in with laughter.

So be universal, let the essential character of your loving nature shine through, and have a lot of fun doing it, because that is the third essential part of your nature. If you do that, you will be very successful, and you will be loved by everyone in return. You are well on your way.

Do you have another question on your paper, or is there something else on your mind?

Enlightenment and Self Mastery

ST: I would like to ask more relating to my question about enlightenment. Will I become enlightened in this lifetime?

PB: Yes, you will. Meditation and study are the way to enlightenment for many people, but your path is more the path of life experience. As you observe and live life, whether in India or Japan or somewhere else, you will reach a level of enlightenment that not everyone reaches. This, and a life of teaching, will lead you to your enlightenment.

You move forward on your path to enlightenment as a result of paying off karmic debt, and when karma is paid, heaven can bring you the highest level of understanding. As you teach, you will be paying off karma and doing your dharma at the same time. Dharma and life mission are essentially the same—the things you were called to do through this body. So, as you pay off karma and do your dharma, the merit for enlightenment will come.

You and I are very similar in nature. I am not an intellectual person, and I don't know a lot of things through study. But I am an intuitive spiritual sponge; things just come to me. I was raised as a country boy, yet many people, especially in the Western world, think I have a couple of degrees because of the vocabulary I use and the way I articulate.

It was only after Saint Germain came into my life that this happened, because he overshadows me, and his nature becomes my nature. His intelligence and vocabulary became my intelligence and vocabulary. It doesn't mean I am a blank slate or an empty container, but it means this was to be my path. You and I have similar paths.

The size and scope of your mission determines how many guides you have. I have four major souls I work with in my inner band, and in the outer band there are maybe thirty more. When I had a radio show, I served 70,000 to 80,000 listeners every week, and I have read for thousands and thousands of people. Because of the size and scope of my mission, I work with many guides.

Did you have a family member who passed over who had a heart problem?

ST: Yes. My grandmothers on my mother's side and my father's side died with heart problems.

PB: They are both here. I know they are here because I have been feeling a heart problem, but now that I have spoken about it, it is gone. When I first became aware of them, my heart was fluttering, and I felt like I was going to pass out. I thought it was because I have been doing so many readings, but then my guides told me that it was your guides' way of getting my attention. They are bringing a lot of love to you, and they are so happy today that you have had this experience; it has been a long time coming. Your grandmother says not to worry. I am seeing her and other ancestors of yours around you.

One of the beings who is going to work with you is Archangel Michael. If you don't have a picture of him, you should get one and put it wherever you pray. He is a protector and guide for you, and I saw him very clearly behind you. Have any other mediums seen him with you?

ST: No.

PB: It wasn't the time, but now it is. Archangel Michael's energies will protect you, but they will also help bridge your awareness from the East to the West. He is universal, but is predominantly known in the Western world. The fact that you have gifts similar to mine doesn't mean you don't have to work at it. You do absorb just by being in a situation as opposed to having to study and approach it intellectually, but you still have to work at it. You especially need to discipline yourself to meditate regularly, so the kundalini energy can rise.

The truth about spiritual self-mastery has to do with kundalini energy rising to different levels of consciousness. From the heart chakra up are the chakras that are in touch with heaven, and below this point are the chakras that are in touch with earth. The heart works as a bridge between the higher and the lower chakras. In order to raise your consciousness, you have to meditate and get in touch with these levels.

Our goal is God. It is all God, but experience tells us that the crown chakra is the place where we finally break through and realize God completely. When that awareness comes, you realize that there is only one energy. You have to work for that, because it doesn't come automatically.

What I teach comes ninety-five percent from life experience and five percent from books. For many teachers it is the other way around, and they simply repeat what they have read. With enough drama, they can convince you that they have arrived, but eventually they fail to get the support of spirit world, and their work declines. Therefore, I always pray, not because I think I am special, but because I know I can't do this work without God.

Does this answer your question? We have time for one more.

ST: Saint Germain said he would come back one more time before the end of the session, which he has never said quite so clearly in the past. I am waiting for whatever information he has for me. I have no more questions, but as long as Saint Germain comes and says what he has to say, that is all I need.

PB: Ok, I will tune in.

The River of Life

SG: I am back. I love your delightfulness. You are rather like a fairy; a little pixie running around the world, and we love it.

Beloved one, life is truly like being in a boat on a river, not knowing where the river is flowing. Sometimes the control of the boat is in your hands, and at other times, when the waters are turbulent, the control is not in your hands. At times, the boat becomes marooned in a harbor, and you go ashore and look at the river from God's perspective; you take a break from the river.

On this river are many boats, other souls who are also flowing on the river of life, and sometimes your boats touch, and you exchange conversation and move on. At other times, the boats stay together for quite a while and, in some cases, they wind up in the same harbor side by side. But ultimately, the boat of life will move on—through turbulent or placid waters, through straight stretches, and down waterfalls. The important thing is to stay in the boat and make the journey to the end.

If you are not always in control, who is? The river is God, flowing and carrying you where he will. He takes you through all kinds of experiences; up and down, back and forth, around and around. He is also the boat, the container or protective element that lovingly carries you along on the waters of life. He is the oars you use to row the boat, and he gives you truth and love so you can move through the waters safely. Ultimately, he is the mystery of life, for you do not know exactly where the river is taking you.

When the river finally flows into the ocean of life, this is death. You are no longer in the boat riding on the river, because you have flowed into the ocean of life. In other words, you exist in the very presence of God. Therefore, the purpose and destination of this entire journey is to wind up in the ocean of God where you will experience limitless love, limitless life, and you will know that you are God.

I am not saying all of this to you to wax poetic, but rather to encourage you to flow with life and know there are no accidents on this river. Whether you find yourself in a safe harbor, in turbulent waters, or in placid waters, it is all God carrying you along. He knows how to flow, how to carry you, and when to bring you home.

In your life's work, keep this river of life in mind from now on. Trust one hundred percent that you are loved, that you are carried along, and that you will arrive home safely. How do I know about the river of life? I have traveled it myself. I know its bends and twists, its torments and its joys, and I also know that one can survive it. From this side, I spend many hours whispering into the ears of students on earth saying, "You can do it!" And I say to you, on this river of life, "You can do it; you can do it; you can do it!"

Our love follows you always. This is Saint Germain.

PB: I don't want to come out of my trance. He is still here and hasn't left me yet. Did you get it all? Was it worth it? Good; I'm happy to hear that. Well, I don't know what he talked about, but I feel like I have been on a trip or something.

ST: That is exactly what he was talking about.

PB: I feel like I am in a boat or something.

ST: That is what he talked about.

PB: Oh really?

ST: Yes. He was talking about the boat of life.

PB: That's neat. I've never experienced that before.

Ok, let's close with a prayer.

Father, I thank you for the blessed privilege of doing this work. I ask that you pour out your love and blessings, so this young woman can realize the fulfillment of your will for her life. I pray this in divine love and gratitude. Amen.

End of recording

ACCEPTING SHYNESS; DEALING WITH ANGER

Yuki K.—Female

Philip Burley (PB): I'd like to begin with prayer:

Beloved Heavenly Father, thank you so much for the faith of this beautiful woman. I am very deeply moved by her effort to come here to get a message from above. Please reward her amply for this kind of faith and effort. I ask first for healing for her heart, so that any kind of pain or difficulty that is there can be taken away during this time. If anywhere else throughout her entire spirit and body needs healing, I ask that it be healed. May her guides and teachers come very close to me to bring through the information she needs. Father, I humbly ask your blessing upon this reading. In divine love, I pray and ask. Amen.

First of all, spirit shows me a gold ring. Do you have a question about a husband or marriage?

YK: I have a question about my husband.

PB: Ok, go ahead and ask that question. They are bringing it up first by showing me the wedding ring.

YK: I would like to know about my husband's spirit guides.

PB: Ok, do you have a picture of your husband? There is a very high spirit, a man, who was not Buddhist or Shinto, but in his own way he was a very spiritual and religious man. He tells me that he was also something of a writer in his day. Does your husband write?

YK: No.

PB: I didn't think so, but this man is telling me he is a writer. Is your husband's father in spirit?

YK: He is alive.

PB: He is alive? Then it's got to be his father's father. He is working very closely with him. Does your husband work a lot with his hands?

YK: Yes.

PB: What does he do?

YK: He exchanges store mats in front of all the shops in Japan. They all have mats, and they are very big, so he goes and exchanges them. He drives a truck around placing mats that have just been washed and taking away to wash the ones that people have been walking on. He is the one responsible for exchanging the mats.

PB: He works with his hands. He is a very good man, very pure-hearted, and you and he will be together until you die. I can't pick up anymore. Usually, when I do readings, it is for the person here with me, but I wanted to try. I do want to say that your husband is the kind of person who was born good. His love and his goodness are almost his religion. You have a good man, a very good man, and most women would feel lucky to have this kind of man.

The Spirit of Buddha

YK: We went to Nepal last year. A place in Nepal called Lumbini is supposedly where Buddha was born. In our hotel room there was an altar, and while I was meditating, I could hear footsteps in the room. I was meditating with my husband, and he heard the same exact footsteps that I heard.

PB: That was Buddha. I haven't read the spirits around you, but as soon as I looked at you, I saw Buddha. The spirit that works with your husband, as I said, is not Shinto or Buddhist, but he is a universal master. Buddha works with you, and they say that the man that works with your husband was a disciple of Buddha. Your interest in spiritual things isn't just because you are Japanese, but because you are a very high spirit. My guide Saint Germain said that your husband's and your own love for God or goodness is what created the condition for spirit to make those sounds of footsteps.

Your aura is pure gold. You don't really need to be here, because you have an innate spirituality that you can really trust. Spirit is all around you. Don't you feel their presence?

YK: No.

PB: There are many around you, and they are naturally drawn to you. Let's go ahead and start with your questions.

Father's Presence in Spirit

YK: I want my father to come here today.

PB: Yes, your father has been standing here, just waiting. Did he grow up in the countryside?

YK: He was really raised in the city, not the country.

PB: He bows to you, and he is so grateful that you could be here today. He says he appreciates all the prayers you've said for him, and they have really helped him. He says, "Please don't stop praying." He is in a good place—not in the highest, highest area, but above the middle area. He is talking to me about your mother and is very concerned that she is okay. Does she live close to you?

YK: Yes.

PB: I don't know if it is the same neighborhood, but I'm seeing her somewhere very close to you. Above all, he wants your mother to know that he came today. He is a very loving man, and when I am in his energy, I feel very, very warm. He's also very intelligent. I see high Buddhist spirits or priests or something like religious spirits with him. Did he die of heart failure?

YK: His liver failed.

PB: Still, it was his heart that ultimately gave out.

Okay, do you have a question on your paper about a child? Do you remember?

YK: No, no questions about a child.

PB: Have you been praying about a child? He is talking to me very clearly about a child.

YK: I really don't want to have children, but I am feeling pressure from people.

PB: Yes, that is coming from him too. He wants you to have a child because he wants to have descendants. But if you don't want to, he understands. He is kind of joking with you, because he knows the situation. Is it because you don't have confidence?

YK: Yes.

PB: Yes, he is talking about that too. Your soul knows what it needs to do. He says not to let other people pressure you to do something against your own desire. Is this a conflict between you and your husband?

YK: No.

PB: No. That is what I thought. From heaven's point of view, it's okay if you don't have a child. I'm seeing Buddha right here, and even he is smiling and nodding yes. Listen to your soul. This question about a child is very important, even though you didn't have it on your paper, because you don't want a child, and your father and spirit are trying to impress you to feel free about not having a child. The purpose of their coming on this topic is to free you, so you can leave from here with a freer heart. They're just confirming that.

There is something else that I don't think is on your paper, about something that happened to you in the past that really hasn't left you. I don't know if it is something you feel guilty about, or what it is, but they are showing dirty laundry. Is there something holding you back, or something you feel guilty about?

Accepting Shyness

YK: Since I've been a child I've always been very, very shy, and I don't do well with people. As soon as I meet people, I want to get away from them. I don't do well with meeting people. My emotions are very strong. They go up and down, and I am not able to control them.

PB: Does this make you feel bad?

YK: Yes.

PB: Yes. I'm going to let Saint Germain come through. This is a very important point for you.

Saint Germain (SG): I am here. This is Saint Germain. God bless you. There is nothing wrong with being shy, dear one. Were more people quiet rather than always speaking, things would be better in the world. You are a special kind of person. Those who are not shy are always pushing those who are shy to be more involved, but you should feel comfortable with being you. Your shyness is also a kind of feminine beauty. Of that you should be proud.

How can you be something other than what you are? Sometimes parents in their insensitivity push the child, saying things like, "You should do this, or you should be that." Then the poor child is confused. It wants to be who he or she is innately. Many children get pressured in the same way. The first and most important thing is to accept yourself just as you are. Do not apologize for being you. Don't feel bad or guilty because you feel shy with people. Unless we accept ourselves exactly as we are, then spirit can't help us. Do you want to be so shy that you are afraid of people?

YK: No.

SG: No. So the ideal person, to you, would be one who is not shy, correct?

YK: Yes.

SG: Yes. So you can see within yourself that sometimes your shyness puts a block in the way of your achieving full realization of self. The more you focus upon being shy, the shyer you become. The more you feel uncomfortable around people, the more uncomfortable you feel around people. My advice is to accept yourself exactly as you are today, and then see what happens. Whenever you feel too shy in a situation, do not become upset. Just say to yourself, I accept myself one hundred percent as I am. I don't care what anyone thinks or says, I have to be me. Then watch what happens.

It is when we fight something that it stays with us. When we accept ourselves and our problems just as they are, they lose power. The secret to your personal overcoming and healing is to accept self just as you are. It is your reality. Work within your reality, not someone else's. If you live this way, your shyness will eventually leave you. It is by accepting our weaknesses and working with them that those weaknesses are overcome. There is guidance on earth that says to face what you fear and the fear will flee. It is the same with your shyness. The uncomfortable feeling you have had in your body and in your heart will leave you. Follow what we are telling you and watch what happens. Now I am going to step away from Philip and I will come back if necessary.

PB: Would you ask your next question, please?

Spiritual Phenomena

YK: I was meditating one day and saw a man in white clothes sitting on the ground near me with his legs crossed. I want to know if he is a spiritual guide, because I don't know who my spiritual guides are or what their names are. I have also seen falling stars in the sky, including one on the right side, and at two different times on the left side. It was like a ball of light or something shooting up in the air. I want to know what that was.

SG: This is Saint Germain. The man you saw is your husband's guide—the one Philip saw with your husband. You will remember that Philip told you he was all in white.

The Buddha works with you, dear one. You also have a Buddhist nun, and the spirit of Kwan Yin. Yes, there are a number of people working with you. In time, they will reveal themselves more and more.

As far as the fireballs are concerned, they are spiritual phenomena. These were literal, real events, and spirit was operating around you that you may know your spiritual power. You also have the ability to go into trance. As we are in your energies, we can feel this reality.

Your life is far from over, and you are far from understanding or knowing your potential. You are a more natural medium than the person I am speaking through. But don't worry about that now. Now is not the time to talk about that. In time, the door will open for you in that area, but for now, let us work with you in meditation. Now I am going to step back again from Philip and allow you to ask the next question.

PB: Okay, please ask your next question.

Dealing with Anger

YK: I have two or three questions and will ask the last one later. In my heart, when I am meditating, I have trouble controlling my emotions, especially my anger. My anger goes up and down, and I am not able to control it. I want you to talk about how to bring peace in my heart. Also, within my third chakra from the bottom up, I feel there's something like a tumor. That is a separate question from the heart question.

PB: Let's go to the first question on peace. Saint Germain is not coming through, but he will be answering the question through me. My voice won't change.

It is not possible to live a lie for very long. If we act one way outside, and feel another way inside, that conflict is eventually going to come out somewhere in our body. All human beings feel angry at times to varying degrees. That comes from the very nature of God, who also feels joy and anger at times. Even as some days we have sunshine and other days we have rain and thunder and lighting, it is all good, and it is all God. Therefore, look at your anger with love. Don't deny it. Don't pretend as if there is no thunder and lightning in your life. The more you deny it, the more you push it inside, such energy is very harmful. It is better to confess to yourself and to someone you trust that you have such feelings. Why? So you can get rid of them.

Anger is a form of energy that is of a certain vibration. It has such a low vibration that it becomes harmful to the physical body. Again, by talking about your anger it will be dissipated or diluted.

Today it is very important that you are talking about your shyness and your anger. Because in this setting with spirit, there will be no criticism or judgment; only forgiveness, understanding, and love. Rather than push your anger down, you need to look at it, analyze it, and understand its root cause. Bringing the light of understanding into the room of anger does away with the darkness.

YK: Lightness and anger are almost the same word in Japanese.

PB: Really?

YK: Yes, almost the exact same word.

PB: Modern psychology is very helpful, Saint Germain says. Psychology doesn't have to deny spiritual truth, and it doesn't have to be looked upon simply as brain or mind examination. Modern psychology seeks to bring understanding of the human mind and heart, and when it does, it is very effective in helping people.

Looking at your anger honestly will lessen it until it eventually goes away. That is the secret. Whomever you can trust to talk to about your anger, even it is only to God in prayer, do so and be honest about it, even if it means getting angry while you talk about it.

I (Philip) was also filled with much anger. I went out in the countryside one day and for two hours yelled and shouted at God about my life. I cried and cried and told him, "You love these trees, and you love nature more than you love me. Otherwise, you wouldn't make me suffer so much." I was angry at life and God. After two hours, my whole spirit was cleansed. I had a very profound spiritual experience in which God revealed himself to me. He told me he was so happy that I let him know how I felt. He already knew how I felt, so who was I fooling? I wasn't fooling anyone but myself. After that, God came closer to me than at any time in my life, and he has remained close. What does all this mean? It means the truth of life will set us free. When we confess to ourselves and others our shortcomings, then we are on our way to being liberated from them.

Saint Germain is laughing, and he's asking if this all makes sense to you.

YK: It kind of makes sense.

PB: Yes. As you work with it, you'll understand it more. Saint Germain says you're so used to pushing your feelings down so as to not bother people that it's hard for you to look at your feelings and deal with them. The center of emotional expression is this area, the solar plexus. You have a backup of emotions, and this is what causes your tension.

After I began to be honest with myself and God, the pain I had there went away. Is this making sense? (Yes.) You can work with this, as you will have the tape to listen to. This is good therapy. Let's go to your next question.

Dealing with Spiritual Sensitivity

YK: I was in the middle of meditating one time and a very large crystal appeared and just spun around once or something.

PB: It spun around you?

YK: The crystal was near me, and I saw it go around. When I saw that, my heart really began to hurt.

PB: The biggest thing in your life is to learn to love yourself. You are so ultra-sensitive that you feel much more than the average person. You have to come to treasure that and to direct it. Believe me, I was just like you. I came to recognize and embrace my sensitivity, though as a boy growing up, I was ashamed of it. When I learned how to use this as a gift to help other people, my life became much brighter and much happier.

You are a born psychic—you were born a medium. You have to learn how to use it. If we have such a gift and don't use it for the sake of others, it's often used against us. You and your husband both have good spirits working with you, and there is no reason that you can't be successful in life. When you get away from being shy to the point of being afraid of people, and your anger is released, you will find you have a very beautiful, positive heart underneath all of this.

Wouldn't you like to be free?

YK: Yes.

PB: You can be free, and you will be. There is no question about it. I want you to be very optimistic about yourself.

What is your next question?

Connecting with Higher Self

YK: I would like you to teach me how to connect with my higher self.

PB: Do you have about ten years? Saint Germain and my guides all just came very close right now because we work on this part together. Saint Germain is not going to speak directly through me, but they are overshadowing me to work with this question. I will have my eyes both open and closed, as I listen to what they say.

First of all, they say your longing to know your higher self is coming from your higher self. The center of that desire comes from your higher self. Saint Germain says the steps on the ladder to the higher self are self-acceptance, optimism, faith, vision, hope, and love. These steps on the ladder to the higher self in themselves open you up to that awareness. The higher self contains everything—every quality—contained within the steps on the ladder.

Saint Germain wants to point out that right now we three are operating from our higher selves because the higher self is always centered upon spiritual, God-centered things. The higher self is the inner core of the self we don't like. In other words, here is the outer person that we don't like and the inner self that we do like. We are all trying to get away from this earthbound self and move toward that higher self.

There is no secret and there is no secret door. The whole self, including the higher self and lower self, exists in oneness. It's just a matter of awakening to that reality as a fact. A Buddha-like or Christ-like person is always operating from the higher self, meaning from the self that is centered upon divine love or God. Awakening to the higher self comes through faith, effort, and meditation. Saint Germain says that the degree of our faith and effort will determine how fast we awaken to the higher self.

Above all, he says, we cannot get there by wishful thinking. You have to walk the spiritual path. Naturally, as we walk the spiritual path, we are going to meet our lower self. But the lower self is just like a covering over the higher self. It is like having a dirty body, and once we wash it, the dirt is gone. The lower self is gone as we focus on the higher self. He says the secret to finding the higher self, therefore, is to constantly focus heavenward, always turning your mind to high things, positive things, loving things, constructive things. That's all they are saying. Is that helpful? Do you have any questions about this?

Meditation

YK: Is it important to do a lot of meditating?

PB: Be reasonable about it. Healthy spiritual life is achieved through a good balance between physical responsibility, physical living, and spiritual life. The ideal spiritual person is one who has their feet firmly on the ground and their head in the clouds. Start with twenty minutes in the morning for three months.

YK: Only twenty minutes in the morning?

PB: Yes. You can meditate longer if you want to, but twenty minutes in the morning, and later twenty minutes in the evening, five or six days a week, is enough. You can't make enlightenment happen. It is by God's grace that we come into this enlightenment. As we demonstrate our desire through faith and effort, then God comes and meets us halfway. He will open the door to the higher levels, so be very patient and take your time. Ultimately, enlightenment is not in our hands. The final steps to full enlightenment are in God's hands. This way, God and man work together. In the final analysis, this is the way we learn who really is in charge.

YK: Say that one more time.

PB: In this way, we learn that God is the one that brings ultimate enlightenment.

Healing as Life's Mission

YK: I am asking about my life's mission. My husband and I would like to work together in the future as healers, and I would like to know if we will be able to do that.

PB: You should go for it. You need to do the inner work first, and you should share this experience with your husband. In the future if he has time, he should get this kind of reading. It can be through me or anyone.

As I started to go deep into trance, I saw the two of you doing healing work as a team. To be an effective healer, you have to begin to work with some of your inner issues, such as your shyness, anger, and so on. Otherwise, you are like a doctor who is sick trying to take care of other sick people. So much physical healing is really based on mental healing, and pain is often the result of needing to be healed spiritually. Evidently, in childhood you were very silent in the midst of some unjust things. Does this make sense?

YK: When I was a little child, my older brother went crazy and went into a mental institution. Maybe you are talking about that?

PB: I am talking about all the forces that were around you in your family. Things happened to you, not physically, but things happened to you that were unjust and unfair. As I look at you, my guide Tiffany says you have healing ability, so you should work on this. You should just work gradually and not think of it as a big ministry in the beginning. Work one-on-one with people. There is plenty of work to do. The Japanese are waking up, from what I can see, in a very big way to this whole field of healing energy, so this is a lucky time. People like you are being inspired. Go for it, and just ask heaven to provide everything. How old are you?

YK: I am twenty-nine and will be thirty soon.

PB: When I was twenty-nine, I was just starting this kind of work. From the age of twenty-nine to forty-four I went through the worst time in my life. I didn't know who I was, what I wanted to do with my life, or where I was going. But now I know I went through all of that so I could come to this day. It takes time, and you have to pay the price.

Let's go to your next question.

Directing the Kundalini Energy

YK: When energy comes into me, my arms and my legs tend to move. What is that?

PB: That is kundalini energy. I had the same phenomena. My whole body moved. It's a good sign. Are you sitting with a teacher? You really need to be with a teacher. Teachers are only temporary doorways to help you find your higher self. We learn what they know and move on. A true teacher will want you to move beyond what they can teach you, but in order to get through a wall we need a door to go through. Teachers can be the door that lets us get through the wall. In order to affect and direct your energies, you need to be in some kind of organized setting.

Are you from Hiroshima?

YK: Yes.

PB: Surely, in Hiroshima there are such people who can be teachers. You have to look around.

YK: I think there are. I have met plenty of people from Hiroshima involved in this. If there are no groups, my husband and I could form a group.

PB: Right.

YK: I don't think there are any spiritual places at all in Hiroshima. Hiroshima is very big, and I could look in places such as natural food shops, little shops that sell crystals, or yoga places. They usually have little pamphlets listing teachers that are teaching things related to spirituality and events that are going on. I am sure they have teachers there.

PB: How strongly does your husband want to do this work?

YK: He hasn't started the work yet, but he has been studying spiritual things for twenty years, and he wants to do spiritual work at some time in the future.

PB: Saint Germain just said, "Tell them I will help them. That's what this is all about."

YK: Thank you.

PB: Let's go to your next question.

DNA and Change

YK: I was meditating and saw a coil. I don't know the color or what it really is, but I saw this coil very clearly and want to know if you can tell me what it might mean.

PB: It has to do with your DNA. Do you understand? If you really understand it, it's the DNA strand.

YK: Yes, I know about it. It's huge in Japan right now.

PB: Well, it is your DNA. There is a lot of golden light around this. It's about your DNA strand, and it means a major shift in your overall being. In spiritual work, changes are very subtle, and this discourages a lot of people. So even though there is a major change for you going on now, right this moment and from now on, this change will be very subtle. Often in spiritual life it feels like things are just standing still, and you can destroy your foundation by just being too impatient.

For most people who want to do this work, their major downfall is impatience.

There are two clear things that must happen to become an authority or teacher in spiritual matters: you must grow as your work grows, and you must be changing into the very person that you are telling other people to be. Otherwise, you are a hypocrite, and it won't work.

YK: I'm trying to understand the word "hypocrite."

PB: Whatever you tell other people that they must be doing, you have to do it first, or heaven can't really bless you. If you tell people they should lead a disciplined life in meditation, you better be leading a disciplined life in meditation. If you say, when healing them, that they need to change their diet, you had better be aware of your own diet. Otherwise, you have no true authority to do the work and you could be called a hypocrite. But you can do it. I am seeing good spirits all around you right now. There are a lot of them.

I can take one more question.

Tibetan Connection

YK: I went to Nepal and Pokhara, and we stayed in a hotel run by Tibetans. There were many pictures of Tibetans there. I want to know if I have some kind of connection with Tibet.

PB: This is so interesting, because before you asked this question, I was going to ask if you have some Tibetan ancestry. I keep feeling Tibet around you. You must have picked up a lot of that, and you were supposed to, because Tibet is part of the spiritual environment and experience you and your husband need for your healing work. What is your question regarding that?

YK: I feel a strong connection with Tibet. Do you think I need to go there?

PB: It's not necessary. You have many Tibetan spirits around you already. It is very important in this work to appreciate your own history, get a sense of your own value, and enlarge the dimension of your understanding of yourself. You are not really this finite human personality but an ever-expanding, limitless being with all the powers of God.

In order for you to come into complete happiness and fullness in life, you have to break out of who you think you are. God wants to use you in a big way, not in a small way, and you and your husband are going to be very effective healers, step by step by step. At the same time, expand, expand, expand your understanding of yourself. You have a lot of wisdom to bring to your work, and you know that. On the outside you may have the appearance of being shy, but inside you know you are very intelligent and very capable.

My wife worked with a young person who is Chinese who is very shy like you. He wouldn't even look at her. But little by little she got him to finally start looking at her, and today he is completely able to do that. When people are shy and look down, for most of them it means they don't like themselves. You have to see your own beauty, and you will. Are you aware that you are a very pretty woman? In my eyes I see a very beautiful face—a classic beauty. I don't know how many people have told you how good you are as a person. Has there been anyone in your life, your mother or father, who has really encouraged you?

YK: Yes, my parents have been encouraging.

PB: Okay. We could go on and on, but we will stop here and close with a prayer.

Father, we thank you for this wonderful time together. When we see each other, we see you. Let your cosmic light shine forth and use this willing soul to help other souls. May the content of this reading have a significant impact upon her consciousness so that she can stand tall and have healthy pride in her value, so that she can go forth boldly into the world and realize her own potential and your potential within her. Again, thank you for this time together. All this I pray in divine love. So be it.

End of recording

Spiritual Reading Twenty-One

FINDING GOD WITHIN

Suki H.—Female

Philip Burley (PB): I ask that you hold the paper with your questions, though I will take it and give it back to you at times.

I will be going in and out of trance or semi-trance. I don't know when Saint Germain will come in. Sometimes he announces himself before coming in, and sometimes he just comes in. If he wants to handle a question, or I want him to handle it, it will happen spontaneously, as everything does.

If I may, I will hold the paper with your questions now.

We will begin with a prayer:

Dear Father, we turn our hearts and minds to you, the all-loving, ever-present intelligence behind all that is created. This person has come today to ask questions, and I ask for those guides and teachers that work with her to come forward and work closely in coordination with my guides and teachers to bring in the answers. Whatever healing is needed for her, or anyone in her family, let it happen today. Let your healing energy go forth.

I ask for you to help me to be totally out of the way, so everything can come through unhindered by my presence. Make me a pure channel for your voice and your thoughts and for those of spirit. Thank you in advance, so very much, for what you will do here today. All this I pray in divine love. Amen.

You are surrounded by a group of six lovely women. I don't know how else to describe them except to say they are very feminine and almost angelic in nature. They are something like sprite spirits, all in white, with red sashes around their waists. They have an energy field that is all pink. They have very black hair and beautiful faces. These women are like guides and teachers for you, but also like an angelic force, and there is a fragrance of roses with them. I have never seen this before. My guide Tiffany says that their white clothing represents your purity and that the red sash around their waists, being in the middle, represents the fact that your life is balanced in love. You were born in love. When your parents conceived you, there was very deep love between them.

Entering the Realm of Enlightenment

I am just watching some of the things happening around you. This is very unusual, but you have much orange and gold color in your aura. When we see this shade of orange, and it is true in this case, it usually represents the highest color in the spirit world. Many people think the highest color is violet, but orange is the highest because it is a combination of red which is the love of God and yellow which is the energy of God. I see this energy primarily around Eastern masters like Buddha or Confucius. This is very good.

As I was looking at this orange color, I saw a healing energy come into you, down through your arms and into your hands. They don't show me whether you are in the healing field or if you are interested in that, but you do have the gift of healing. As I am looking spiritually at your fingers, there is blue light coming out of each fingertip.

You are at a strategic and opportune time of your life right now. Spiritually you are standing on this side of the river of enlightenment. For most people this river is very wide, but for you it is only about one-third as wide as it is for most. As it passes by, the river is very blue, a beautiful blue. The crossing of the river before you has nothing to do with death, lest you think that. This is the river of life. You will not go down into it, but cross over it to the land of enlightenment. Some people must spend a lot of time in deep thought and meditation to reach enlightenment, and while you can do those things, you're almost at the point where you will arrive at the awareness of enlightenment just by being you. I see you helping many people in your life, almost like a nurse does, but not as a nurse. I see you reaching out to people and helping them, and this will happen more and more as you grow older.

The master Jesus is here for you and stands directly behind you. I don't know what this means in relation to you, but he is talking about the necessity of bridging East and West. He is using his hands (Philip demonstrates) to say that you have certain abilities to help make a bridge for others in spiritual matters. You don't know it yet, but God has given you great potential, far more than the average person. They are showing me a container of milk, coming from God, and it is poured into you. The milk is for you and for others to drink as your life unfolds.

I see the master Kwan Yin, immediately to your left, surrounded by a magenta or reddish-pink color today. She just walked around you and touched your lips, and I have never seen her do this with anyone else. She also touched your third eye and your throat, these three centers. She says that, as a master, she is working with other masters to help open the third eye. She also says that you are born to speak what you understand and what you receive from spirit, and you have the potential for channeling.

You were born to be a universal person, not just Japanese. Do you know that?

SH: I know it a little bit, yes.

Born for Spiritual Work

PB: This island nation is too small for you. Eventually you must travel to many parts of the world, for two reasons. You are to receive spiritual things, and you are to give spiritual things to others. I don't know if you are in some kind of a spiritual school now, but I am seeing courses that you have taken or will take. You are going to get some kind of credential to work spiritually. As far as your purpose in this life is concerned, you are multifaceted, so there are different things you will do. In any case, you are not born to exist just for the physical world. You were born primarily for spiritual work.

You have a grandmother standing here. Is your mother's mother in spirit?

SH: Yes.

PB: Yes. That is what I thought. She is so solidified that it's hard to tell whether she is on earth or in spirit, because sometimes when a person is sleeping, they are taken out of their body. She is very much a part of your energy, and she is talking to me about how she follows you around. Have you ever sensed her near you? You will.

While on earth, your grandmother wasn't a particularly outspoken or expressive person, but in spirit she is quite capable. She was a very honest woman, and the energy field around her is all blue. It is not a deep blue, but more like the color blue in this dish. The blue around her has a lot of white lines in it, which is unusual, and it means that she was a pure soul who embodied truth because she was an innately honest person. She didn't have to work at it.

Have you felt that spiritually you have been going in circles, looking and searching? That time is coming to an end. This is why I saw you crossing the river of life. It is time for a major change. They really want you to trust your inner voice and not question or doubt it. You are much like I am in that you are led very precisely. You often doubt yourself; but the most important thing is for you to say what you see and feel. Speak it out, especially to yourself.

Saint Germain wanted me to say this: God is in all positive manifestations. Therefore, any thinking, feeling, or action that is positive is all God. When you make that the ruling idea which guides all your thoughts, feelings, and activities, it is much easier to walk the spiritual path.

In other words, God is with us not only when we pray or when we cry out in an emergency—but one hundred percent of the time, all the time, everywhere.

Saint Germain wants to drive this point home: Everything is God. He says that if you feel drawn to do something positive which is not harmful to you or anyone else, then do it. That is God guiding you. If you feel a strong desire to travel somewhere, you have the money, and you feel joyful about it, that is God's guidance. He says that for you, particularly, this practice will serve you greatly. Know that wherever you are, God is. That is how they are trying to train you. That is a large part of your path to self-enlightenment.

Let's start with your questions.

Relationship with Mother

SH: The first question I want to ask is about the relationship between my mother and me. I feel like I have experienced trauma from the time that I was in my mother's womb, and I still have anger toward my mother. I have the feeling that the operation I had last month has to do with this anger toward my mother. I'd like to know how I should relate my anger to her. I am not sure what to do, so please tell me in detail what to do in this case.

PB: I perceive spiritually that your situation is much like that of another person whom I read for, whose relationship with his mother also seemed to cause a problem in his body. A major reason why your mother's mother is with you is to compensate for your mother's inadequacies and weaknesses. Your grandmother is your guide, but she is also trying to say, "I'm sorry."

Your grandmother says that your mother fundamentally does not like herself and as a result takes that out on other people. Do you understand?

SH: Yes.

PB: Even though you were born from the love of your parents, you came to her at a time when she wasn't emotionally ready for you. Because she felt so inadequate, part of her didn't even want a child. Have you ever felt that she didn't want you?

SH: All the time.

PB: The truth is that she wanted children, but the timing was not good for her, and she held on to the narrow idea that things should happen only when she thought they should happen.

Sometimes in life, we come to realize that we can want someone to be different from the way they are, but it is nearly impossible to cause someone else to think and act differently or as we think they should.

Saint Germain says, here in my right ear, that it is best to be open, tolerant, and considerate of others' points of view but that, at times as individuals, we need to do things our way or we are not being most honest, loving, and fair to ourselves. Yes, *we can compromise where compromise is possible*, he says.

You might approach the problems with your mother by saying something like this, "I hear you mother, and I appreciate what you are saying, *and* I must do things as I see them. Otherwise, I am not honoring myself but always honoring others and doing what they say and want. I can't and won't do that anymore.

You won't be here forever and so I need to become self-reliant and genuinely confident in my own decision making. Please understand."

We eventually learn that we have to want the best for someone but not to expect them to think and act as we do or, again, as we think they should. That is what individuality and uniqueness are all about. It is your life and your path you need to walk and not someone else's. Additionally, because of your difficulty with your mother you may love your mother but not like her, or even appreciate her, except for the fact that she gave you birth. For that, Saint Germain says, you can be grateful and honor her.

Love is a two-way path and when it is not returned in kind, it is, after a while, very difficult to keep loving that person except unconditionally which at times may be a compromise. It is case by case.

Learning the Lessons of Love

The issue is not what your mother did or didn't do, but how you responded to it. As hard as it may be, you need to look at your mother's life with compassion. She is not a mean or negative person by intention, and in her heart, she is not conscious of doing wrong. She was a victim of her own mother, and she made you a victim, but none of this was intentional.

Saint Germain says that if you look at it that way, you can have compassion and can even forgive her. In the end, because your mother is the way she is, you know that you don't want to be like her. In this way, she is like a great master in teaching you exactly what you don't want to be like. It is partly because of her that you try to practice not hurting other people like you have been hurt. I'm going to let Saint Germain come through now.

Saint Germain (SG): I am here. Can you hear me all right?

SH: Yes, I can hear you.

SG: God bless you. What I was trying to say through Philip was that if you had a mother who was loving and positive, you might be very happy and at peace, but you would never have aspired to a higher level of living. Your desire to get away from your mother and leave home gave God an opportunity to come into your life more fully. Because your life was unhappy, you searched for answers.

One important reason you came to this medium is that through him you could receive some insight, consciously and unconsciously, to solve your problem with your mother. There are no accidents in life, and everything unfolds just as it should. One could say that if you had forgiven your mother earlier, you may not have had the problem in your body. That is wishful thinking, because the reality is that you didn't forgive your mother, and you did have the problem.

The idea about what should have happened is purely in your imagination. Reality, from God's point of view, is always what is happening now. To live in reality and embrace it as it happens is to live wisely. For example, someone with a problem like yours may think, "This shouldn't have happened," or "There is some mistake," but there *are* no mistakes. What happens each moment is reality. We need to understand what we are supposed to learn from reality.

Life on Earth is not a perfect life without problems, but rather a classroom for learning about self and God. In addition to forgiving your mother, and even more importantly, you need to ask what you can learn from all of this about yourself.

Jesus looked at the world that caused him to suffer and asked the question, "What does this teach me about me?" He forgave all those who brought about his downfall, and used his experience as a stepping-stone to understand himself. From the time Jesus was a child he was considered to be illegitimate, and his brothers and sisters made fun of him all the time. He had no place to go but inside himself, and because he was an advanced soul, when he went inside, he found God. He returned to that inner place again and again throughout his entire life. By doing that, Jesus discovered himself and learned that he was not his body, his feelings, or his thoughts. He was a divine, eternal being in whom God existed fully, and he tried to teach us what he had discovered. If you understand the meaning of these words, they will carry you forward throughout your life.

Life will be what it will be, and everything is in God's hands. The most important thing in walking our spiritual path is to learn about ourselves and change in necessary ways in order to perfect the soul and our relationship with ourselves and God. That is the ultimate, perfect, and practical solution to all problems. If you will practice what we are saying here, you will find much peace inside and ultimately with your mother too. Be assured that your mother's mother is working hard in the spirit world to support you in solving all these problems. I am going to leave Philip, so that we can move on to your next question, but I will come back later.

Life is Worth Living

SH: I want more than anything to feel worthy of this life and to feel that my life is worth living. There are many weak points within me which affect my life and purpose. My problems and lack of a sense of self worth have affected all areas of my life. I have much desire for love, but because of many traumatic experiences, I don't have self-confidence. I wonder if I will find a partner in this lifetime. I would like more understanding about this and want to be able to move forward and advance in my lifetime. I feel I received much of the answer a moment ago from Saint Germain, but I would like more advice if it is available.

PB: Let me shake your hand and welcome you to the club of humanity, because this is what we all go through! In my many years of working with people, I find this is universal. Very few people feel worthy, and few know who they are. I see this so often that it brings tears to my eyes. I feel that this is one reason God has given me this kind of work to do, because man's biggest problem is his lack of connection with God. This has been said so many times that it is almost worn out, so people say, "Yeah, yeah, yeah, I have heard that before," but it is absolutely true.

The second problem is that people are looking for God in the wrong places. Most are looking for God outside of themselves, and some make gods of other people. Christians worship Jesus, Buddhists worship Buddha, and in India, people worship their guru and a pantheon of spiritual beings. For people at that level of development that is okay. It's all they know. But remember what I told you about where you are standing in relation to the river of life?

For a soul like you, it is time for you to find God within you, totally, completely, and absolutely. God is already there. You don't have to go anywhere or do anything special. God is always, always present. The kind of thing that you feel right now, a mixture of joy and sadness, is bittersweet. It is your own divine heart crying out to let yourself know that God is already present.

The question is *how do we find God in ourselves?* I cannot fully address this question without sharing information that most people are not entirely ready to know or to hear. I can say however, that the presence of God is not separate from our own. The essence and overall presence of *our energy* is not separate from God's *essence and overall presence.* When you truly find your Divine Self you will simultaneously find God.

The path to this experience, originally intended to happen right here on earth as it did with the Master Jesus, is the path of meditation. Right meditation, which is basic and simple meditation minus many trappings, if practiced earnestly and regularly can't help but eventually lead you to your own Self-realization and, at the same time, God-realization.

Simply speaking, it is a vibrational, scientific process similar to turning a dial on a radio going from radio stations at lower frequencies to higher frequencies, each with its own distinct radio station vibration or frequency.

Primarily I can say that what you are looking for in searching for God is within and meditation is the means of taking you within to discover God. It is not an ultra-sensational experience but quite the opposite: as if eternal spring has, at last, dawned, and all is eternally well and filled with an immeasurable, deeply healing love and peace.

As I am talking to you, I am seeing blue. Mother Mary is manifesting behind you, and she is beautiful. Her presence is beautiful. She is all in blue and sends a great amount of love toward you. She is helping you, and says, "Listen; he knows what he is talking about."

As I have told others, Jesus works even more with me in my inner life than Saint Germain does, and I have had many dreams of Jesus. In one dream, when I met him, it was like meeting an old, old friend. He grabbed me, pulled me to him, and started crying on my shoulder. He couldn't stop crying, and said, "They still don't understand. I tried to teach that God lives in you and in every human being, but they are still looking for God outside. I am very sad because they still haven't understood."

I can see clearly in you that you were born to understand—to get it—and you will. The way to find God within is to want God more than anything else. That is my most important teaching.

Have you read Yogananda's teachings? He referred to the mother side of God more than the father side. Jesus, Yogananda, and Saint Germain all understood what I am talking about. They loved because they *were* love—pure love itself. They longed for the source of life.

Next to being serious in your search to find God, the second biggest secret is to love other people as yourself, including your mother. God loves everyone unconditionally, and if you do that, the God presence in you will come out. More than anything else, in your journals, in your thinking, and in your prayers, ask yourself, "How can I love everyone?" This doesn't mean that you have to love everyone personally, because that is impossible; but when you look at another person, don't judge that person. Regardless of what they look like, what their skin color is, or however they appear, don't judge them. God is in every one of them.

I have practiced this teaching for many years. When I see people, I just see God, so I can well appreciate what Jesus felt. That is such a wonderful blessing, because that is true spiritual sight. To see God in every person is more important than being able to see or hear spirits. If you practice this, it will bring out the God that is in you, and you will find God. You, especially, don't have to spend long hours in meditation. Just practice loving everyone as yourself.

You are the first person here in Japan with whom I have shared so many tears. You brought a lovely spiritual atmosphere with you, so I thank you for the privilege of reading for you.

Let's go to your next question.

Mother Mary and Unconditional Love

SH: About ten years ago, I had a very big experience with the light. At that time, I felt myself become one with Mother Mary and really felt the light and compassion of Mother Mary.

PB: I can see that.

SH: Yes, that is why I was waiting for Mother Mary to come today. After I had this experience, regardless of what else happened during the next ten years, I have been able to overcome everything in my life. One of my questions is about that experience and what it really meant for me. I felt that I had the experience so that I could step up to the next level. As you said earlier, I also feel that this is a time of transformation in my life. Ten years have passed since that experience, and I would like to have general information on what might happen during the next ten years.

PB: You don't want very much, do you? (Laughter) First of all, the experience was exactly what it was, and everything that you got from it you were supposed to get. Mother Mary has been standing beside me speaking. She said that there are many things that you and she have in common, both strengths and weaknesses. After we receive a high revelation such as when you saw the light ten years ago, we are often tested. Your biggest test has been your relationship with your mother. Mother Mary says that if you can love your mother unconditionally, you can reach self-mastery. It's easy to love a stranger, because we don't have all the history with them, but God uses the people closest to us to test and teach us.

Mother Mary says that your mother and she have something in common: "As I opposed my son, your mother opposed you." But Jesus was also tested as to whether or not he loved his mother. He was so upset with her at one time that he said to her in public, "Woman, what have you to do with me?" The reason he said that was because she didn't understand him, and she opposed him. He could have said, "If you were really with me and understood me, you wouldn't have treated me the way you did."

Mother Mary says (I am listening), "Because of the way in which I conceived Jesus, it made it appear that I have conceived him out of wedlock. Joseph had a very hard time accepting Jesus because he seriously thought that Jesus was an illegitimate child and that I had slept with another man. If the angel had not come to him to tell him that Jesus was from God, Joseph would have rejected me and left me. Whenever we looked at Jesus, Joseph and I both felt heartache and conflict. I loved Jesus with all my heart, but I wasn't really free to love him because of all the criticism surrounding his birth. Our life together was miserable, and I grew bitter as I got older. When Jesus became a public person, I still had all of those feelings inside. Only much later did I realize what and who Jesus really was."

"There is a story behind my wrongdoing and there is a story behind your mother's wrongdoing. You can see that I repented and turned my life around. In time, your mother will do the same thing. Meanwhile forgive her. The next ten years for you are in the making now. Please apply what Philip told you today, particularly about making a relationship with God inside, and also about practicing the loving of others as yourself."

"Consequently, your whole path will be smoother and easier, and you will go faster up the mountain. Don't think so much about the next ten years; just think about the day in front of you. If you look too far ahead, you may miss what is important today. Those who become true masters are those who focus, focus, focus upon the now. By focusing on the now, every day will unfold correctly."

Regarding a man in your life, the answer to that is still up in the air. Part of you is not fully decided, because in you there is a sense that maybe you should devote your whole life to spiritual things and to God. On the other hand, you want to be fulfilled as a human being and that may also be God's will for you. You have to decide, and it is not yet decided."

SH: Do you mean that it hasn't been decided by me or it hasn't been decided by God?

PB: God already knows.

Finding God Within

SH: I have one question: Last year I had a dream about my partner. At first, the number zero appeared, but it turned and twisted until it became a ring. Then the number eight appeared, and I thought that this usually is the symbol of eternity. Then the numbers of the day and the month of my birthday appeared. I thought that maybe God had already prepared my partner and that's what the dream meant. Do you think that this is a possibility?

PB: The zero represents that which is in your soul that is not yet totally known to you. It also shows that you can decide to keep it a zero or turn it into a figure eight. The figure eight not only represents infinity, but in the spirit world it also represents new beginnings. For example, on the eighth day a new week begins. Your dream portends a relationship that can be eternal and also a new beginning for you. Your soul is still trying to decide. Your outer self has the desire, but your inner self isn't sure yet.

When someone with Mother Mary's nature works with a person so directly, that person's soul often questions whether to live a celibate life devoted totally as a bride to God or to be married to a partner on earth. This question often comes up.

I am speaking personally now. When I first prayed for you, I saw a man coming to you. I don't want to influence you, and in fact, I am not allowed to influence you, but I clearly saw the potential for you to have a partner in life.

The more important question right now is about how to find God within. The release of that power within you will solve many of your problems and will answer the question of marriage. Trust that inner reality one hundred and fifty percent, seriously. You are a person that I would trust to definitely come to the right answers.

Saint Germain wants you to know he works with you as well. You have a number of masters with you. But the most important question is not who works with us, but rather, do we master our own life? Can we stand before God in the spirit world and say, "I did it"? We will not ask, "Did the Mother Mary, or Saint Germain, or Jesus do it for me or through me?" but, "Did I do it?" That's exactly what all the true master teachers would say. Guides and teachers are there to help us on the path, but not to do our work for us.

Are all of your questions answered?

SH: Until now I have not been able to get any information from my soul or make contact with my soul. I am asking for any information you can give me about my soul, including what kind of soul I have. Is there anything that you can tell me?

PB: I will remind you, for the third time, of the river I saw. This is a very, very historical moment for you. You are going into the big time.

(I am listening.) Saint Germain just said, "When you find God inside, you will find your soul. You have the wrong idea about what a soul is. That which thinks and speaks, that which longs for and aspires to, is the soul—the essence of the essence of the essence. Most importantly, the soul is not different from God. It *is* God. The final awakening is when we realize, 'Oh, I am not the little person I thought I was; I am God!'" Saint Germain is laughing now. He is watching your face, and he is really enjoying himself. Go for God, and you will find your soul.

I'm going to close with a prayer.

Father, thank you so much that we could have this wonderful, wonderful spiritual time together. You honor me with such high-level spirit. Go with this young lady and show yourself to her quickly. As she does her part, I know you will do your part to meet her halfway. Nothing more need be said except thank you with all our hearts. Amen.

End of recording

www.ingramcontent.com/pod-product-compliance
Lightning Source LLC
Chambersburg PA
CBHW032032080426
42733CB00006B/64